ON LISTENING TO
HOLOCAUST SURVIVORS

38215580

9/29/99
Ingram
$24.95
C. Rachanay

ON LISTENING TO HOLOCAUST SURVIVORS

Recounting and Life History

Henry Greenspan

Foreword by
Robert Coles

 PRAEGER

Westport, Connecticut
London

Library of Congress Cataloging-in-Publication Data

Greenspan, Henry, 1948–
    On listening to Holocaust survivors : recounting and life history
/ Henry Greenspan ; foreword by Robert Coles.
        p. cm.
    Includes bibliographical references and index.
    ISBN 0–275–95718–7 (alk. paper)
    1. Holocaust, Jewish (1939–1945)—Personal narratives—History and
criticism. 2. Holocaust survivors—Interviews—History and
criticism. I. Title.
D804.195.G74 1998
940.53'18—dc21   98–4944

British Library Cataloguing in Publication Data is available.

Library of Congress Catalog Card Number: 98–4944
ISBN: 0–275–95718–7

First published in 1998

Praeger Publishers, 88 Post Road West, Westport, CT 06881
An imprint of Greenwood Publishing Group, Inc.

Printed in the United States of America

The paper used in this book complies with the
Permanent Paper Standard issued by the National
Information Standards Organization (Z39.48–1984).

10 9 8 7 6 5 4 3 2 1

Copyright Acknowledgments

The author and publisher gratefully acknowledge permission for use of the following
material:

Excerpts from *If This Is a Man (Survival in Auschwitz)* by Primo Levi, translated by Stuart
Woolf, Translation copyright © 1959 by Orion Press, Inc., © 1958 by Giulio Einaudi
editore S.P.A. Used by permission of Viking Penguin, a division of Penguin Books USA
Inc.

Caption of a drawing by Warren Miller; © 1979. Used by permission of The New Yorker
Magazine, Inc.

The pain does not touch upon something human, on another's heart, but rather is something incomprehensible, linked with the cosmos, a natural phenomenon like the creation of the world.

Oskar Rosenfeld, *Notebook E*, Lodz Ghetto

Contents

Foreword

During the 1950s, in my early twenties and a medical student, I got to know Ilona Karmel, a Holocaust survivor—the first such person I had ever met. She had written a novel, *Stephania*, which drew on her experiences in a concentration camp. Her writing had gained great approval, and even then she was contemplating the plot of another story. I recall asking her about what she had in mind, and I can still hear her brief, pointed reply, spoken (I later realized) across the huge psychological distance between her life and mine: "The camp—it will always be the camp." In due time her second novel, *An Estate of Memory*, appeared—also a critical success and true to her word, a narrative that took readers into a world that, really, defies rather than expands (the traditional role of fiction) the imagination. Talented, vivacious, a born-storyteller, Ilona Karmel tried hard to bring her terrible experiences to our attention (again, the novelist's quite ordinary and generous activity), but she seemed in her bones to know the difficulty, maybe the impossibility, of such an effort on her part, as she indicated once with these words: "I think I'm writing to learn for myself what happened. To be truthful, I can't imagine what you [American-born to parents whose families were never immediately threatened by the Nazis] would make of certain scenes in *Stephania*."

As I read Henry Greenspan's unique and remarkably compelling book, I kept remembering Ilona Karmel's two novels and her remarks about writing that summons the Holocaust as its central subject. In his own way, Professor Greenspan—an extraordinarily patient, knowing, dedicated psychologist—has struggled with the very dilemma Ilona Karmel tried to evoke rather than resolve: how to put into words (that is, render in a human way) something that is beyond words because of its utter inhumanity? True to his vocation as a committed, respectful listener, Professor Greenspan lets Oskar Rosenfeld warn us from the start about the obstacles in our way: how difficult it is for you, who are holding this book, and me, who has written these words, and, yes, this book's author, and even those whose experience and memory it seeks to honor—how impossible it is for any of us, finally, to grasp what took place in Europe in the middle of the twentieth century.

Still, the essence of our humanity is to try to make sense of things, even to make sense of the senseless. We are creatures of language, who insist on retelling, who try to figure out the why of things, who can't let go of the past, who give it, constantly, the narrative life of memory, of reveries by day, of dreams by night, of stories told silently to ourselves or spoken to others or relayed on paper for still others unseen, though—in the larger scheme of things—very much companions. That being the case, we cannot avoid trying to accomplish what we also know is so often beyond our ken—hence, our probes into the stubborn mysteries of our origins and, yes, our probes into the nature of the evil to which we are heir, notwithstanding all of our scientific and even our cultural achievements. So it was that the Germany of Goethe and Schiller became the Germany of bestiality and murder—beyond, at first, the belief of so many; beyond our full moral or psychological understanding even now.

Nevertheless, we are brought nearer to such understanding in the pages ahead, not of the peculiar evil that informed the lives of Hitler and his accomplices, but of their victims, each of whom, however, deserves to be acknowledged as much more—as, in fact, the particular man or woman or child he or she was and ought (in our thinking) to continue to be. It is to such people—precisely to the textured, individual voices of those who somehow survived—that Henry Greenspan has listened. And what he aims to offer is an account, as it were, of what has been recounted: an effort of remembrance that goes further, much further, than the confines of a day's, a week's, even a month's recall. The issue is not simply time. Rather, as Freud well knew, it is the claim of human subjectivity itself—its irreducible complexity, ironies, and contradictions—and hence our right to be heard, and heard, and heard, so that the variousness of our individuality, of our experiences and their retelling, be truthfully comprehended.

In the pages ahead we are offered that kind of human inquiry—years and years of human relatedness: a psychologist who dared give the heart and soul of his working life to certain fellow human beings who were fated to enter a world utterly elsewhere, as it were, and who returned to us with Conrad's "the horror, the horror" not waiting on the tips of their tongues for someone readily to hear, not waiting for someone to categorize or turn into an earnestly well-intentioned moral or educational or psychological or social lesson; but rather as something *there*, in all its immense, unprecedented, layered presence, at once outside the bounds of memory, if occasionally within the grasp of the repeated exertions of thought and feeling that Henry Greenspan has in mind when he speaks of "recounting" in connection with "life history." What follows, then, is the story of a long journey, indeed, taken by a wise clinician, a careful and clear-headed writer, who wants to bring us as close to a kind of human truth as those men and women whom he attended so long and hard will enable us to get. The result is a psychological document of enormous significance—we learn not only something (a lot, but not all, almost by definition not all) about certain lives, but, very important, we learn about (psychological) learning itself: what it takes to study well and justly the lives of others—the time needed, the tact, the perseverance, the dedication, the consideration, the contemplation, and, not least, the moral energy.

Robert Coles

Acknowledgments

Developed over two decades, this book has several disciplinary homes. It is a work of psychology in its situating Holocaust survivors' recounting within their individual life histories and in its insistence, a clinician's bias, that important communications take time to emerge. The work is sociological or social-psychological in its also contextualizing survivors' recounting within the expectations of survivors' listeners. It is historical in its locating those listeners' expectations within the cultural discourses about survivors that have evolved over what is now many years. Finally, the book is part of narrative study through its focus on the forms of recounting itself: the ways that survivors find words and make stories for memories, which finally negate all words and stories.

The friends and colleagues to whom I owe much also inhabit several disciplines and homes.

Within psychology and psychiatry I have benefitted immensely from the reflections of Henry Krystal, Francois Rochat, and George Rosenwald, all of whom, with extraordinary graciousness, read both early and late versions of this manuscript. I am also indebted to Joseph Adelson, along with the Michigan Society of Fellows and the Ford Foundation, for making it possible for me to come to the University of Michigan in the 1970s and begin the work that became this book.

During my graduate study in the Department of Sociology at Brandeis University, Kurt Wolff contributed immeasurably to my thinking both about survivors and about my own purposes as a writer and researcher.

Much more recently, sociologist Kai Erikson kindly read the final version of this manuscript.

Among colleagues in Comparative Literature and interdisciplinary Holocaust Studies, Michael Andre Bernstein, Karin Doerr, Elliot Ginsburg, Alvin Rosenfeld, and David Schoem contributed to this project in important ways. Theatre scholar and translator Claude Schumacher provided the benefits of both his insight and his remarkable editor's eye. Philosopher John Roth's generosity, integrity, and care are a continuing inspiration.

My students in the seminar that, for a decade, has borne the same name as this book have contributed to my thinking more than most of them know. Some have become fellow teachers and friends on whose percep-tions I continue to rely—especially Victoria Brescoll, Corinna Derman, Darone Ruskay, and Felicia Tripp. I am forever indebted to the Residential College of the University of Michigan, both for introducing me to such extraordinary students and for supporting my efforts in all ways.

My editors at Praeger have handled this project with superb attentive-ness. I would mention Elisabetta Linton, Ellen Louer, Norine Mudrick, and Nina Pearlstein.

My primary colleague among historians, Sidney Bolkosky, is more than a colleague. Several of the survivors whom we both know and have interviewed recount the Holocaust mainly as a story about brothers. During the years that Sid and I have been listening to their stories, we have also become brothers.

The survivors whose recounting is at the core of these pages have honored my life with their trust and their insights for more than twenty years. What I owe them goes far beyond thanks. So I only say, "Dayenu."

This book is dedicated to my wife, Nancy, who is in our garden with the orioles while these pages are being written. Some of us need quests like long books and projects. Others need seeds and soil and the fruits all seasons bring. There is, she calls out, a yellow warbler in the pine tree. I will go and look.

Introduction: From Testimony to Recounting

At a recent public talk I was asked to comment on the differences between the work I do, as an interviewer of Holocaust survivors, and interviewing for testimony collections such as the Survivors of the Shoah project that Steven Spielberg initiated in 1994. For a while I treaded water, trying to explain contrasts in approach and purpose that were evident but not easy to summarize. Suddenly, a colleague who was moderating the program came to my aid. "The Shoah Foundation wants to interview 50,000 different survivors once," she reflected. "Hank wants to interview the same survivor 50,000 times."

As will become clear, this is not a quantitative study—anything but. But to begin with a pure assertion of quantity, even when invoked with ironic exaggeration, seems right. This is a book about immersion in details, returns and revisions, and taking the time that sustained talk takes. It is far less concerned with the things some say come out of survivors' testimony—lessons and legacies, teaching or tolerance—than it is preoccupied with the question of how we get *into* survivors' recounting. It is also driven by the related convictions that more and more talk *about* Holocaust survivors (which has characterized recent years) does not necessarily lead to better talk *with* them, and that nothing is more common than to think we follow survivors' retelling only to discover, in a later conversation, that we do not. Needless to say, the revelation depends on having the later conversation.

Whatever revelations these pages contain reflect twenty years of conversations and later conversations. Those meetings have certainly not numbered in the thousands. But they have been part of sustained acquaintance with a group of survivors whom I first interviewed in the late 1970s. This was for a study on the forms and contexts of recounting—how survivors speak about their memories and the influence of listeners on what survivors do, in fact, retell—and those questions remain at the center of my work.[1] With a number of the participants, this initial study led to continuing conversation and reflection, and the present volume is an attempt to summarize the core of what has emerged. It is a report on two decades of listening to survivors—and to some survivors in particular.[2]

Later Conversations

Even within relatively short periods of time, having the chance to talk with the same survivor more than once enables one to learn things very difficult to discover any other way. In general, first interviews tend to evoke versions of experience that are "proven"—ones we already know are tellable by us and hearable by our listeners. This is true for everyone and applies to the retelling of all kinds of experience. In the context of survivors' experience, however, finding what is both tellable and hearable is not a typical challenge. Every version is not only "selective" but precarious, often contested by memory at the same moment that memory is given voice. As listeners, however, we hear what we hear—which includes what we anticipate hearing and what survivors, anticipating our anticipations, have constructed to be hearable. As a result, what we take as "the testimony" may turn out to be radically unlike the terror actually recalled.

As a single example that is later reviewed in detail: Leon, one of the survivors whom we will get to know well, retold the story of a prisoner's execution in each of three different interviews I conducted with him over two months in 1979. It was apparent in each retelling that he did not remember having told me the story before, and this was the only episode that he repeated in this way. The story, therefore, seemed to be quintessentially Leon's testimony—a recounting that appeared to have a mind and a memory of its own. In fact, however, what may be most notable about this episode is how *untypical* it is of Leon's memories of the destruction. And, indeed, when I asked Leon about the significance of this story, which I began to do at his third retelling, he came to speak about the ways *all* his stories are unrepresentative; about the inadequacy of the story form itself. In a phrase that has remained essential to my understanding of survivors' recounting, Leon insisted: "It is *not* a story. It has to be *made* a story. In order to convey it. And with all the frustration that implies.

Because, at best, you compromise. You compromise." Beyond the compromises and behind the stories was what Leon called a "landscape of death"—a simultaneity of terrors in which not only stories but "even sound was out of place," an enclosing nightmare in which even screams were silenced. It was that landscape to which his story ultimately led—and to which it pointed through its own repetitive insistence—but one would not have known that from the story alone. The story alone does not retell it.

Testimony as Recounting

Leon's repeated story is an example of what later conversations may reveal—in this instance, a discussion that literally depended on returning to his recounting several times. This example also helps explain why I speak of "recounting" in most of what follows, rather than "testimony," which is the more usual term. Perhaps reflecting its use in judicial and religious contexts—declarations of witness or of faith—"testimony" suggests a formal, finished quality that almost never characterizes survivors' remembrance. "Recounting," it has seemed to me, better connotes the provisional and processual nature of retelling—a series of what are *always* compromises that always point beyond themselves. "Recounting" may also better suggest the emergence of retelling within conversation, in contrast with testimonies as one-way transmissions that listeners simply "get" or "gather." The roles of recounter and listener in the interview dialogue are not the same. A good interview is a process in which two people work hard to understand the views and experience of one person: the interviewee. Within that focus, however, the exploration can become fully collaborative. As the example from Leon conveys, recounter and listener can work together to understand the significance of a particular story and, in this case, of "stories" in general.

Indeed, this example does make it clear that recounting often includes more than specific episodes from the destruction (to which "testimony" usually refers) but may also involve, for example, reflection on the processes of remembrance and retelling themselves. I will argue, in fact, that *everything* survivors say in the context of their remembering the Holocaust should be considered part of their recounting: reflections on the destruction as a whole no less than retelling specific events; retelling their experiences now (such as the challenge of retelling itself) no less than retelling experiences from within the destruction. Perhaps most controversially, I suggest that even what are usually understood as psychological "symptoms" of survivors' experiences—accounts of guilt, for example—

should be considered part of recounting. Most essentially, this is because *all* these accounts can be understood as ways survivors "make a story" for what is "not a story." Pained as such stories can be, relative to the agonies toward which they point, they remain tellable by survivors and hearable by their listeners.

As we shall often follow in these pages, shifting reflexively from experiences during the destruction to experiences after—experiences *as* a survivor—is one typical way that the tellable is constructed. Returning to Leon, along with the story he repeated from within the terror, he most often retells his own story as a struggling recounter—what it is like to *be* a person who must "make stories" for a "not-story." The story of the frustrated storyteller is communicable. The great part of Leon's direct memories of the destruction are not.[3]

Life Histories

Immersed in recounting as a process, we begin to follow the creation and destinies of stories—survivors' specific stories of the destruction as well as their own stories as survivors. We also discover that both these kinds of stories are contextualized, in turn, by the wider story of each recounter's life history as a whole. The very act of "making a story" depends on using plots and meanings that are essentially alien to the destruction itself. They must be retrieved from elsewhere: from all the rest of who survivors are, what they have lived, and what they remember.

A good part of this study is devoted to tracing the emergence of survivors' recounting—in particular, their stories and narrative voices—from *two* sets of memories: salient themes and identifications salvaged from what survivors themselves often call "the normal circumstances of life" (and which they share with all of us) and memories of the reduction and finally dissolution of those meanings (and much more) within the Holocaust itself. On one side, then, recounting is "personalized"—it is, indeed, partly structured by the "normal" stories and circumstances of individual lives. But this kind of structuring is also a "compromise"—and, in the context of the rest of what survivors have lived and remember, it is always a failed compromise. It is precisely that failure that we learn to follow. Meanings that are salvaged are eventually reduced again; analogies are introduced and then negated and abandoned; stories are cut short or are insistently repeated.

We thus learn "in practice" what we perhaps knew in theory: that the Holocaust had nothing to do with the inwardness of individual lives, it was enacted on an entirely different scale. "The pain does not touch upon something human, on another's heart," wrote Oskar Rosenfeld from within the killing.[4] "The dimensions of our suffering could not be fully expressed in an individual soul," wrote Aharon Appelfeld afterward.[5] And yet for stories to be made, and memory to be touched at all, it is precisely on the expressions of individual hearts and souls that recounters must draw. The contradiction is irreducible and permanent: all recounters inhabit it; no recounter resolves it.

In order to reveal that contradiction and its vicissitudes most vividly, the survivors introduced in these pages are themselves presented as distinct individuals. They are not abstract "voices from the Holocaust" or initials attached to fragments of testimony, but recounters whom we come to know as particular people, as we might come to know them in an actual, sustained conversation. We thus follow *someone's* struggle for words—and someone's failure to find them. Indeed, by the final chapters, we should know these recounters well enough that we can anticipate—in style, in emphasis, and in heart—the kind of contribution to the conversation each is likely to make.[6]

The recounting of one survivor, Victor, is presented in quite unusual depth and detail. I devote two full chapters to etching out the fate of his voices (he has more than one) and stories within the two worlds of memory from which they emerge. These chapters are a shift in interpretive magnification and perhaps reveal, more than any other part of this book, what I mean by immersion in recounting over time, in detail, and in individual particularity. In an age of collecting testimonies by the thousands, usually in single interviews, these chapters may also serve to remind us how far we remain from getting "the story" even when we devote this much attention to a single recounter. Echoing Leon's conclusion about stories and "not-stories," Victor came to assert: "What is not told is also true; what is not in the book is also true." We best gauge the truth about the truth not told, I think, when we pursue it with unusual persistence.

Participation

Immersion in recounting reveals that survivors' retelling is a continuous effort to give voice and stories to truths that live on as the negation of voice and stories. Immersion in recounting also brings us to our own role as listeners. On one level, this is because survivors talk about us. As we shall hear, the longer we do listen, in fact, the more survivors tend to say about listeners' importance and, for so many years, listeners' absence. And while some writers suggest that survivors recount in order to "integrate" their memories, or to create form and meaning for their own sakes, the essential truth is that survivors recount in order to be heard. Indeed, without at least a remnant of that hope, survivors do not recount at all.

From the beginning, then, we are implicated. As I have suggested, even when listeners are present and willing, survivors anticipate what will be hearable by us as well as what is tellable by them, and both negotiations are reflected in what they do, in fact, retell. How listeners' expectations affect recounting, and the wider history of our assumptions about survivors, are thus also central in what follows. As noted, the very terms that are most typically associated with survivors and their retelling—"testimony," "stories," "legacies," "survivor guilt," and more—reflect the public discourse within which recounting takes place. That discourse is also analyzed as a structure of expectations with which survivors must negotiate.

At core, however, this study aspires to do something more than analysis. Along with being *about* the forms and contexts of recounting, these pages are written to be, within their sphere, a locus *of* listening to survivors. That is, the hope is to re-create a certain sense of evolving conversation within the text itself. That goal is an additional reason why recounters are presented as particular people whom we get to know as we might know them over the course of actual, deepening acquaintance. It is why I refer to those recounters, not as "subjects" or "informants," but as "participants"—originally participants in conversations with me, now participants in the widening conversation intended here. Finally, this is the reason that the work's most conceptual chapters come at its beginning, comprising Part One, "Initiations." The purpose of the two opening chapters is to prepare us for the much more detailed presentations of recounters in the chapters that follow, perhaps the way a grammar prepares for more advanced texts. Already knowing something in general about the forms and vicissitudes of recounting, the subject of Chapter 1, we should be ready to enter more fully into the fate of particular voices and stories. Likewise, already knowing something in general about the role and impact of listeners, the subject of Chapter 2, we should be more self-conscious in our listening here. On one level, the reflections of recounters certainly remain "data"—there is no denying that. But, within the trajectory of these pages, they are always destination as well.

Part I

Initiations

Chapter 1

The Forms of Recounting: Tellable Beginnings

How guileless they were, those surviving tellers of tales. They sought to confer a retroactive meaning upon a trial which had none.
                                    Elie Wiesel, *One Generation After*

WHO CAN RETELL?

"Who can retell?" The question comes from the English translation of "Mi Y'Malel," a traditional Hebrew song sung during the Jewish festival of Hanukah. "Mi Y'Malel" calls on its listeners to remember the salvations of the Jewish people, specifically the victory of the Maccabees over the Syrians, and to rededicate themselves through the inspiration of that history.

> Who can retell the things that befell us?
> Who can count them?
> In every age a hero or sage
> Came to our aid.
> Hark! At this time of year in days of yore,
> Maccabees the temple did restore.
> And now all Israel will again arise
> Redeem itself through act and sacrifice.[1]

In continuity with past redemptions, Israel is called to a new awakening. Telling and retelling the tale will help make it so.

In evoking an image of Jewish memory and its retelling, "Mi Y'Malel" is a fitting opening for this chapter. We shall be attending to other attempts to find continuity with the Jewish past, particularly through efforts to recount it. At the same time, in the context of our specific topic, remembering and recounting the Holocaust, the spirit of "Mi Y'Malel" is immediately out of place. Indeed, it is bitterly ironic. For in remembering the Holocaust, we recall not salvation but extermination. While there were certainly heroes and sages among the Holocaust's victims, few are remembered and none stand elevated and apart from the collective annihilation. And unless historical awareness is limited to drawing connections between the Holocaust and the establishment of the modern state of Israel, the destruction likewise provides no restoration to recall nor redemption to anticipate. Unmitigated atrocity, mass murder, the eradication of several European Jewish cultures—all in the context of the world's general indifference—are what the Holocaust provides.

Still, the very contrast of implications of "Mi Y'Malel" when Hanukah and Holocaust are juxtaposed serves to introduce what follows. "Who can retell the things that befell us? Who can count them?" In the context of Hanukah, the questions are an invitation, perhaps what a teacher would say to eager students or a parent to children. Who can retell? Anyone who has learned to recite the traditional narratives. Recounters are limited only by their knowledge of the ancient stories and, so the exclamatory tone of the song suggests, by the degree to which they may be awed by the sheer number of tales to be told. Either way, both the questions and their answers remain essentially rhetorical. Formalized in traditional texts and ceremonial contexts, "retelling" is quite literally that. One recites one's portion among the generations of others, known and imagined, who have also gathered to retell and listen and retell again.

Who can retell? How different are the echoes of the question when the Holocaust is its background. There may be knowledge enough—numbers of dead, names of places, a chronology of events—but each fact mocks as much as supports our capacity to speak "knowledgeably" about such things. Marshaling emotion does not help to break the sense of pretense. How much despair, how much rage, how much of silence itself, is enough?[2] What we know does not fit with what we are able to feel. Neither fits with intimations of a pain that seems to go on forever. Confronting the Holocaust authentically, there is always a problem of scale—too big, too terrible, too many—and a failure of grasp.

Finished and Unfinished Testimony

"Who can retell the things that befell us?" We are tempted to exchange distress for humility. Perhaps only those who actually endured the destruction can retell it: the survivors and those who left some record—a letter, a diary—but did not survive. Their accounts, invested with the authority of direct experience, may then become chapters of a new inviolable text to be reread and retold. Such was George Steiner's recommendation in an often quoted passage:

> These books and the documents that have survived are not for "review." Not unless "review" signifies, as perhaps it should in these instances, a "seeing-again," over and over. As in some Borges fable, the only completely decent "review" of the *Warsaw Diary* or of Elie Wiesel's *Night* would be to re-copy the book, line by line, pausing at the names of the dead and the names of the children as the orthodox scribe pauses, when re-copying the Bible, at the hallowed name of God. Until we know many of the words by *heart* (knowledge deeper than mind) and can repeat a few at the break of morning to remind ourselves that we live *after*, that the end of the day may bring inhuman trial or a remembrance stranger than death.[3]

Steiner proposes an obscure ceremony, but it is structured by the traditional model: reciting a fixed and hallowed text "over and over" with the cycle of the seasons and the sun.

Steiner is not alone in his wish to sanctify the testimony of those who actually experienced the Holocaust: the survivors and, through them, the millions who neither survived nor left any record of their agonies. This sort of veneration may have several different functions, as we shall consider further on. But, for Steiner, it is clear that such deference stems from a genuine acknowledgment of the enormity of the loss. It also serves to remind us that remembrance, simply as remembrance, must precede any attempt to derive lessons or meanings out of what the victims endured. Still, as an answer to the question, "Who can retell?" this response also fails, and the reasons for its failure go to the heart of the logic of the present study.

To say it most simply: Survivors' testimony taken alone does not solve the problem of retelling because, in the end, survivors are no more able than we to retell the essence of what they endured. For all the irreplaceable status of their accounts, even these cannot encompass so much. Thus Elie Wiesel insisted that "between the survivor's memory and its reflection in words, his own included, there is an unbridgeable gulf." Describing survivors' inability to retell, as well as others' inability to comprehend, Wiesel continued:

> Their sentences are terse, sharp, etched into stone. Every word contains a hundred, and the silence between the words strikes us as hard as the words themselves. They wrote not with words, but against them. They tried to communicate their experience of the Holocaust, but all they communicated was their feeling of helplessness at not being able to communicate the experience.[4]

If this is true, then to freeze survivors' words, to repeat them "line by line" however many times, in itself may bring us no closer to "knowledge deeper than mind" than without such reverent discipline. Wiesel suggests that survivors' words are themselves survivors of a struggle with a hundred other words and no words at all. To set such words apart as a fixed and finished text is to screen out the agitated, still uncertain process of their selection. And it may be that only by attempting to enter into survivors' struggle for and against words—exactly through some mode of review and interpretation—that we *can* approach what those words seek, and by themselves fail, to convey.

Indeed, it may be precisely the unfinished, contested, and *not* definitive character of survivors' recounting that offers us fullest access to its significance. That is, it is only as we learn to follow survivors' accounts *as* they become disfigured and finally fail—because the destruction is too vast, because the loss is too unbearable, because meaning becomes undone, because stories fall apart, because voice starts to strangle, because death again invades the recounter—that we begin to approach the Holocaust itself.[5]

Rather than self-sufficient texts handed down by custom to initiates, or eyewitness to outsiders, therefore, survivors' testimonies are here understood to be the most provisional of constructions. Far from being outside review and interpretation, they must be reviewed and interpreted in the most painstaking way. The purpose of such interpretation, of course, is not to uncover what survivors "really" mean or to substitute our words for theirs. Rather, it is to enter into the process by which survivors find words and meanings at all in the face of memories that undo their words and meanings.

For the most part, the struggle between meaning and memory has been survivors' private one. It is suggested by the rhythm of words and the "silence between the words" that may strike us "as hard as the words themselves." Still, it is not predictable how that silence will strike. The words alone do not reveal what they cannot convey, and the silences, in themselves, do not reveal their source. Here, therefore, we learn slowly, indirectly, always insecurely—a painstaking task in the literal sense, as even the most agonized words, recognized as our words as much as survivors', only point to more, still unrecounted.

Who can retell? Any of us who allow ourselves, with survivors, to become participants in the effort; each in terms of the other; going as far as we can go.

PARTIAL AND PROVISIONAL FORMS

The Holocaust can be approached only through what it destroyed, and what the Holocaust did destroy goes beyond the lives and collective ways of life erased forever. The relationships we normally presume between imagination and reality, experience and its retelling, being alive and being dead—these, too, have been radically and morbidly transformed. Claims like these are so broad in their scope that they are almost inevitably dismissed as rhetorical. They are meant, however, to be taken literally, and a central aim of this study is to aid our comprehension of them in a serious and literal way.

Even the individual words we use to speak about the Holocaust are surrounded, not only by silence, but by a permanent echo of irony and of pathos. Ideally, our speaking and writing on this topic should proceed differently than it manageably can. Key terms should be in quotation marks—"murdered," "survival," "the aftermath"—to convey that their referents are radically unlike what we usually mean by "someone killing someone else," "living through and after," "the repercussions of an event now past." In *Survival in Auschwitz*, Primo Levi reflected on the problem of words and the need for quotation marks:

> Just as our hunger is not that feeling of missing a meal, so our way of being cold has need of a new word. We say "hunger," we say "tiredness," "fear," "pain," we say "winter" and they are different things. They are free words, created and used by free men who lived in comfort and suffering in their homes. If the Lagers had lasted longer, a new, harsh language would have been born.[6]

In fact, however, a new language was not born. There is only the old language, sometimes in quotation marks. Most typically, the quotation marks are also missing, so that only the "silence between the words" marks what the words themselves do not convey—a silence then filled by whatever our own imaginations, as listeners, allow it to contain.

Survivors do not have such a choice. The struggle that we may only sense between the reality of the Holocaust and the old words and concepts is, for them, an immediate presence. And it starts to become apparent how easy it may be for us to hear as the "last word"—already agonized enough—what, for survivors, is only the tellable beginning.

Salvaged Words

As a single example related to the immediate discussion, the poet Tadeusz Rozewicz reflected on the fate of language in the wake of the destruction. After the war, Rozewicz wrote, he would have to compose his poems "out of a remnant of words, salvaged words, out of uninteresting words, words from the great rubbish dump, the great cemetery."[7] Rozewicz's despair is evident, but his thoughts may not initially strike us as unfamiliar. We might be reminded of other poets following other wars, such as T. S. Eliot's evocation of a "heap of broken images" abandoned to "stony rubbish" in the opening of *The Waste Land*.[8] Are not Rozewicz's "remnant of words" salvaged from the "rubbish dump" and Eliot's "broken images" scattered amidst the waste land (and amidst his poem) the same? On one level they *are* the same. Each poet is attempting to describe the fate of language and culture in the aftermath of war. There is a continuity of concept and imagery between them, just as there is a continuity between the two world wars to which they respond.[9]

But there is also a difference, and it is critical. That difference turns, first, on the fact that images that are "broken" are not the same as words that must be "salvaged." Although damaged and disordered, "broken" images retain a discrete integrity. Like ancient artifacts, they can be gathered up by the practiced collector and secured against a totality of destruction—fragments "shored against" ruin, wrote Eliot, suggesting private faith if little public hope.[10] By contrast, "salvaged words," words that have been *in* "the great rubbish dump," are already ruined. They may be dredged up, but the stain is indelible and their disfiguring permanent. And the turn from Eliot's stony waste land to Rozewicz's rubbish dump cemetery is complete when we realize that, in the world to which Rozewicz refers, rubbish dumps *were* the cemeteries. There, garbage, waste, and people were thrown out together—same goal, same method. Here is what Victor remembers from his second day in the extermination camp, Treblinka. He

had been selected to sort the belongings of those from his transport who
had already been killed:

> The next day we were working on the clothes—to look in the pockets, to
> sort out money to money, gold to gold. . . . They have a place, they call it a
> "Lazaret," that means "infirmary." It was behind the trees so nobody should
> see it. And everybody takes a suitcase of rubbish there and puts in the
> rubbish. . . . So here was fire. And here was always burning rubbish. And
> there were some dead bodies burning over there, with the skin folded and
> the bone showing, that I could see. . . . I went over there to put in my rubbish.

Would we still confuse the world that Eliot invokes—a metaphoric plain
of stony rubbish but retaining real cemeteries—with that of Rozewicz: a
place like Treblinka where only the rubbish dump was real and "the great
cemetery" (like the "Lazaret") metaphoric?[11] The juxtaposition is cruel.
But certainly it is no more cruel than the similar juxtapositions that
survivors always carry between memories like Victor's and "normal" assumptions about cemeteries and rubbish dumps. Evoking such juxtapositions, and echoing almost every survivor's description of life in the
aftermath, Isabella Leitner reflected: "We live by constant comparisons. It
is hard enough to live in one world. We are destined to live forever in
two."[12]

To have survived the Holocaust means, at core, to live in two constantly
compared but never integrated worlds. And to recount the Holocaust
means, most essentially, to try to employ the terms of one world (the world
survivors share with all of us) to describe the terms, and the negation of
terms, of the other. It is always a translation, and it is always ultimately
futile.[13] Still, that very juxtaposition of worlds—and especially the futility
to which it leads—become useful. The ways that Eliot's and Rozewicz's
visions *are* analogous, for example—in imagery, tone, and context—are
what put into perspective the distance between them. Here the juxtaposition was contrived in order to make the point. As a number of interpret-
ers suggest, however, alternating assertion and then negation of analogy
and precedent are typical within many individual works on the Holocaust.
"The fundamental anguish which is at the heart of all Holocaust literature," notes Sidra Ezrahi, is "the challenge of generating words that can
measure up to the enormity of the devastation, while the very voices
which violate the silence after the destruction are signs of its antithesis—
of remaining life and possible bridges to the future."[14] The only way out
of the dilemma (and the escape is only partial) is for writers to show that
their words and voices *are* now "remnants"—more accurately, "re-

mains"—the decomposition of which is re-created within the literary composition itself.

Thus Alvin Rosenfeld, in his seminal study of Holocaust literature, described the "revisionary and essentially antithetical nature of so much of Holocaust writing, which not only mimics and parodies but finally refutes and rejects its direct literary antecedents."[15] Although analogies and antecedents are explicitly or implicitly introduced, "it emerges in almost all cases that the gains in perspective are only temporary and provisional," that "such analogies are introduced only to reveal their inadequacies."[16] Taken as a whole, the literature of the Holocaust becomes "a literature of fragments, of partial and provisional forms," tending toward erasure at the moment of inscription.[17]

Still, partial and provisional forms remain forms. Their use, their articulation at all, does reflect "remaining life and possible bridges to the future," however compromised and reduced. Likewise, Rozewicz's decision to continue to write is significant as his determination to remain a poet—as *continuance* if not continuity—even with such an injured stock of words. Such poetry, Rosenfeld writes,

> survives to remind us of all that has been destroyed. And also to remind us of what has not been destroyed, for while it is true that Holocaust literature is nothing if not language in a condition of severe diminishment and decline, it is still capable of articulating powerful truths—if none other, then those that reflect life in its diminishment and decline. We have lost so much, but not yet the power to register what it is that has been taken from us.[18]

"To register" does not mean to fully integrate or comprehend. It simply means to assert the ongoing presence of some perspective, perhaps only the memory of a perspective, provisionally salvaged from the cemetery, from the rubbish dump.

RECOUNTING EMBODIED: STORIES, VOICES, LIVES

In the pages that follow, the literature of the Holocaust—its recounting in memoirs, histories, and novels—will be of only peripheral concern. The words and silences presented here come mostly from interview dialogues, from situated *acts* of speech and silence, rather than from finished texts. Still, the concepts discussed in relation to writing about the Holocaust remain central. We shall continue to follow the introduction and then negation of analogies and antecedents. Likewise, we continue to trace the fate of all such forms as "salvaged remnants": their ongoing capacity to "register," if only *through* their recurring dissolution, what it is that has been destroyed. Now, however, it is not literary works that take form between meaning's creation and dissolution. It is the lives and voices of individual recounters.

In the remainder of this chapter I turn to the relationship between survivors' Holocaust recounting and their individual life histories. When, later in the work, we listen to each of the survivors in greater depth, the concepts presented here will be individually embodied. Here, the idea toward which I write is that recounting, in its essence, is embodied. That is, it is not only that the stories and voices survivors choose for their retelling are rooted in their particular life histories. Equally important is the realization that, for survivors, recounting draws on the roots of ongoing speech and ongoing life themselves.

Making a Story of What Is Not a Story

Along with its grounding in dialogue, a key difference between this work and most literary studies concerns the kind of analogies and antecedents to which we shall attend. Rather than self-consciously chosen metaphors or literary genres, the meanings in recounting of greatest interest here are those that can be shown to be more intrinsically grounded in survivors' individual life histories. These include salient themes and identifications, characteristic aspirations or doubts, that survivors draw on when they retell who they are and what they have lived, just as we all draw on such themes when recounting our own lives. And, in fact, there is nothing about such meanings that is unique to survivors. But given what survivors *have* lived, there is certainly something unique about their fate. For while such constellations of meaning continue to give form to survivors' retelling, they, too, are "remnants." Even in the course of recounting, they can be consumed again.

As a single example, it may be noted that even Victor's account of the rubbish pit at Treblinka is not a pure engram, engraved into his memory and later retold without mediation. As we shall hear when the full context of its retelling is presented, even this memory is partially structured by, and its significance to Victor partially derived from, other organizing themes of his life: themes having to do with other secrets revealed, and pretense unmasked, both in reality and in fantasy. Of course, we are right if we ask what normal kind of unmasking, or normal fantasy of unmasking, can possibly compare with witnessing the reduction of one's people to rubbish, with the absolutely unsymbolic "unmasking" of "skin folded and the bone showing." The analogy is itself incinerated; itself reduced to pretense. But that is exactly the point. For memories like Victor's derive a part of their specific terror precisely in the obliteration of the normal transaction between inner meanings and outer facts, between even one's worst imagining and the normally mitigating circumstances of lived reality. Along with the particular incident described, the retrospective recounting of such incidents is always also a report about the transformation of that relationship—about the day a worst nightmare became actual and after which, therefore, one would never fully wake up (to some other "reality") again.[19]

Still, never fully waking up is not the same as not waking up at all. And what is perhaps hardest to grasp is this: that the very meanings destroyed as analogies in experiences like Victor's somehow live on, though now as altered remnants, to give form even to the memory of that destruction. Meanwhile, however, the destruction also lives on, often enough becoming, once again, the only "meaningful" reality. We are dealing, therefore, with a *simultaneity* of continuity and radical break. The wound heals *and* it does not, the pain moderates *and* it remains unqualified; to follow survivors' retelling, we must hold on to both truths at once. Thus provisionally mediating forms and their recurrent dissolution may superimpose themselves upon each other in rapid oscillation. Survivors' recounting emerges from some unstable locus within these shifting fields.[20]

Victor's account of the rubbish pit is of a kind that seems to take form precisely between the poles of meaning's creation and dissolution. Along with its thematic continuity with other organizing memories of his (having nothing to do with extremity), personal mediation is reflected in the *way* Victor retells this memory. It emerges as part of his recounting a more detailed incident that is itself retold in traditional story form: with identified actors, a specific place and time, and a coherent unfolding of action, reaction, and development. Such a narrative form itself suggests mediation. For, in general, retelling a memory as a story implies the narrator's ability to take some perspective on experience and *give* it significance and form—if only by choosing to tell this story in this way. Likewise, because the end of a story is always somewhere in view the moment it is begun, retelling a memory as a story implies the narrator's faith that his recounting will cohere through some personally mastered trajectory of logic and meaning. In fact, stories like Victor's seem to express this sense of mastery with unusual insistence. As I have suggested, survivors often recount such stories more than once over a series of interviews, and there is an unmistakable quality of personal ownership that characterizes their retelling. It is as though the recounter were saying, "This is *my* story," salvaged in memory for some particular reason and later retold in order to make some particularly vital point.[21]

All this, then, is on the side of the self's mediation. But what also becomes apparent in the course of recounting is that such stories are, in a sense, the last episodes that can be retold "as stories." Both their inner and outer borders are compressed by a hierarchy of deaths that stories cannot integrate or convey. And the story reveals itself to be, not only "partial and provisional," but created on the very edge of its own dissolution.

As suggested, there is, first, the reductive transformation of the story's constituent meanings. Themes of "normal" unmasking terminate in a vision of peeling flesh; "normal" indifference becomes total oblivion; "normal" vulnerability reduces to absolute terror and helplessness. The seeds of the story's undoing—memories of the worst possible made actual— are thus carried within it. And when they emerge, the story ends.

This is the second death: the dissolution of the story itself. For, in place of narrative unfolding, we now hear a pressured staccato of snapshot images. Recounting takes on the language of immediacy and simultaneity rather than remembrance and duration: "*Here* was fire," said Victor, and *here* was always burning rubbish and *here* were always burning people. Reading from a diary entry in which she was recalling Birkenau, Paula spoke similarly:

> *This* is impossible. That I am here, on this earth, all by myself. That there is fire. That there are people. That there are bones. That there are the suffocated innocents. This is impossible: that ours, that mine, are there.

These images are terminal images. Each is suffused with the contradictory convictions of being both indelibly factual and "impossible": that is, impossible to accept as having anything to do with fact. Fully in the grasp of such memories, one either sees everything—and attempts, impossibly, to name it—or sees nothing. But the guiding perspective and selectivity we normally take for granted in seeing as in storytelling—distinguishing foreground and background, focus and periphery—are here dissolved. In the course of his recounting, Manny also came to terminal images—as in Victor's memory, of corpses and rubbish. Retelling his arrival at Auschwitz, an account he had given many times before, Manny abruptly paused:

> How do I describe the—, [long pause] corpses that were lying around there, like, like, like garbage? Or the stench. Or not knowing if you will be one of that group, marching. And tears, the separations from, from parents, from children, the agony—, the, the, the, the—, the sorrow. [pause] I don't know if there is a word. For the pain. [long pause] To describe—

And then he simply stopped trying.[22]

The death of the story can also rekindle the recounter's personal dissolution: a beginning to drown in awakened sorrow and agony that many survivors describe as dying itself. "You don't want to get into it to a deepness that you feel you cannot get out," Paula insisted. "The more you pull yourself into nonexistence—just, like being in midair—you don't always have the inner strength." In the diary entry in which she had remembered Birkenau, Paula described the "deepness" more fully. Following the images of bones, fire, and suffocated innocents, she wrote:

> My pen wants to go on and on by itself. It is sliding from my hand. At times like this my strength leaves me. It leaves me when I see it all again. When I see the truth once more.

If it were possible, Paula would continue to record what she recalls. But she is pulled too far into nonexistence. Seeing it all again, recounting falters and strength fails. Aharon Appelfeld wrote of such moments: "When the individual attempted merely to become aware of his own consciousness, he collapsed."[23]

The collapse of the recounter leads out to the deaths of all the others, although they were killed in such a way and on such a scale that remnants of personal meaning, rather than being obliterated, are here left strangely untouched. The suffering recalled in this circle of memory—mass, anonymous, unmitigated—is simply outside the scope of forms grounded in individual lives even provisionally to mediate, beyond leaving some mark of a horizon stretching beyond their own. "It was a landscape of death where, in effect, no one beheld it," said Leon, trying to indicate what remained outside all his stories and even outside their dissolution. For all that survivors strive to retell, no survivor conveys more than "the closing in of darkness for one particular individual," wrote Wiesel, "nothing more and perhaps much less."[24] Likewise, after completing his recounting of his second day in Treblinka, Victor repeatedly insisted: "But what is not told is *also* true; what they don't tell you is also true," trying to suggest a whole universe of atrocity of which the rubbish pit was only the tellable beginning.

For survivors, such tellable beginnings are as persistent as they are fragile. On one side, they are an assertion that something *can* be recounted with meaning and coherence. "It has to be described in human terms," said Leon, "It cannot *be* described otherwise. . . . So it has to be described in terms of the experiences of individuals." Through whatever "human terms" they can salvage, survivors compromise. They "make stories," Leon added, out of what is "not a story." But, along with their particular content, these stories are also stories about the death of stories, a death often re-created within them. And even that death is itself only the most provisional analogy for a vastly more encompassing end of creations.

Voices and Unfinished Sentences

To this point, we have considered recounting in terms of survivors retelling particular memories of the destruction. That is how we usually think of survivors' recounting, especially when formalized as "bearing witness" or "giving testimony." In fact, however, survivors retell more than specific incidents they witnessed and endured. They also convey what it is to *be* a survivor—to be a person who has such memories to retell—which includes what it is to be the particular survivor they each, individually, are. In the course of recounting, such self-presentations emerge in various ways: in survivors' direct reflections about who they are and what they have become; in the narrative identity each assumes while retelling; and, most implicitly, in the tones and cadences of their speech itself. Whether directly or indirectly, all these levels convey *who* is speaking when each speaks as a survivor—a dimension of recounting I refer to as each survivor's "voice."

Survivors' voices vary as much as survivors themselves. We shall hear some recounters who stand accusing and others who feel condemned; outspoken critics and those who speak for quiet compromise; defenders of continuing faith in either God or humanity and confessors to a totality of despair. Most of the participants, in fact, present both sides of such polarities, the initial opposite becoming more prominent as our conversations deepened. Here the point is that, whatever their content, survivors' voices are also "partial and provisional" forms that mediate their recounting. And, like survivors' stories of particular episodes, their voices, too, can be traced in two directions: both toward their rootedness in survivors' individual life histories and toward their reduction and, finally, dissolution within the Holocaust itself. Indeed, in their voices, survivors most directly juxtapose the words and meanings belonging to one world of memories with the screams and silences belonging to another.

On one side, then, survivors' voices are rooted in self-images and identifications, both positive and negative, that survivors carried well before they became "survivors." Their self-presentations as a rebel or an ingenue, an unmasker of tradition or its faithful inheritor, derive from relationships and memories of relationships with quite other authorities than their persecutors, and from quite other times. In fact, the whole realm of conflicts and identifications with parents, teachers, and communal tradition comes into play when survivors construct their own role as transmitters of memory. Their voices (like all voices) are an inheritance from other voices; really, from a whole world of voices to which they once belonged.

At the same time, here, too, we come to the following kinds of questions: What happens when an established and already conflicted identity as an "unmasker" meets, in Treblinka, both its confirmation as a requirement for survival (i.e., being able to "see through" the infinite ruses of the killers) *and* its terminal enactment by the killers (i.e., reducing one's people to rubbish)? Likewise, what happens to the "belle indifference" of an adolescent girl when such suppression of inner and outer data becomes, at Birkenau, both the only way of maintaining sanity while sorting the clothes (including her family's) of those already gassed *and* indelibly linked with the indifference of a world, looking on while the gassing and the sorting took place? And finally, what sorts of situations are these—at Treblinka or at Birkenau—where opposites like "seeing through everything" and "not seeing anything" can both represent survival within the destruction while, on another level of dissolved opposition, they can both represent the destruction itself?

Even while trying to find a path through such examples, we begin to feel an enclosing disorientation—the collapse of some distinctions and the oppressive hardening of others. For Paula, the survivor of Birkenau, being able, as she says, to "pull down the shade" and remain productive in her "own little world" continue to inform her voice and her reflections. She speaks for limits, for modest self-restraint, for "focusing on the good"—facets of her self-presentation supported both by her earlier development and by her experience of surviving. Yet none of this prevents her from also having flashes of accusatory rage when suddenly the "shade" is up. Usually in response to the indifference of others, this rage also has roots in Paula's personal past. But its expression provides no lasting relief. For, in the end, anger is no less reduced by association with the destruction than indifference. Distilled down to their most malign possibilities—the ones that Paula came to experience—both indifference and denunciation lead to the same ends: people being turned into stone or into ash or into both.

Within the closed circles of those memories, when Paula can no longer bear the self-constriction, and sometimes the guilt, of "pulling down the shade," her voice temporarily joins that of Victor, stripping away the masquerade. When Victor, as unmasker, can no longer tolerate a world devoid of faithfulness and trust, his voice joins that of Paula, choosing shadow over sight. Meanwhile, neither Paula nor Victor can drown out the

echoes of other shouts and silences—including those of the killers themselves.

Survivors' voices are thus compound voices. In some uncertain balance,
each contains both earlier identifications and their reductive transformations; both a primary theme and its opposite; echoes of both the murderers
and the dead. No wonder, then, that even the tones and rhythms of
survivors' voices often have a uniquely orchestral quality, reflecting that
complexity. They may be vibrant, intense, larger-than-life—as, in a certain
sense, they are. Yet the fuller they become, the more they risk breaking
against memories that no single voice can articulate. At these moments,
the silence comes not so much "between the words" as erupts within them,
sometimes taking them over again.

Lydia quite literally lost her voice during the destruction and only
gradually regained it during the years that followed. First, she recalled, she
had to learn again to scream. Over time, her screams again became
words—"salvaged words" in the most literal sense. And even now Lydia's
speech is punctuated by unexpected gaps and pauses that seem to pull at
her words and at her breath.

Lydia's experience is unique. But many other survivors similarly suggest
that the "closing in of darkness" was also a closing in of silence—ultimately,
a lived nightmare in which even screams were strangled. Wiesel's depiction
of the enclosing darkness, in fact, began as a description of suffocated
speech. Survivors' efforts to retell, he wrote, "are feeble, stammering,
unfinished, incoherent attempts to describe a single moment of being
painfully, excruciatingly alive—the closing in of darkness for one particular
individual, nothing more and perhaps much less." Beyond the individual
recounter's muting terror, a whole world of darkness remained, remembered
but not retold.

In an extraordinary series of reflections, Leon suggested that the very
essence of that world was silence—a "dead silence" in the literal sense. He
was recalling the day his work kommando was returning to the Radom
ghetto only hours after a murderous round-up. Suddenly, he paused:

> The scene coming back from the arms factory into the ghetto. And the
> grayness of the morning. And those dozens of bodies wherever you turned.
> We were scared and confused. Even the Ukrainian guards were scared and
> confused. . . .
>
> You're supposed to react! You're supposed to run up! And race! Yell!
> Scream! Utter! Emote! Show *anything* about it! Anything, whether it is—,
>
> Entering the ghetto in a dead silence. Those columns marching in. . . . It
> appears to be devoid of the human element, of the redeeming feature of a

human emotion. Maybe a poet can evoke something approaching it. But even sound, even sound would be out of place. There is no sound actually. There is no sound. It would have to be a silent poem.

Leon's explosion of words about the death of words is itself a responsive cry, and the redeeming emotion, of the sort that was suffocated at the time. He can talk about not being able to talk about it, and on that he is, in fact, brilliantly articulate. But the memory of the ghetto itself is essentially not described and, forever soundless, remains irreducibly alien to such attempts to invoke it. This was the context in which Leon concluded that it was "a landscape of death where, in effect, no one beheld it."

"The very voices which violate the silence after the destruction are signs of its antithesis," wrote Ezrahi, "of remaining life and possible bridges to the future." It should now be clear how radical that antithesis is. Leon revises Adorno's famous formulation (before Adorno's own revision): Auschwitz opposes poetry, not because it is poetry, but because it is sound.[25] And the opposition remains for other survivors as well. Ever present but unrecounted, the memories that inhabit survivors' silences can pull against their speech even when they are not speaking specifically about the destruction. Discussing one of the continuing costs of guarding herself from the "deepness"—a loss of many of her memories from *before* the Holocaust—Paula commented:

> I pull down the shade. I'm not able to sort out the good and the bad. Because everything becomes, like, under one heading. The whole life is one category. The past, my wonderful childhood, and the nice memories—it's just wishful thinking but not a vision. . . . So it's all blocked out. It's not sorted out. It's kind of incoherent, just like my thoughts. It goes from—it's an unfinished sentence. I can write just a simple letter, and I never feel the sentence is completed. Because I'm ahead to the next one already. So I don't know if I come across clearly. Even in everyday. I know what I want to say, but I don't know if *you* know what I want to say.

Further on, we shall see that Paula has more access to her earlier memories than "wishful thinking" or "imagining" suggest. Likewise, her thoughts are far from "incoherent" much of the time, especially when she feels she is in the presence of listeners who want to hear what she does want to say. Still, as a general expression of survivors' sense that there is perpetually something left unspoken—memories demanding articulation but undoing any such attempt—Paula's metaphor of the chronically "unfinished sentence" cannot be surpassed.

Lives as Texts: Retelling and Enactment

Every story survivors retell implies a voice: the voice of its recounter. Similarly, every voice implies a wider story: the story *of* that voice and of the individual life it articulates. In these pages, those wider stories, survivors' accounts of their ongoing lives, are also considered to be part of their recounting. Here they attempt to retell not only their experiences during the Holocaust, or their identities as recounters, but the status of their survival itself. In Ezrahi's phrase, they tell us what, for them, does constitute "remaining life and possible bridges to the future." As would be expected from what has preceded, they also tell us about remaining deaths and recurrent returns to the past. For, like their stories and their voices, survivors' accounts of their continuing lives also take form between meaning's creation and dissolution—ultimately between life and death themselves.

As noted with regard to survivors' voices, these wider self-presentations are typically not viewed as part of survivors' recounting at all. Survivors' reflections on their continuing faiths or aspirations, for example, are usually summarized as just that: survivors' "reflections" or "philosophies of life" or developed "ways of coping." Alternatively, survivors' expressions of guilt or despair are typically viewed in psychiatric terms—as symptoms of what they endured. Once again, it is only their retelling particular events—their directly "bearing witness"— that is taken as their recounting.

Undoubtedly, these categories have a certain usefulness. However, it is essential to the understanding of recounting developed here that we move beyond them. For if it is true, as Leon said, that at the heart of his memories "even sound" is "out of place"—or, as Paula said, that "even in everyday," her sentences are left unfinished—then *all* survivors' words evoking those memories are balanced against that silence. Those words include survivors' accounts of "symptoms" now no less than their accounts of episodes then; their reflections on the destruction as a whole no less than their retelling particular events. All of these are ways of giving voice and meaning to what lives on, for survivors, as the negation of voice and meaning. Still following Leon, all are part of recounters' efforts to "make stories" and find "human terms."

In the case of survivors' accounts of their ongoing lives, Leon's descriptions are particularly apt. Compared with the memories that are their background, expressions of guilt or despair, for example, *are* comprehensible "human terms." Notwithstanding their own anguish, they stand as still communicable cries of the heart salvaged from a terror in which even screams were strangled. Likewise, even at their most disfiguring, they remain analogies *for* that greater death. As I shall elucidate, they are remnants of personal meaning, rooted in memories in which guilt and despair *do* have meaning, which persist to give form to memories in which they do not.

Indeed, retelling some aspect of their own story, as survivors, is a very common way that survivors construct a tellable account. Leon cannot directly describe the scene in the ghetto, but he can convey his own story, as a man of words, who cannot find the words to retell *that*. Commenting on such reflexive shifts from the incommunicable memory to the efforts of the recounter, Elie Wiesel has noted how often the "story of the messenger" becomes the story "of the messenger unable to deliver his message."[26] This is true, in fact, in Wiesel's own writing, which far more often tells the stories of struggling witnesses than it attempts to describe the destruction to which they were witness.

Recounters' stories about their ongoing lives—their struggle with guilt, for example, or their struggle to retell—thus serve a function similar to the stories they "make" about particular incidents: the creation of accounts that are tellable at all. At the same time, there is often a more specific relationship between survivors' stories that retell specific episodes and those that retell a wider life. As we shall hear, especially as we listen to Victor's several stories, the story of an incident and the story of a life may be, in essence, the same story—structured by the same salvaged meanings, unfolding according to the same trajectory, containing the same cast of characters. Thus the destinies of an unmasking prosecutor, and of those unmasked, figure in all the stories that Victor retells. Evidence is brought forth, secrets are revealed, whether they are the secrets of the killers, of an absent God, or of Victor himself. Whatever the context, what we hear are Victor's repeated attempts to retell his own story—or, more accurately, his attempts to make a single story out of all that he remembers.

For some survivors, the attempt to find "human terms" for memory involves more than stories that are told. It also involves stories that are lived: *enactments* of personal guilt or rage that use, as their media, the contents and contexts of survivors' ongoing lives themselves.[27] Thus Reuben gives form to his memories of one ghetto through his daily visits to another—and through his now self-imposed inability to leave. Wondering why he has not moved his store out of a decaying area of the inner city, he reflected:

> Sometimes, I was thinking to myself, you know, unconsciously, maybe I didn't want to move out. I could have moved out. I could have moved out during that time. I mean, to a different neighborhood . . . because over there

it's very depressed, you know, the boarded-up buildings. From the riots in the city. After the riots in the city . . . I don't know. It reminds me sometimes of the ghetto—, everything like, it's a—, a lot like in the ghetto. Everything was boarded-up. And ruined. You know what I mean. Maybe, maybe I'm punishing myself. I don't know. It could be. I don't know.

As Reuben both lives and retells his story of the ghetto (and of his guilt), so Victor lives, as well as recounts, his story of unmasking. He confided that over the past several years he had been repetitively rereading the Bible, searching for contradictions, omissions, damning evidence. Victor explained:

I read it over. I read it over twelve times, the Old Testament. . . . I feel that when I sit down at the Bible I am a prosecutor. And the Bible is the material that I am trying to find something to criticize it, to criticize . . .

I was still interested in my background. But besides this, I say, "God, where are you? Are you dumb? Are you deaf? You don't see nothing! Are you blind? Or are you *not at all?*"

So why does these people fool me? Why so many thousands of generations want to put down the knowledge of religion, the authority of God, and the knowledge of everything about the way to live? Why the Ten Com - mandments? Why *everything?* Why was this bluffing going on?

Determined not to be fooled again, Victor makes his own war on narrative tradition. *His* story becomes the tale of a prosecutor of stories, and his life becomes his text.

How should we understand these sketches of Reuben and Victor? Reuben himself suggests a psychiatric interpretation—that he "unconsciously didn't want to move out" because of unconscious self-punishment—and certainly that is the way we most typically do understand stories like Reuben's. Indeed, as will be considered at length in the next chapter, constructing psychological narratives about survivors—and especially about their guilt—has become one of *our* most typical ways to "make a story" about what they have endured.[28] Thus we are inclined to agree with Reuben. His daily visits to the inner city and his inability to leave do appear to be a striking example of "survivor guilt." In the same vein, we would suggest that Victor may be "acting out" his aggression through his prosecution; perhaps also "identifying with the aggressor" in making himself the prosecutor in the first place. Through such interpretations, we do, indeed, have stories for what Victor and Reuben tell us—stories which are familiar, coherent, and above all, finished.

I emphasize these points in order to underline how different are the consequences when we view lived stories like Reuben's and Victor's, not as "symptoms" of the Holocaust, but as part of their attempts to recount it. Once again, instead of having finished texts and complete stories, we would be only at the beginning of understanding. For, within the recounting perspective, the significance of these accounts is not in what Reuben and Victor *can* retell or *do* enact. It is rather that, notwithstanding their own real pain, all such stories and enactments point to agonies that are *not* thereby retold. Ultimately, we realize that we are listening to analogies: metaphors, sculpted out of the shapes of individual lives themselves, for memories that are far more terrible than one man's self-punishment or another's prosecution.[29]

For all the continuing pain that Reuben's and Victor's stories do suggest, they remain analogies in exactly this sense. While the ruins Reuben does not leave "remind" him of the ghetto, and are even "a lot like in the ghetto," the inner city is *not* the ghetto. Likewise, however "unconscious" the forces that hold him, Reuben tells us he stays by choice: "I could have moved out"; "maybe I didn't want to move out." No such choice characterized his original imprisonment. Indeed, Reuben tells us that the very capacity to "want" was then destroyed:

> First you were weak. You were half-dead. You didn't have no, no strength anymore. No desire to fight. Even to live anymore, you know what I mean? . . . I mean, that's the way they did it. You had no desire, no strength, nothing. You lost your courage. You lost everything.

Emerging out of this totality of loss, Reuben's story is an act of will *against* the terminal despair. At its core, it is an act of loyalty and willed remembrance modeled on other such acts that Reuben recalls—ones in which guilt and self-questioning *do* retain their meaning. Reuben cites as antecedent for his own story another story of recurrent returns to a grave. He recounted:

> Have you heard of Rabbi Nahman of Bratslav? He was the only Hasidic rabbi, the grandson of the Baal Shem Tov. He was buried in Uman. Uman, that's in Russia, you know. So his Hasidim, they used to call them "Teute Hasidim." You know what "teute" means? Dead. The "Dead Hasidim." After he died, maybe two hundred fifty years ago, the Hasidim never named another rabbi. Usually, if a rabbi dies, they name his son, or grandson, or somebody as a rabbi, somebody as the leader. After Reb Nahman of Bratslav died, they never named another rabbi after him. They used to go only to the grave.

That's why they call them "Teute Hasidim," because they have a dead rabbi. They used to have a song. In Yiddish it rhymes, "Why should we worry what's going to be tomorrow? Let's worry what we did wrong yesterday." Maybe we can do right, what we did wrong yesterday. Maybe we can do right about it.

However compromised the analogy, Reuben has a story in which to situate, and through which to retell, his own. There have been other unprecedented losses, leading to precedented refusals to move on or to move out.

Victor's story also has its antecedent, just as it, too, is only analogic. For all the intensity of his prosecuting, it remains qualified by a fidelity and a possible reconciliation totally absent from the terminal unmaskings he remembers. Above all, between Victor and God, the confrontation is *not* terminal. Quite unlike that between killer and victim, here there is still time and the possibility of a healing future that time allows. And that means that Victor still *can* ask his questions. At least that story, the story of such questions, is not completely meaningless and finished. In fact, Victor tells us it is a quite ancient story. Many others have questioned the loyalty, and the existence, of the other partner in the Covenant. Victor identifies with Maimonides, another "revealer of secrets." Said Victor:

> When Maimonides wrote his books, he revealed a lot of things that Jewish geniuses—ones before—did not reveal. But Maimonides said, "Since no one before me revealed it, and I know it, if I will not reveal it, maybe I will die with a heavy heart, that I didn't reveal it. So I take it upon my body, and my soul, the sin. And I will open the secrets now. And put it in print."

As Reuben finds continuity in the legend of those who question themselves, Victor draws on the tradition of those who question outwardly. Following Maimonides, his story becomes an experiment in how much fact can be revealed and fidelity remain intact. More particularly, it is an experiment in how much death can be revealed and the story itself survive.

The answer, for both Reuben and Victor, is only so much. As in survivors' voices and their stories of particular incidents, the capacity to give form to the nightmare is strictly limited. If survivors attempt to retell more, meanings become burdened, reduced, and sometimes fully consumed. When lives are texts, that reduction and dissolution are that much more palpable, and that much more disfiguring.

In Reuben's story, this process of reduction is particularly evident. Originally he had wanted to recount his memories in the form of an actual story, a narrative written rather than lived. It was this, a novel he had begun, that was to have been his act of remembrance. Said Reuben:

> To me, writing the story, would be, like a monument to the—, to the Jewish people. The way they lived, and the way they worked, and the way they dealt with people. I mean, how it was. How happy they were, how sad they were, at different times.

Within the world he remembers, what Reuben calls the "whole life" of Jewish culture before the destruction, he sought his "human terms." Indeed, these memories from normal times were quite literally to be a mediating frame that Reuben hoped to build around the other memories he carries. He explained:

> I tried to write a few times. Not a, history, or documents. But I tried to write a novel around it, *around* it . . . I tried to write a novel, not about the Holocaust, just about the whole, *the whole life*, before the Holocaust, with the Holocaust included. You know what I mean, the whole life. How it was . . . a novel around different characters. How it was.

Reuben never wrote his novel. He said he stopped partly because of the pure pain of trying to remember: "You have to live it through, back again. You have to concentrate, and go back in again." In particular, he suggests that the totality of his loss—the destruction of an entire people and their world—was simply beyond the scope of his story or his strength: "You're uprooted—completely. You're lost—completely. Everything. The Jewish people—it's never going to be like it was anymore. . . . It's lost. . . . I'm lost too." Finally, Reuben suggested that, even if he could have written his novel, he would not easily have found responsive readers. "Who knows what goes on in people's minds?" he asked—but he did not hesitate to list pity, indifference, and outright rejection as some of the responses he anticipated.

Thus, between the depths of an inner silence and the expectation of an outward one, Reuben's pages lay unfinished. Yet this did not mean that his effort to give form to his memories came to an end. Rather, as I have suggested, the shape of his *individual* "whole life" became the medium of his recounting. The story Reuben now lives became his testament and his monument. Mediated by his guilt, his ghetto, and the legend of the Dead Hasidim, this *is* still a story. A whole world of agony is translated into a pain (self-punishment) that can be given voice; one set of ruins stands for another; a single grave in Uman represents millions of graves that exist nowhere. But, as a result of these translations, the story Reuben lives is more obscure, more private, and certainly more personally disfiguring than the one he might have written.

Death as Context

Stories like Reuben's bring us back to the concepts and contradictions that have been central from the beginning of this discussion. Meanings are salvaged from their own dissolution. They somehow live on to frame even the memory of that dissolution, to give it voice and form. But, even in the course of those re-creations, voices and forms continue to be disfigured by the memories they attempt to convey. Stories lead to a staccato of snapshot images. Words are distorted by screams and silences. Lives become replicas of deaths.

There is, finally, one last concept and one last "even" that needs to be repeated: that the deaths survivors know also live on. They persist, not only as re-created, but as the irreducible antitheses of all the modes of recounting; so that even when survivors' retelling is most burdened and disfigured, it remains only the tellable beginning of much more. Thus the dissolution of stories points to a more profound ending than the breakdown of narrative. Unfinished sentences point to a more consuming silence than their own gaps and pauses. Guilt or despair, however disfiguring to their bearer, point to more encompassing agony than anything still expressible through the language of individual hearts and lives.

What is it to carry such memories and never be able to retell them; for *all* one's sentences to be essentially unfinished? Such a situation jeopardizes our most basic assumptions about the integrative potential of human communication: that, somehow and eventually, even the worst terrors can be conveyed. But even more difficult to hear truly is what survivors tell us about the integrity of lived experience, of life itself. "Torture blocks out the contradiction of death and allows us to experience it personally," wrote Jean Amery, and "whoever was tortured stays tortured."[30] Wiesel insisted: "The problem is not: to be or not to be. But rather: to be and not to be."[31] Elsewhere, Wiesel wrote of one of his characters:

> Michael felt suddenly that someone was standing behind him. He turned abruptly: no one. And yet he felt a presence in the room, even an odor, an awareness. Only then did he understand that death is something other, something more, than the simple absence of life. Life may quit a body, a consciousness, but death does not necessarily follow. Just as death may invade a creature even though life has not yet departed.[32]

The personification of death as "other" is older than literature itself. But what is crucial to hear in this passage are the transformations of that metaphor. Someone becomes something. The language becomes increasingly sensory and organic—a presence, an odor, an awareness. Death is no longer the inheritor of life or simply life's absence. Rather, death itself is lived. It is an independent co-presence palpable at life's core. Writing about her struggle to awaken from a nightmare, Charlotte Delbo described death's awakening as well: "The pain is so unbearable, so exactly the pain I suffered there, that I feel it again physically, I feel it through my whole body. . . . I feel death seizing me, I feel myself die."[33]

I have suggested that the "closing in of darkness" was a closing in of silence. It may now be added that it was also a closing in of death: the physical death that is the terminus of trauma; the deaths of meaning and belonging; the deaths of all the others; immersion in a "landscape of death" that many survivors describe as the death of everything, "the death of creation."[34] As experienced, these levels tend to fuse, so that the terror of the soul's disintegration resonates immediately with the terror of the imminent destruction of the flesh, and one's individual death evokes the death of a people and a world. But however manifest, death remains active, constitutive of memory, and ready to consume again the life with which it co-exists. Thus there is one more irreducible contradiction that we must manage to accommodate. It is not only between meaning's creation and dissolution or between speech and silence that survivors' recounting takes form. It also takes form between ongoing life and ongoing death themselves.

Of all the images that might be made or borrowed to express these contradictions, and to suggest the fate of recounting within them, the most vivid is, once again, one of Paula's. It comes at the end of this section because, in one simple series of sentences, Paula captured virtually all that has been discussed in many complicated ones: the simultaneous persistence and dissolution of forms in survivors' recounting, the resulting transformation of those forms into "salvaged remnants," and the unprecedented quality of the new relationship between those remnants and their ever-present negation. Further, to make her image, Paula drew on the symbol that has most universally represented persistence of form and life in individuals, families, and creations: "a beautiful tree."

I saw a beautiful tree the other day, all chopped up. But the curves are still there. The inside is completely hollow. It's still beautiful. And it's a beautiful sight to me. Whenever I drive by that street, I look for that tree. And they don't cut it down. It's still there. For years. It's an odd-shaped tree, with no roots, and completely hollow. I don't know if I make the comparison—, the tree doesn't speak. It's living there. I mean, living without living. It's hollow inside. There's no vigor to it. But the shape is still there.

A beautiful tree / all chopped up / curves still there / completely hollow / still beautiful, a beautiful sight / odd-shaped, with no roots, completely hollow / living there / without living / the shape is still there—nine turns, nine contradictions, all there and all true. Here, they are miraculously captured within a single image. But they are not resolved in any of the stories and voices we shall hear or in any of the lives we shall come to know.

FROM MOUTH TO EAR

Elie Wiesel has said of recounting: "The truth will never be written. Like the *Talmud*, it will be transmitted from mouth to ear, from eye to eye."[35] To the degree that *Talmud* suggests a traditional image of transmission like "Mi Y'Malel," it is one more analogy that will not hold. For the Holocaust, we have no sacred text to recite and no laws of conduct whose meaning might be enlivened by interpretation. Rather, the only stories and meanings we have are remnants of those we already knew, now more burdened than before. We have whatever "curves and shapes" are "still there," even while the tree is rootless, hollow, and dead.

Still, out of such remnants, the attempt to retell has continued. For survivors, it continues in all their efforts to create some text for their memories. Thus they construct stories for what cannot be retold by any story. They initiate sentences that remain unfinished. They strive to give voice, and sometimes the "curves and shapes" of their lives themselves, to what lives on as the negation of voice and life. They re-create deaths and silences through the media of other deaths and silences.

The forms of recounting that result are provisional and precarious, completely unlike immutable scripture. Yet I think it is precisely this incompleteness that *is* at the heart of Wiesel's analogy. "The truth will never be written." Nor, finally, will it be transmitted in any other way. But, through words that come from mouths rather than books, there is at least the possibility of pointing more tangibly to what cannot be retold. In actual speech, we hear silence as an abrupt halt, a gasp for breath, the agonized deliberation around the choice of a single word. The problem of "the unspeakable" becomes someone's struggle for words, and someone's failure to find them. Encountering the efforts of a particular person to juxtapose memory of the Holocaust with the meanings of a single life, and recognizing those meanings as the "human terms" of our own lives, we begin to enter into the impossible juxtaposition of any single life with such destruction. The intimate particularity of the former throws into starkest relief the absolute impersonality of the latter.

Within these pages, it remains impossible to re-create the experience of listening to recounting in embodied immediacy. But, as much as may be possible, this work does emulate listening "eye to eye" and "mouth to ear." That is why it moves *toward* encounters with particular survivors rather than away from them. The discussion to this point is preparation: an attempt to ready us as we listen to survivors more and more directly.

It is this demand for sustained engagement that is most talmudic. Adin Steinsaltz has written of the *Talmud*: "It is impossible to arrive at external knowledge of this work. . . . The student must participate intellectually and emotionally in the talmudic debate, himself becoming, to a certain degree, a creator."[36] Here it is survivors' recounting, and the inner debate between words and memory, for which there is no real "external knowledge." To learn genuinely its forms and inhabit its contradictions—its "principles of incoherence" in Lawrence Langer's excellent phrase[37]—we, too, must participate; becoming, to a certain degree, fellow recounters.

Chapter 2

The Context of Recounting: Survivors and Their Listeners

The need to tell our story to "the rest," to make "the rest" participate in it, had taken on for us, before the liberation and after, the character of an immediate and violent impulse.

Primo Levi, *Survival in Auschwitz*

STORIES *ABOUT* SURVIVORS

"I saw a beautiful tree the other day, all chopped up," says Paula. The tree was "living," though "living without living." What sense do we make of sentences such as these? Is it the tree's beauty, its continuity of curves and shape, or its devastation that we should attend to? Is it life or death that the tree predominantly suggests? Can we say the tree is half-dead? Or only half-alive? Clearly, it is neither. The tree, rootless and hollow, died long ago; it has been dead "for years." And yet it is "living there," an object of beauty and personal affirmation that Paula always looks for when she drives down that street. In the midst of such contradictions, we search for some resolution—a compromise, a synthesis, a third way out.

In this chapter, I turn to some of the ways we have sought resolution. That is, I will discuss some of our own "stories" about survivors and about what they have to tell us. Like the previous chapter, this chapter is also preparatory. Its bearing on our overall purposes is two-fold. First, if we are to enter into survivors' struggles with irreducible contradictions, we ought to consider how we have made sense of the life and the death which, to us, their survival represents. "Represents" is the right word. For holding on to both sides of the antithesis has not been easy, and we have tended to identify survivors with one side or the other and make it the whole. Thus, focusing on death, survivors have been depicted as silent victims—guilty, ghostly, and estranged. Focusing on ongoing life—the fact of survival itself—the same survivors are celebrated as heroic witnesses, tellers of tales, redeemers of the human spirit and of hope. As I shall describe, each of these poles has generated its own discourse, rhetorics that are now invoked almost automatically in public reference to survivors. But whichever side is emphasized, the actual antitheses within which survivors live, and out of which their recounting emerges, are missed. And that means, lost behind a wall of fearful or hopeful images, survivors and what they have to tell us are also missed.

Notwithstanding the surge of interest in survivors' testimony in recent years, this tendency to turn survivors into symbols of the Holocaust—really, symbols of our own fears and wishes in response to the Holocaust—remains strong. Indeed, I will suggest that popular response to survivors may be becoming increasingly ritualized, with more and more talk *about* survivors but not necessarily more sustained talk *with* them. Thus we still have a very difficult time entering into survivors' recounting, and that is the second reason for this chapter. For I shall argue that, for survivors, finding listeners *is* the issue. That is, they do not search for form and meaning for the sake of form and meaning.[1] They do so in hope of being heard. And without some faith in that possibility, survivors do not recount at all.

In this chapter, then, we add a level of complexity to our discussion of retelling the Holocaust. Survivors' recounting now emerges within a *double* transaction: an inner dialogue, always embattled, between survivors' speech and survivors' memories, and an outer dialogue, almost as contested, between survivors and their listeners.

The Tellable and the Hearable

Survivors do not recount in a vacuum but always to an actual or imagined audience of listeners. What survivors say, how they say it, whether they say it at all, will depend, in part, on their perceptions of those listeners, as well as on the ways the listeners have made their own hopes, fears, and expectations known. A consideration of listeners—like a consideration of meaning and form—thus becomes essential to the interpretation of survivors' recounting.[2]

Of course, to say that survivors' retelling is affected by survivors' listeners—or by survivors' perceptions of their listeners—may be a truism of only limited usefulness. Do survivors sometimes shape their recounting to meet what they perceive their listeners need or want to hear? Yes, sometimes they do. Do survivors sometimes retell with relative indifference to their listeners' expectations? Yes, sometimes they do. Do survivors, at times, shape their retelling directly to challenge—indeed, to protest—their listeners' presumptions? Yes, that is also sometimes true. Survivors' recounting is affected by survivors' listeners and by survivors' perceptions of their listeners. But it is very difficult to predict how those effects will play out in any individual case.

Understanding this, however, one can still discuss specific examples of the interplay between survivors' search for *some* viable way to give voice to their memories and their choice of a *particular* way in light of their reading of their listeners. Further, because listeners never appear to survivors completely *de novo*, but, accurately or not, will tend to be perceived as more or less typical of listeners of that time and place, certain ways of resolving the double transaction also become typical. To say it more simply: Certain forms of recounting tend to evolve that are, simultaneously, more or less tellable by survivors and more or less hearable by others.

"Survivor Guilt" in Narrative Context

As a single example, survivors' accounts and expressions of guilt may be exactly such a form. Aaron Hass has noted that "for many social scientists, survivor guilt has been an integral aspect in their sketches of the postwar Holocaust survivor." However, a number of studies, including Hass's own, raise doubt about the ubiquity of survivor guilt—"not quite so widespread as we have been led to believe," Hass himself concludes.[3] Indeed, the best known instance of a survivor's own reflection on guilt, Primo Levi's extraordinary chapter, "Shame," in *The Drowned and the Saved*, becomes less and less about guilt or shame at all—at least in the usual individual-psychological senses. While Levi opens with the kind of reflections often associated with survivor guilt—that one's life came at the cost of others' deaths, that one might have done more to help or to resist—he arrives by the end of the chapter at despair on an entirely different scale. Reminiscent of Leon's landscape "devoid of redeeming emotion," Levi speaks of the "atavistic anguish" of an abandoned Creation itself—a "deserted and empty universe" void of *any* human responsiveness or care—and then of the "vaster shame, the shame of the world" in which the taint of such betrayal and such destruction was now irrevocable.[4] His discussion thus moves from individual self-questioning to a failing at a completely other level. It is also near the end of the essay that Levi specifically protests one-dimensional invocations of survivor guilt to explain survivors' motivations—and, in particular, their impulse to retell. "I do not believe that psychoanalysts (who have pounced upon our tangles with professional avidity) are competent to explain this impulse," Levi wrote. "Their interpretations. . . seem to me approximate and simplifed, as if someone wished to apply the theorems of plane geometry to the solution of spheric triangles."[5]

Why, then, such avidity on the part of survivors' listeners—professional and otherwise? And, conversely, why *do* many survivors express guilt, as many certainly do, even if less frequently than we tend to assume? With regard to the survivors' side, I have suggested that survivors speak in such terms in part because they are, in fact, speakable. As I noted in the context of Reuben's stories, guilt can function as a metaphor in survivors' recounting. Notwithstanding all its own anguish, it may also be an analogy for agonies that are not so easily retold. Thus it is not unusual, in the course of recounting, for a survivor to approach the memory of an unredeemed outward horror and then suddenly to switch to a memory evoking self-recrimination or self-doubt.[6] The pain of such questioning is real. But it also seems that the inner, moral horror recasts the outward, mortal horror into a somehow more bearable and retellable form. Perhaps this is because there simply are no words for the latter—even Primo Levi struggles and finally stops. Perhaps it is also because, relative to the absolute negation of traumatic terror, guilt provides some leeway. Guilt does not leave one completely without agency and is not itself completely without meaning. Some future atonement, reconciliation, or redemption are still at least conceivable—however distant they may seem. Within deadly terror, however—all-consuming helplessness, unqualified hopelessness—meaning, personal agency, the future itself, also die.[7] Thus Shamai Davidson suggested that, through guilt, survivors reestablish continuity with *non*-Holocaust memories. Guilt can provide, he noted, a "restoration of the pre-Holocaust psyche, with its old conflicts, clashes, and hopes" and a re-creation of "the internalized world of childhood that was obliterated during the Holocaust."[8] In the terms of this discussion, survivors' self-questioning is a remnant salvaged from memories in which guilt still *does* have meaning, partly in order to mediate the retelling, and the bearing, of memories in which it does not.

To borrow Levi's metaphor, then, survivors themselves must sometimes use "plane geometry" to describe "spheric triangles": Key dimensions are lost, the essence may be missed, but it may also be the best one can do. Narratives of guilt thus become a typical way that survivors "make a story" for the "not-story," even, as Leon added, "with all the frustration" such compromises entail.

On our side, as listeners, we do not experience the frustration. We, therefore, tend to accept such compromised constructions as the *whole* story. Further, when we accept them with particular "avidity," as Levi describes, there may be other motives at work. On one level, guilt is simply a more familiar emotion than the extremity of terror and loss that most survivors know. It is also a less challenging one. For certainly it is easier for us to accommodate the guilty survivor than the utterly abandoned survivor or the rageful, indicting survivor. The pain that the guilty survivor directs inward is kept outside for us—it neither directly shames us nor directly shames the world, indeed the Creation, of which we are a part. However empathic we may be, survivors' guilt remains their problem, not ours.[9]

Further, as I have suggested, the concept of survivor guilt is itself part of a more general psychiatric discourse that has defined one of the primary ways survivors have been perceived during the years since liberation. Following Hass, one could say that survivor guilt has not only been "integral" in sketches of the postwar Holocaust survivor, it has been virtually constitutive. From *The Pawnbroker*, a film that ends with a survivor's self-crucifixion, to the doomed and agonized Sophie of *Sophie's Choice*, to the self-destroying couple of *Enemies: A Love Story*, the survivor guilt story is the story *about* survivors we have been prone to retell. Survivors' own expressions of guilt thus confirm this central paradigm.[10]

Narratives centered on guilt, then, may be one instance of the way a form of testimony emerges that, relative to other possibilities, is particularly speakable by survivors and particularly hearable by us. In so evolving, the phenomenon of guilt, though certainly real for many survivors, may take on an exaggerated significance in some survivors' accounts and, even more so, in our own accounts *about* survivors' accounts. Aware of the resulting distortion, some survivors, like Levi, will protest. As listeners, we will tend to ignore such protests or dismiss them as simply rhetorical—perhaps one more ceremonial bow to "the unspeakable" with little substantive import. We thereby mistake the part for the whole, the analogy for the thing itself, and, once again, take as the "last word" what would otherwise be only the tellable beginning.

A correlate of this is that when the contexts of recounting are especially constricted or ritualized—one-time "oral history" interviews, for example, or formal "bearing witness"—retelling is particularly liable to remain superficial. Without a developing and deepening conversation, and the revising and elucidating that conversation brings, we are most likely to conclude that our presumptions have been confirmed. Hearing what we expect, we are unlikely to hear anything more.

A Context of Expectations

In the remainder of this chapter, I turn to a more general review of our expectations of survivors as these have evolved during the half-century since liberation. Inevitably, this means painting with very broad strokes. I speak here of tendencies—habitual ways we orient ourselves when we know we will be listening to survivors. I say "habitual" because so much in these ways has become ritualized, as I shall describe. Still, my aim is to suggest overall trends rather than attend to the variety of manifestations and exceptions they always embrace.

This also means I will be focusing increasingly on our side of recounting rather than on survivors'. For the task here is to trace the broader contexts of expectations within which survivors, as recounters, have had to dwell.

THE EARLY YEARS: CRYING ALONE

As is becoming better known, there was very little interest in survivors or in their recounting during the first decades after liberation. The widespread collection of survivor testimony, the creation of commemorative programs, and most of the academic and creative projects related to survivors did not significantly begin until the late 1970s—more than thirty years after the destruction.[11] What is perhaps less well known is that there was not simply an absence, a vacuum of responsiveness, in the earlier years, but an active process of suppression and stigmatization. Perhaps also less known is the response of survivors themselves to the silencing they experienced.

Before survivors became "the survivors," they were known by other names. For many years in this country, they were "the refugees," the "greeners" (greenhorns), or simply "the ones who were there." Associated with the horrifying newsreels of the liberated camps (even though many had survived in hiding, in the armed resistance, or under a false identity and had never been in a camp), they evoked a shifting combination of pity, fear, revulsion, and guilt.[12] In general, they were isolated and avoided. Elie Wiesel summarized:

> As they reentered the world, they found themselves in another kind of exile, another kind of prison. People welcomed them with tears and sobs, then turned away. I don't mean parents or close friends; I speak of officialdom, of the man in the street. I speak of all kinds of men and women who treated them as one would sick and needy relatives. Or else as specimens to be observed and to be kept apart from the rest of society by invisible barbed wire. They were disturbing misfits who deserved charity, but nothing else.[13]

During these years, then, to be singled out as a Holocaust survivor meant to be singled out indeed. Manny recalled the way he was singled out and known:

> People would meet me and say, "OHHHHH! Did you know that he was in a concentration camp?!" That's all it was left to! Nobody asked about it. Nobody asked, "How was it there?" Just, "He was in a concentration camp." It was pity; that was that. "This is my nephew," my uncle would introduce me, "you know, *he* was in a concentration camp."

"That's all it was left to," one must assume, because in these years, that said it all.

Clearly, nothing in these attitudes would have encouraged survivors' recounting or any of the kind of public occasions for "bearing witness" that were to evolve later. While there was a flurry of testimony in the immediate aftermath of the war—and again during the period of the Eichmann Trial in 1961—the receptivity of listeners was short-lived.[14] In fact, many survivors recall being directly silenced, even when—in spite of all—they did try to talk about it. Manny continued:

> I personally would have felt much better if I could have talked about it. I didn't feel that I couldn't. Nobody cared. I mean, people, everybody was talking that they didn't want to hear about it. They didn't want to listen. No, they said, "We heard about it." Or, "We don't want to hear about it because we saw the newsreels." . . .
>
> We felt very uncomfortable suppressing it all the time. And dreaming about it. And having nightmares about it. It may sound silly, but I heard this expression when I first came to this country: "When you laugh, everybody laughs with you. When you cry, you cry by yourself." And that's exactly what we did.

Strangely enough, quite a number of survivors recall this particular song lyric about laughing together and crying alone. It must have epitomized the spirit of adjustment, putting the past behind one, moving on—the spirit, in short, of the times.

The Dream of Recounting

Typically, these years of silencing are discussed in terms of a "conspiracy of silence"—the notion that, just as others were not yet ready to hear, survivors themselves were not yet ready to speak. It is difficult to generalize. Without question, most survivors were hesitant, for all the reasons that have been discussed. Recounting meant finding words and voice where words and voice fail. It risked reentering "the deepness." It led to listeners' misunderstandings, resistance, and, sometimes, outright rejection. To many survivors, therefore, the prospect of recounting suggested futility and, potentially, real agony. But equally agonizing was the prospect of *not* recounting. Primo Levi insisted that, even before liberation, the drive to retell was "an immediate and violent impulse," a "primary need."[15] And we have heard Manny say that he would have wanted to speak about it; that he himself could have spoken about it.

Ultimately, we contend here, as elsewhere, with contradictions that are never resolved. Thus it is neither the case that survivors "wanted to talk about it" or that "they didn't want to talk about it." In most instances, survivors wanted both, both at once, without resolution or synthesis. Elie Wiesel said of his memories: "It is as impossible to speak of them as not to speak of them."[16] Within these twin impossibilities, survivors' recounting takes form, as it takes form within the other contradictions we have considered.

Indeed, there is a closer relationship between the forms of recounting and the motivation to do so. Survivors' recounting is not only made of remnants but is itself a kind of remnant. Whatever the specific motives in retelling—to remember the dead, to warn the living, to indict the killers, to document the crime—every act of recounting, really by definition, is premised on the possibility of responsive listeners. But since it is the landscape of death and silence that is remembered, that premise is not given, or supported, by the Holocaust itself. Like the forms and meanings in survivors' recounting, the belief in listeners must also be salvaged from other memories, from elsewhere.[17]

In the midst of the destruction, therefore, the hope of being heard was salvaged most often in imagination: in dreams and daydreams in which listeners and meanings were recurrently salvaged, and lost, together. Primo Levi retold such a dream from his time in Auschwitz. His account is worth reviewing in detail because of how clearly he captures the relationship between his surviving ability to give form to his experiences—in this case, to recount them through the meanings and stories *of* a dream—and his surviving capacity to imagine listeners.

Having described the nightly scene of prisoners crowding into the block's wooden bunks, Levi recalled:

> So I adapt myself to lie like this, forced into immobility, half-lying on the wooden edge. Nevertheless I am so tired and stunned that I, too, soon fall asleep, and I seem to be sleeping on the tracks of a railroad.

The train is about to arrive: one can hear the panting engine, it is my neighbor. I am not yet so asleep as not to be aware of the double nature of the engine. . . . My sleep is very light, it is a veil, if I want I can tear it. I will do it, I want to tear it, so that I can get off the railway track. Now I am awake: but not really awake, only a little more, one step higher on the ladder between the unconscious and the conscious. . . . I can register noises: I am sure that the distant whistle is real, it does not come from an engine in a dream, it can be heard objectively. . . . This whistle is an important thing and in some ways essential: we have heard it so often associated with the suffering and the work of the camp that it has become a symbol and immediately evokes an image like certain music or smells. [18]

Levi's dream thus begins as a normal dream: The sounds of his sleeping neighbor are, through the dreamwork, at least partially assimilated to the dreamed image of the panting engine. The sounds have a condensed "double nature"—they emerge between imagination and reality or, as Levi says, "between the unconscious and the conscious." Soon, however, Levi is pulled toward the conscious and objective side of the narrow ledge in which, as on which, he sleeps. His dream is interrupted by the real whistle, a "symbol" but not in the way that dream forms are symbolic. Rather, the whistle is a trigger, a stimulus, like "certain music or smells." And what it evokes is the wider reality of the suffering that Levi *cannot* weave back into his sleep or into his dream.

Abruptly, however, this entire oscillation between mediating imagination (in which things can have a "double nature") and outward fact is framed by a second, and deeper, dream. Levi directly continues:

There is my sister here, with some unidentifiable friend and many other people. They are all listening to me and it is this very story I am telling: the whistle of three notes, the hard bed, my neighbor whom I would like to move, but whom I am afraid to wake as he is stronger than me. . . . It is an intense pleasure, physical, inexpressible, to be at home, among friendly people, and to have so many things to recount.

In this second dream *of* recounting, the struggle between dreaming and waking becomes itself a recountable story—the "very story" Levi dreams himself retelling. Just as survivors, in the aftermath, sometimes "make a story" reflexively—the messenger's story becoming the story of being a messenger—here Levi reflexively "makes a story" about his dreaming that he is able to dream retelling. Most important, Levi is swept up by the inexpressible pleasure of being home again, surrounded by friends, and having so much to retell. Forms for recounting and an imagined context of responsive listeners are thus salvaged together. In a sense, Levi dreams that what was actually happening to him could be retold almost as though it *were* a dream: a terrible dream, but one that led to a secure awakening.

But exactly the opposite awakening takes place. The dream of recounting dissolves. Its story and the wish for listeners that is its foundation cannot be sustained within the nightmare actually taking place. As reality overtakes imagination, "inexpressible pleasure" is overcome by "desolating grief." Immediately after evoking the image of being at home and having "so many things to recount," Levi continued:

> But I cannot help noticing that my listeners do not follow me. In fact, they are completely indifferent: they speak confusedly of other things among themselves, as if I was not there. My sister looks at me, gets up and goes away without a word.
>
> A desolating grief is now born in me, like certain barely remembered pains of one's early infancy. It is pain in its pure state, not tempered by a sense of extraneous circumstances, a pain like that which makes children cry; and it is better for me to swim once again up to the surface, but this time I deliberately open my eyes to have a guarantee in front of me of being effectively awake.

Unable to hold onto the image of responsive listeners, Levi finds no other way to mediate his anguish. It is "pain in its pure state," unqualified by perspective or "extraneous circumstances." The best he can do is awaken. Levi then notes that this was not a "haphazard" dream; since arriving in Auschwitz, he has had it many times "with hardly any variations of environment or details." He has even learned from his friend Alberto that "it is also his dream and the dream of many others, perhaps of everyone." Levi then compares this dream to another universal dream in Auschwitz, a dream of eating—or, more precisely, of being fed:

> This is also a collective dream. . . . You not only see the food, . . . you are aware of its rich and striking smell; someone in the dream even holds it up to your lips, but every time a different circumstance intervenes to prevent the consummation of the act. Then the dream dissolves and breaks up into its elements, but it re-forms itself immediately after and begins again, similar, yet changed; and this without pause, for all of us, every night and for the whole of our sleep."[19]

Such, then, was the rhythm of meaning and the end of meaning, hope and the dissolution of hope, even within the destruction. Within those oscillations, the dream of recounting took its place among other salvage-

able remnants of nurture and connection—forming, breaking up, re-form-
ing, dissolving again. Paula retold a similar dream in which the capacity to
sustain an image of care was not strong enough to withstand recurrent
invasions by Auschwitz reality. The dream itself kept dying. She recalled:

> During the war itself, the dreams, the only dream I ever had was that I was
> sitting in my mother's lap. I was sitting in her lap. But at the same time the
> fence, the barbed wires were there. The dream always ended with that. And
> it was very short. The good feeling, the good feeling was, the fence overpow-
> ered the good. So that was the only thing I remembered out of it. The feeling
> itself, the good sheltered feeling, was very temporary. It was very minor. In
> other words, that was it. That's how far you could go. Even in a dream.

The "good, sheltered feeling" of a mother's lap; someone bringing food to
famished lips; the "physical, inexpressible pleasure" to be at home, among
friends, with "so many things to recount"—these are essentially synony-
mous dreams of desperately imagined responsiveness and care. The exqui-
site images of nurture they salvage stand for everything the killers
systematically—and successfully—destroyed. Even in dreams, they were
perpetually undone. Carried into the aftermath, they remained precarious,
especially when survivors encountered, in Wiesel's phrase, "invisible
barbed wire" of a new and unanticipated kind.

Liberation and Isolation

One of the striking things about the survivors whom we hear in these
pages is that almost all of them recall a time, shortly after liberation, when
they tried to talk about what they had so recently endured. Not surprisingly,
these attempts were particularly memorable for those who found at least a
few interested and willing listeners. As noted, Lydia emerged mute from
the war, but her screaming in her sleep, during nightmares, provided a
doctor evidence that her voice could be retrieved. Through his care and
regimen, her words were salvaged from her screams—she began to retell
her memories rather than only relive them.[20] Although full of doubt about
his capacity to convey the landscapes he remembered, Leon was encouraged by a French army captain to write about his experiences. He was then
"young and naive" enough, as he says now, to have believed that a "whole
world" might become his listeners. Even before he attempted his novel,
and certainly before his life became his text, Reuben did successfully write
articles about his survival. He had been encouraged by a Jewish major
serving in the Polish army, who forwarded Reuben's writing to a Yiddish

newspaper. Manny, too, while remembering all the lack of interest he encountered, also recalled exceptions. For him it was a Christian chaplain in the American forces to whom he recounted in some detail.

There was, in fact, a significant amount of survivor testimony published in the immediate aftermath of the war, although this period was brief and is a part of the history of recounting that is usually forgotten.[21] What is perhaps most interesting, for our purposes, is that it is sometimes forgotten even by survivors themselves. That is, even survivors who initially recall they had not wanted "to talk about it," often recall—in a later interview— that this was actually not the case. Here, then, is another instance of the way sustained conversation can revise initial accounts. It may also be an example of the influence of listeners' expectations, which typically are that survivors were not "ready" in the early years.

Paula's experience is particularly instructive in this regard, in part because she kept a diary during the first years that could be compared with her later memory of that period. Initially, in our interviews, she remembered not having been able to speak of her experiences: "I hid it from myself, for many years." She was thus surprised when, in our third interview, she reviewed diary entries she had written during the first days after liberation, literally within forty-eight hours of having survived a death march. Then fifteen years old, Paula wrote in 1945 about the extraordinary care with which she and a few other Auschwitz survivors were received in a former prisoner-of-war camp in which they happened to be liberated:

> The men look at us with astonishment. We are still in our dirty camp clothes, so it is not surprising they are shocked by our appearance. . . . We don't understand each other's languages, but we do understand their kindness and compassion. Soon we are able to take warm showers and sink into bed. How good it feels!
>
> The room fills with inquiring Frenchmen, Yugoslavs, Britishers, and others of many nationalities. They are soldiers, former prisoners-of-war, who had not seen anyone like us before. They are interested in our fate. . . .
>
> Even at this moment, the crematorium remains our nightmare. We are telling everybody about it, whether we want to or not. Our stories are only about the crematorium, whether we want to or not. Because either in my dreams or when I am awake, I can only see the flames in front of me. And the vision never fades.
>
> Too much talk is tiring. The visitors are courteous. They would like to stay longer, but the doctor makes them leave.

Even when Paula did *not* want to talk about it, she talked about it. Her entry suggests recounting as the primary impulse, the "elementary need," that Primo Levi described. It also suggests the significance of listeners. Amidst the compassion of those around her, Paula now experienced what Levi dreamed, and the dream did not dissolve. As Paula herself came to say, the responsiveness of these men also brought back her own dream of shelter—the dream of her mother—to which she had clung in Birkenau. Under the protection of those memories, she began to recount the others.

Despite the nightmare that continued to consume her, Paula recalled this time at liberation as one of the most confirming in her life. She was surrounded by a warmth and a solidarity that were scarcely conceivable after the terror and degradation she had just escaped; and she responded with hope. A day after she wrote the entry above, she noted, "We talk about the past and the future. And the future and the past. Now good will come . . . I think we could get back very fast to a regular life—a normal, human way of life—as we were used to years before." Buoyed by others' care, it was apparently possible in 1945, not only to know both an ongoing death and an ongoing life, but also to retell both.[22]

Scarcely two years later, however, Paula expressed an entirely different mood in her diary. She was now far from the group she had known at liberation and had become isolated and frustrated, unable to share her memories or her distress. Indeed, this was the period when Paula's diary itself became more and more important as an alternative, private context of recounting. "God, what's wrong with me?" she wrote. "I'm choked with my own cry. I'd like to cry but I can't. Today I came home all angered, for no reason." In a related entry, she suggested more about why she may have choked her cry and why she was so angry. "It's hard to be smart," she noted. "But it's harder yet, with a smart head, to live as though ignorant." However she acted outwardly, Paula did not hide her thoughts in her diary. This was the time she wrote the entry recalling the flames and suffocated innocents and describing her pen wanting "to go on and on by itself," even though it was falling from her hand.

Three years later, in 1950, Paula felt even more isolated. She now expressed much greater conflict about how she had and had not followed her "smart head" and why she lived "as though ignorant." By this time, she had arrived in the United States, and had discovered the mood—even the song lyric—that Manny also remembered. Twenty years old, writing on the fifth anniversary of her liberation, Paula confided to her diary:

Five years is like half a century when you live your life with bitterness and reminiscing. . . . Is this anger? Is this conscience? Is this self-awareness or self-criticism? . . .

Five years. It's not long to write it down. And it's easy to pronounce it.
But when I remember, I am carried back even more clearly than anytime
before. But why?

I don't know what I am. I don't know when I'm doing right or wrong. Am
I right when I'm thinking? And for what I am thinking? Many times, I think
I was just born for trouble. To be a burden and sorrow to everybody, because
I cannot laugh. They say, "If you laugh, everybody laughs with you. And if
you cry, you cry alone." Yes my diary, here I am—in America! . . .

But nobody's right and nobody's wrong. Only the truth is right. But that
is so rare. Now I'm pushing the years back. For me, that's like putting the
clock back a few minutes. Time elapses. But the impossible does not fade
from my eyes.

As remains characteristic of her, Paula now questions herself as much as
she questions outwardly. She is only certain that "the truth is right," and,
exactly as she had written at liberation, the truth was an impossible that
would not fade from her eyes.

Looking back at these entries more than thirty years later, Paula expressed mixed feelings. "It scares me to think how angry I was then," she
noted, "how desperate and how frustrated." But she was also still attached
to the young woman she had been and relieved to discover that she had
not succumbed to the silence without a struggle. She reflected: "Now I look
back. It's frightening. But I am able to realize that I still had feelings. I
wasn't dead altogether. There was still a soul deep down that wanted to
come to the surface." This was also the context in which Paula first spoke
about the stigma and silence imposed on survivors. She recalled:

I had to really suppress it. To me, I was right. . . . But the other side would
say, "Keep it to yourself because you will be locked up!" Because everybody
lived, "This is to forget!" You know, "Hush up your bad dreams!"

We were ashamed. We were made to feel ashamed. So I covered up. "I'm
fine, Joe! *That's* not me! How are *you*?" Because we were trying to find a place
in the community. We had to survive again, in a new country. We tried to
get along, you know, "I'm an American too!"

Paula's style is not to complain outwardly. Reinforced by the natural
inclinations of her character, her experience of surviving, and her experience of having to "survive again," she speaks of learning to cope, to make
do, to "improvise with the given materials," as she says, rather than dwell
on their limitations. And so she spoke that way about her constricted
recounting:

I decided, well, I can still do it for myself. I don't have to do it for anybody else. And it was helpful. I always had people in my life that I could really write to; I had close people that I could communicate with. And that was very helpful to me. For many years, I scribbled to myself in the diary. Or I scribbled to them. And it was a comfort. We carried on a very interesting correspondence! It was there. It existed.

Like the curves and shapes of Paula's tree, the remnants of recounting were thus salvaged—"It was there. It existed." But clearly it persisted in a more modest space, and on a more limited scale, than Paula and her "smart head" would have chosen.

Surviving Again

Like Paula, Manny also recalled learning, in the United States, to "survive again." His personal style is *not* self-constricting—he loves to "*oyzreden*" as he says in Yiddish, to "speak out"—and so he spoke out with characteristic intensity and vigor:

So, so, what are we going to do? Ask the people for sympathy?! "Come on! I'm a survivor from the Holocaust! Have some sympathy!" *NO!* We had to adapt ourselves to the mainstream of the country. To make a new life. To fend for ourselves.

Like before: Here is this people. They surround you and they throw you into a hole—into a hell hole! And then, suddenly, you are here. In the most gorgeous country in the world. In the most beautiful country in the world! And you are *back* in a hell hole! No! No! It's not the same. But our experience has taught us. You have to survive. . . .

Not just me. It's everybody. You come to a big country like this, you're a drop in the bucket. You have to make your own way of life. Here, it's different. It's individual. *Everybody* is for themselves! And you have to survive!

Manny does not want to overstate the connections between one "hell hole" and the other. But it is clear that, early on, he learned how to survive—and to be "a survivor"—in a more typically American sense.

Still, even when survivors did "adapt themselves to the mainstream," as so many successfully did, most discovered they were still isolated. In Wiesel's phrase, the "invisible barbed wire" remained. And what he and other survivors recall can only be described as a continuing need, on the part of others, to view them as "sick and needy relatives," objects for observation or for pity. Thus Manny notes that he remained the "nephew from the concentration camps" even after years of being well established.

However contradictory, to be an appropriate representative of the horror could be as much a demand on survivors as to be "an American too." Thus Jack Goldman recalled:

> I was always uncomfortable when people would expect me to be the emaci-
> ated, depressed survivor every minute of my day. "Oh, you look so well," they
> would say, surprised that a year after liberation I no longer weighed eighty
> pounds, as I did when the Americans rescued me. And having a dull job, and
> loving music, I used to whistle or hum a tune, without even knowing what
> I was humming or what the tune was, and people would say, "How can you
> whistle after all you've gone through?" Such questions seemed so ridiculous
> to me.[23]

Notwithstanding the song lyric, then, when survivors laughed or hummed a tune, the "whole world" did *not* laugh with them—perhaps because, if that much fellowship was granted, the potential fellowship of fate might also have to be granted. Either way, it is no wonder that Manny concludes: "I was, as they say, 'part of the mainstream.' But I was not *in* the mainstream. Because I was very much alone. Very much."

THE ROMANCING OF SURVIVAL

Looking back from the perspective of the present, it is easy to be indignant about the silencing and stigmatization that survivors faced during the early years. Their exclusion from the common life, even while being enjoined to adapt to it, was simple and direct. The general refusal to listen to their recounting was blunt and undisguised. Yet perhaps there is also a sense in which these responses, exactly because they were so direct, can also be recalled with a certain nostalgia. Certainly they do reflect a genuine dread and revulsion in the face of the Holocaust, which are exactly the appropriate responses. And few could have imagined, during these earlier years, that those who survived the destruction would eventually be greeted as celebrants of life, redeemers of the human spirit, and voices of heroic affirmation.

That, however, is precisely what happened. In an interview from the late seventies, Sally Grubman, a survivor of Auschwitz and Ravensbruck, described the transformation:

> There is a tremendous interest in the Holocaust that we didn't see when we
> came. . . . I see an awakening of consciousness, but also some confusion about
> the reality. American Jewish teachers invite me into their classrooms to

speak, but they do not want me to make the Holocaust a sad experience. They want me to turn us into heroes and create a heroic experience for the survivors. There is this book they use, *The Holocaust: A History of Courage and Resistance*, but the Holocaust was never a history of courage and resistance. It was a destruction by fire of innocent people, and it's not right to make it something it never was.

We are not heroes. We survived by some fluke that we do not ourselves understand. And people have said, "Sally, tell the children about the joy of survival." And I can see that they don't understand it at all. If you're in a canoe and your life is in danger for a few minutes and you survive, you can talk about the joy of survival. We went through fire and ashes and whole families were destroyed. And we are left. How can we talk about the joy of survival?[24]

In the first years after liberation, the Holocaust evoked terror, guilt, and a general unwillingness to believe. And, so soon afterward, "making it something it never was" was less an option. The destruction and its implications could only be denied more directly, and the direct silencing and exclusion of survivors reflected that denial. Only much later did a "tremendous interest" in surviving the Holocaust develop. Strange as it may seem, once treated as the most alien of men and women, survivors were greeted more and more often as the most representative.

1978

The changed response to Holocaust survivors reflected a surge of public interest in the Holocaust generally, and the timing of that shift can be given with some precision. In his book, *Preserving Memory*, Edward Linenthal reflected that 1978 was "a crucial year in the organization of Holocaust consciousness" in the United States.[25] He recalled the public reaction to the Nazi march in Skokie, Illinois; Jimmy Carter's establishment of a President's Commission on the Holocaust that would eventually oversee the creation of the U.S. Holocaust Memorial Museum; and the airing of NBC's miniseries, *Holocaust*, watched by an estimated 120 million people over four evenings that April. The television drama especially was a watershed event and began a trend that has continued. "From 1962 until 1978, Hollywood made almost no films directly related to the Holocaust," historian David Wyman observed. Since *Holocaust*, he noted, there has been a steady stream.[26] Raul Hilberg, reflecting on the transformation, also pointed to the significance of 1978. Along with all the other developments, he described the surge in academic study of the Holocaust that began at that time:

> Here, in the United States, something happened. We can almost pinpoint when. It was roughly 1978. Naturally such developments don't really have a precise date on which they begin. And yet, here was a television play that the author, Gerald Green, could not have sold to any network five or ten years earlier. Here was a nationalization of the Holocaust by Executive Order establishing a President's Commission. . . . Here we see the multiplication of books about the Holocaust, of courses about the Holocaust, of curricula about the Holocaust, of conferences about the Holocaust. [27]

Here, too, we see the emergence of Holocaust survivors in American public awareness. Through their participation in the newly formed commemorative activities and institutions—and particularly in their increasingly celebrated role as witnesses—survivors also began to be heard in the late seventies, often for the first time.[28] In Joan Ringelheim's 1992 survey of survivor testimony collections in the United States, for example, virtually every project—37 of 43—had been founded since 1977. The great majority of these were established by the mid-1980s, less than a decade after, as Hilberg noted, "something happened."[29]

What happened? Unquestionably, many factors contributed to the upsurge of interest in survivors and in the Holocaust more generally in these years. The passage of time itself, the evolving self-confidence of the American Jewish community, the changing political climate in Israel, and American self-questioning after Vietnam have all been implicated.[30] In my work, I have argued that it is essential also to consider the much wider preoccupation with public and private disaster, destruction and victimization, surviving and survivalism, that became pervasive in America in the 1970s.[31]

These issues are extraordinarily complex, and I can only be schematic here. Suffice it to say, then, that beginning in the midseventies, images of "survival" and "survivors" emerged everywhere in American popular culture, manifest in all sorts of seemingly disparate contexts. As Christopher Lasch was the first to describe, everyday persistence and coping as much as actual life and death struggle were suddenly portrayed in survival terms. Applied so broadly, the rhetoric of extremity served both to express a persistent sense of crisis and, by overstatement, to dilute it. But whether invoked with irony or with dead seriousness, being "a survivor"—more specifically, being known as "a survivor"—became a kind of fashion.[32]

Thus, while a wave of docu-dramas depicted life after mass disaster—natural and nuclear, environmental and genocidal—the new people-magazines headlined as "survivors" almost everyone whose careers had staying power: Lauren Bacall, David Brinkley, or B. B. King. As victims of genuine terror entered everyday public discussion—rape survivors, domestic violence survivors, survivors of childhood incest and abuse—there was an explosion of "How to Survive" guides covering every life contingency from the loss of a love, to falling in love, to getting a job, to "surviving" the job once you got it. While paramilitary "survivalist" groups formed to prepare for civilization's end, virtually every civilian sphere—from work life to family life, fiscal health to physical health—was framed in the new language of surviving and survival. A cartoon by Warren Miller that appeared in *The New Yorker* in 1979 perfectly captured the cachet that being "a survivor" had suddenly acquired. Depicting an archetypal two men stranded on a desert island, its caption had one exclaiming to the other: "That's what we are, all right—survivors! People will say, 'Hey, those two are real survivors! Talk about survivors—look at those two!' Yes, sirree, no doubt about it, when it comes to survivors, we really . . ."[33]

Holocaust survivors are "real survivors." And I am suggesting that the "tremendous interest" in Holocaust survivors that Sally Grubman described may be more helpfully understood in the context of these cultural trends than simply in terms of some new readiness, on survivors' part or ours, "to talk about it." In addition, the irony of the desert island cartoon highlights a paradox at the very heart of the new survival rhetoric. On one side, it is clear that "surviving"—as an ideal or a fashion—represents a *constriction* of hope and horizon. In Lasch's phrase, it reflects "an age of diminishing expectations"—an age of downsizing, insecurity, cynicism, and distrust. Being "a survivor," in other words, is what you hope for when the spheres of cultural, interpersonal, and political life seem consistently to discourage hoping for much else. At the same time, like the two men on the island, it is possible to make a virtue out of such necessity. Survival can be hyped and romanced. One can search, in its extremity, for lessons and legacies, affirmation and inspiration, new models of salvation or simply of success.[34]

So, in essence, we began to do with Holocaust survivors. As survival eclipsed adjustment as a primary virtue in American culture-at-large, our response to these survivors also underwent a transformation. Out of "the ashes" or "the darkness" or "defeat," we began to look for heroes and victories and "the joy of survival."

A DIVIDED DISCOURSE

The new rhetoric of survival as triumph and redemption has not meant, as is sometimes assumed, that we have not continued to view Holocaust survivors exclusively as victims. Indeed, reinforced by an increasingly popularized mental health discourse about survivors, and about traumatic victimization more generally, representations of survivors as guilty, despairing, shattered, or dead have become more fixed than ever.[35] The old language of "sick and needy" has become more clinical, but no less persistent. "All of these people walk around like human wrecks, like ghosts," exclaimed a discussant at a psychiatric conference on survivors' trauma, perhaps forgetting for that moment that the conference was itself organized and run by survivors—hardly a job for wandering spirits.[36] Likewise, in more recent years, only the naive would ask a whistling Jack Goldman how he could "do that after all he had been through." More likely, the significance of his behavior would be assumed: perhaps as his way of "coping" or "denying" or—in the most likely phrase—as Jack Goldman's way of "surviving."

Thus two quite distinct ways of imagining survivors have evolved since the late 1970s—a ceremonial rhetoric in which we honor survivors as celebrants and heroes and a psychiatric rhetoric in which the same survivors are depicted as ghosts and wrecks. Between the two sets of images, both the ongoing life and the ongoing death that survivors know *are* represented. But the problem, as I have suggested, is that each of these ways of representing survivors has evolved into a separate and self-sufficient discourse. And indeed, so self-sufficient have these discourses become that they are increasingly detached—not only from each other—but from remembering the Holocaust itself.

On one side, then, survivors are now everywhere invited to "bear witness." The interest in testimony that Sally Grubman noted continues to accelerate, and its collection and distribution—in the greatest possible quantity, through the most contemporary possible means—have become a modern crusade. The accompanying rhetoric, however, remains traditional, even folk. We honor the "tales" and "stories" survivors retell, the "legacies" they bestow, their courage and heroism in speaking at all. Indeed, so much have we come to celebrate the *act* of testimony—congratulating survivors for giving it and, perhaps, ourselves for getting it—that the specific content of that testimony is left as mostly background. That is, survivors' speech tends to be esteemed in the abstract—as the *idea* of testimony rather than the reality. At times, it seems specifically to be acclaimed instead of being listened to.

Meanwhile, another rhetoric is also heard. There is seemingly knowledgeable talk of post-traumatic stress, survivor guilt and shame, nightmares and depressions. Here, too, the perspective remains abstract. Just as the particulars of testimony become background when we celebrate witnessing itself, so the specific personal and historical content of survivors' pain becomes secondary when memory is reduced to symptoms. As consequences of the Holocaust—psychological by-products—symptoms need only be noted and counted. Even when survivors themselves speak of their guilt or their depression—as they often enough do—this is more likely to be taken as diagnostic confirmation than as an invitation to further discussion. In that way, the psychiatric discourse on symptoms, like the celebratory discourse on testimony, remains self-sufficient and uninterrupted.

The Oscillations of Rhetoric

At times, the oscillation between these two rhetorics can be particularly striking. Several such instances occurred during the American television coverage of the first World Gathering of Jewish Holocaust Survivors, held in Jerusalem in 1981. The reporters' comments are worth reviewing because of how clearly they demonstrate that even well-informed listeners, guided by the best intentions, can be compelled by celebratory and psychiatric discourse.

For example, after the lead-in photographs of corpses, crematoria, and terrified victims with which all the programs began, one of the commentators made the following introductory remarks to the first broadcast of the series:

> In the opening sequences we showed you a glimpse—even a glimpse is enough—of the savagery of the Holocaust. We didn't do this to shock you, although it is shocking. We did it so that you better understand the triumph of the human spirit. One cannot understand what it means to have been a survivor unless you know *what* they have survived.
>
> These heroic people who are gathered here today have not come to resurrect the nightmares of the past. They have not come to mourn. They have come to celebrate life. To bear witness. And to pass it on to their children and their children's children. This is more valuable than all of the material assets they could pass on. *This* is their true legacy.[37]

From the start, one might wonder how it is possible to "bear witness" *without* mourning and *without* resurrecting "the nightmares of the past."

In fact, the scenes from the Gathering that immediately followed—survivors grouped around message boards and holding up signs in search of those they lost—seemed to have everything to do with mourning and resurrection.[38] But these remarks alone already suggest much greater involvement with the idea of "heroic people" gathered to "bear witness" than with the content that witnessing is about. Of that—represented by the opening photographs—"even a glimpse is enough." And what we are really seeking to understand, in any case, is something else: "the triumph of the human spirit."

Still, as notable as this celebration of survivors as heroic witnesses, themselves engaged in "celebrating life," was the appearance further on in the broadcasts of a quite different way of discussing survivors and their legacies. The shift was particularly apparent as the commentators turned to those whom they called "the bearers of the legacy," the children of survivors. For what had earlier been applauded as a sacred transmission was now portrayed as the passing on of psychic burdens and universal affliction. Indeed, within this rhetoric, the nightmarish past was not only resurrected but had gained virtual possession of the intergenerational future. Thus one reporter introduced her interviews with children of survivors:

> Throughout the world there are tens of thousands of young people who have never met. And yet they dream the same nightmares, share the same fears, and deal with the same emotional problems. Although they live separated by continents, they shared an experience which has marked them for life.[39]

If this change of discourse was not clear enough, the questions that the reporter then asked the children of survivors who were interviewed—an Israeli, an American, and an Australian—left no doubt about the transformation. They proceeded:

> "Do you have any particular nightmares?"
> "Do you think there is a problem between survivors and their children in an inability to communicate?"

And, finally, a question that seemed to finish off the previously invaluable legacy once and for all:

> "Do you feel that you'll ever get rid of the legacy of the Holocaust?"

For their own part, the children of survivors had no difficulty coming up with exemplary nightmares, family tensions, and related problems. But they also appeared discomforted by the direction of the questions and seemed to be pushing to speak about something else. For all, this had to do with more essential ways that the Holocaust had entered into their awareness. Thus the Israeli said that "the Holocaust is part of me, as everything is part of me. As my hands are part of me. As my eyes are part of me." Referring to the nightmare she had remembered, the American was quick to add: "More than that—those are only things that happened a few times—more than that, it's something that goes with me through my everyday life." Likewise, the Australian agreed that she would never "get rid of the legacy of the Holocaust." However, she continued: "Nor do I want to. It's part of my history . . . it goes back to the whole Jewish history." At least in the segments of the interviews that were broadcast, these comments were never followed up with further questions or discussion. They were left as simple assertions, perhaps as protests, which did little to modify the primary theme that nightmares, fears, and emotional problems were now what "the legacy" was about.

Even so, the matter was not left within psychiatric discourse either. Toward the end of the broadcasts, while discussing the fact that there would never be another such gathering of survivors, the commentators again raised the theme of redemptive rebirth through the passing of the legacy. One said this in final summary:

> It is true that this is, this was, a one-time event, a moment in history. But I do not think it will disappear. There was a legacy that was passed on, there were seeds that were sown, there will be flowers that will blossom forth from this, through the second generation, through the children of survivors, and through all of us who have observed this week. [40]

It was left up to us, the viewing audience, to determine what sort of flowers these might be and how to understand their rootedness in a legacy presented alternately as priceless and pathogenic. Meanwhile, we might also wonder how much more, excluded by the language of both veneration and diagnosis, remains unheard; perhaps unspoken.

Two Monologues

There should be no misunderstanding: Survivors should be honored and their testimony cherished. Likewise, whatever the struggles of survivors or their children in the aftermath, these ought to be understood in the most serious way. The problem with the celebratory and psychiatric discourses discussed here is that testimony and the realities of survivors' and their children's lives are *not* seriously engaged. Rather, as I have emphasized, in place of entering into actual testimony, celebratory discourse fixes on the *idea* of "bearing witness." As typically invoked, the psychiatric discourse functions similarly: charting "emotional problems" substitutes for entering into the impact of the destruction for anyone in particular. That is why, I think, the children of survivors who were interviewed protest. Their knowledge of the Holocaust is not a checklist of symptoms, they each insist, but something complexly lived: "part of me," part of "my everyday life," "part of my history." And that is also why, I think, their protests are ignored. To pursue them would require the kind of developing dialogue that discourses like these preclude.

In the end, then, the split between celebratory and psychiatric discourse overlays an even more profound division—a "division of labor" within the process of recounting itself. On their side, survivors' "job" is to talk about the Holocaust: to *be* witnesses or testifiers or passers-on of legacies. Our "job," by contrast, is to talk about survivors—either as heroic people who have such a task to fulfill or as haunted victims of the destruction. Whichever rhetoric we invoke, two discrete and disconnected monologues are now created *between* survivors and ourselves. Survivors provide witnessing and testimony about the Holocaust; we provide observations—or testimonials—about survivors.

Legacies as "Last Words"

In recent years, the rhetoric of intergenerational transmission, of "true legacies" passed on "to children and to children's children," has become particularly salient in discourse about survivors. Indeed, whether speaking of a legacy of trauma, of testimony, of Hitler, of Schindler, of night, or of dawn, there is probably no word used more often in connection with survivors than the word "legacy." Companion references to survivors as "storytellers," "tellers of tales," or—more postmodernistically—"weavers of narrative tapestries" are almost as ubiquitous. Both "legacies" and "stories" evoke primary images of a people's narrative tradition and its transmission—exactly as in "Mi Y'Malel," imagery of meaningful continuity in historical time and coherent retelling of historical times. Enticed by such language, it is easy to miss the irony that the coherence of stories and the continuity of legacies are precisely what remembering the Holocaust undoes.[41]

To speak of legacies is also to evoke the idea of endings—of final messages delivered, last words uttered. The commentary on the 1981 Jerusalem gathering was thus typical in declaring it a "one-time event, a moment in history" that would never happen again. Other gatherings of survivors likewise tend to be described as unique and never to be repeated, invoking the image—not only of testimony—but specifically of *final* testimony, of testament. And, indeed, the notion that the survivors are all dying was repeated almost as often twenty years ago—in the seventies—as it is (with more statistical justification) today; partly reflecting—and partly reflected in—all the legacy talk.[42] Thus it seems that, at the same historical moment that survivors' words were suddenly in demand, they were in demand specifically as "last words"—what you pass on to children, what you leave before you leave.

It is this orientation to "last words" that is at the heart of the two discourses that have developed since the late seventies. On one side, there are survivors' "last words" as they are invited to tell their story, leave their legacy, and—by implication—disappear. On the other side, there are our own "last words" as we eulogize the heroes and pity the victims—that is, as we put ourselves in the role of those who will survive the survivors and bid them farewell ("there were seeds that were sown, there will be flowers that will blossom forth"). Neither survivors' final testament nor our final testimonial brooks interruption or elucidation. They lead, once again, to monologues—worlds of discourse that are one-way, self-sufficient, and closed.

Now survivors *do* have legacies, and there is a great deal that they, like all parents, do pass on to their children. But—exactly the converse of our usual expectations—these legacies are rooted not in the Holocaust, nor in having survived the Holocaust, but in what can be salvaged and re-created *in spite of* the Holocaust. In other words, survivors' legacies—like survivors' voices and stories and their dreams of recounting and shelter—are rooted primarily in the other memories they carry.

Listen to Paula as she struggles to define her own legacy within and against the prevailing rhetoric, including its imagery of one-way transmission and its suggestions of imminent demise. She reflected:

> But, you know, my wish is always, as I'm getting older—I mean, I'm not dying yet! I hope I'm not dying yet!—but what did I achieve in my own little circle? In my own family? What was I able to leave for them? What is the word I want to use? The word they always use? "Legacy." What is my "legacy"? I don't know.

> Do they look at me as a quote-unquote "survivor"? Do they have compas -
> sion because now they understand what happened? And so they understand
> *me* instead of I understanding *them*? You know, it's a bothering thought!

For Paula, being a "quote-unquote survivor" is here what contributes *least*
to her sense of "legacy." She is talking about the complexity of particular
relationships—a mother and her children—and against whatever one-way
presumptions go with "quote-unquotes." Paula continued:

> But, on the other hand, every parent, every person who leaves a legacy in this
> life, it's a very little minor thing. I'm thinking of my own parents, especially my
> father, because unfortunately my mother I remember only vaguely. . . .
> When I go to the synagogue, which I don't do that often, but I always
> hear my father's voice. And I always recall, at certain prayers, how much joy
> he got out of singing that particular one. He wasn't extremely religious. He
> was just good-hearted, believing, so pure within his world. . . . And he
> enjoyed singing "En K'elohenu." And he excelled! You know, his voice
> just—!! And every time I sing that, I feel that this is why I enjoy it—because
> my father enjoyed it. . . .
> So, actually, what is a legacy? It's a very, it's one little thing if you are going
> to make it a legacy. I can't. I can work on it, but it's up to you what you take
> out of it. How you translate it for yourself. And for that you have to be
> fortunate. To be able to enjoy these little things that are given.

Contrary to what her listeners might expect, the legacies Paula describes
do not emerge from the destruction, from triumphing over the destruction,
or from suffering after the destruction. They are simply the normal things
of life—a father's voice, a favorite hymn, a remembered pleasure—the stuff
of survivors' legacies as they are of all of ours; even if survivors also carry
knowledge of such legacies' terrible fragility.

PRIVATE NIGHTMARES

Like Paula, Leon also thinks about his legacy, and he does so in terms
that are closer to our usual understanding of what survivors' legacies entail.
He worries about his recounting. What has he managed to communicate?
What difference has it made? If he cannot convey memory itself, Leon
powerfully conveys the problem of the messenger.

> Will it ever come out? That someone else will understand? I wouldn't mind
> if I could paint it. I wouldn't mind if I could do it in any fashion at all. Because
> I'm living, almost, in a certain—, my bitterness is that the Holocaust, actually

the lesson of the Holocaust, will never be learned. And maybe it's not going to be learned because it's too horrible. The mind revolts from grasping it. The mind is incapable of grasping it.

And, therefore, the illusions under which we labored—that learning the reality of the Holocaust will maybe prevent another one from happening, will maybe cure mankind of this madness—I think it doesn't come to pass. It is not the case. It is hardly the fact. It is not likely to come to a realization. Because no words are adequate to acquaint the people with the Holocaust.

Leon begins by emphasizing the inherent incommunicability of the Holocaust. Along with this inner silence, however, Leon also speaks of an outward one. He continues:

No words are adequate to acquaint people with the reality of the Holocaust. But then another thought comes in. Supposing they could. Isn't there going to be a certain reluctance to submerge yourself in it? Who, on his own volition, will want to absorb the horror of it all?

Leon has answers to these questions. He expects to find responsive listeners as little as he expects to find adequate words, and the problem goes beyond "a certain reluctance." "Deeply ingrained within me," he notes, "is the conviction that the world didn't learn anything from the Holocaust, and definitely doesn't regret anything about the Holocaust." Leon once had greater hopes. In response to my asking him whom he does view as his listeners, he answered:

Truthfully, when I was young and naive, I thought the whole world. But it is a good indication of advanced age—of being jaded and cynical and maybe realism—that I feel defeated before I start. The world just doesn't care. My goal would be more modest: to impress Jewish generations to come on the Holocaust. . . . Do I hope thereby to avoid a repetition of it? This is all futile! At least, at least they will not be caught unaware . . . as we were, when the Holocaust caught up with us.

Leon thus finds a smaller circle for his recounting: future Jewish generations and, in particular, his own children. But this is a far more "modest" circle than the one he had anticipated, and it is surrounded by a far more terrible futility.

Perhaps for that reason, Leon only rarely does speak of his memories with his children. Certainly he wants them to know about the destruction, but, as in Paula's reflection on her legacy, what Leon values most is his children coming to their own understanding of this history:

On the one hand, I feel frustrated at not being able to convey to them the Holocaust . . . this horrible heritage. On the other hand, I take great pleasure in the fact that they are growing up completely normal children. They love sports. They have their music. This is a source of great solace to me. That my private Hell won't be their portion also. That they won't be forever marked with the horror of these memories which I cannot escape. . . .

So there is an ambivalence: the normal existence in which I rejoice, and the thing that I deem it my duty to expose them to. . . . Maybe that's why I am permitting nature to take its course. They will have to incorporate it into their own sense of values. Their way. Not necessarily my way.

If there is a legacy here, it is woven out of the full complexity of Leon's ambivalence: his capacity to take pleasure in his children's own pleasures, his wish to warn and to transmit, his awareness of the conflicts thereby created, and his ability to live within them. There is both continuity and discontinuity in such a legacy, and neither comes at the cost of denying the horror or turning its retelling into some kind of celebration or final testament.

In the end, if recounting to his children is Leon's legacy at all, it is a legacy by default, a result of Leon's having found so few genuine listeners elsewhere. Leon's own term for the result is "private nightmares"—memories that grow in horror exactly because they *are* private, in his phrase, "outside the public domain." He noted:

Some things people know about, or think they know about. There are the same scenes in every movie, and they are more or less in the public domain—the liquidation of a ghetto, a shooting, the arrival at Auschwitz, "*Arbeit Macht Frei.*"

But there are also private nightmares, which require a completely differ-ent scenario. Some individual horror stories—, it becomes almost—, I remember reading somewhere about somebody having a nightmare. And he feels like screaming, and no words come out. You know, this horrible feeling—if only I could scream and call for help! I'd be all right! But no words come out. And somehow you feel the same way.

Memories that are "private nightmares" are doubly unspeakable. First, the nightmare itself strangles speech, even screams are silenced. Second, beyond a few iconic images ritually repeated, and a few contexts of recounting that are themselves highly ritualized, the horror is relived in isolation. The voices, stories, and enactments that survivors find for their recounting are conditioned by both kinds of constraints, both kinds of silencing.

Part II
Voices, Stories, Enactments

Chapter 3

A Gathering of Voices

Suddenly, as if at a signal, they all began to scream. A scream that
swelled, mounted, mounted, and spilled over the walls. . . .
  Silences and screams cut into the hours.
                                    Charlotte Delbo, *None of Us Will Return*

VOICES AS GATHERINGS

Compared with the gatherings of thousands of Holocaust survivors in
Jerusalem and elsewhere that have taken place since the 1980s, the
gathering presented here is minute in scale. Including seven primary
participants, it contains only enough voices to make a conversational
circle. Also unlike Jerusalem, this gathering never actually took place. It
is rather a conversation that we must imagine as we juxtapose each
individual voice against the others and against the memories they strive to
retell.[1]

At the start, the most important thing to emphasize is that it *is* individual
voices to which we attend. The participants in this gathering speak not as
emblematic witnesses but as particular people, each with his or her distinctive style and tone. Thus, in these pages, it is only a partial truth to say of
survivors, as did Des Pres:

> Their immediate past is collective rather than personal, a past identical for
> everyone who came through the common catastrophe. Memory and selfhood
> are rooted, often traumatically, in events which define the individual not as

an individual but as a participant in, and the embodiment of, decisive historical experience.[2]

For the survivors whom we shall hear, memory and selfhood *are* rooted in the Holocaust. But they are also rooted elsewhere: in pasts as personal as any of our own. As we listen to their words, therefore, we hear more than voices from Auschwitz or Treblinka, let alone confront "embodiments" of such places. Rather, along with the echoes of screams and silences, we also hear the distinctive accents of Bialystock, Budapest, and Lvov. Within and around memories of collective destruction are fully personal memories of one who had been a schoolgirl in the Carpathians and of another who was once a factory worker in Galicia, who dreamed, and still dreams, of planting trees in Palestine.

Survivors' voices are thus themselves gatherings. In some precarious balance, each contains both the rhythms of its origin and the cacophony of its dissolution. Each must draw on words and cadences that once belonged to entire communities, even while retelling how those communities were destroyed. This complexity within survivors' voices is most evident when they speak specifically *as* survivors: when they take the role of witness or recounter and attempt to retell what they remember. At these times, survivors must directly juxtapose meanings grounded in one world with their reduction in the other. At the same moment, they must also juxtapose their own perceptions of themselves with their perceptions of their listeners' expectations about who they are "as survivors" and what they have to retell.

In this chapter, we enter further into the fate of survivors' voices within this double juxtaposition. We shall hear how each participant establishes his or her identity as a recounter and how that identity changes as conversation deepens. And, indeed, one of the striking things about these conversations are the changes that do take place. However much a gathering, each participant's voice first emerges as a single piece and tone. Only over time, do tensions appear and separate strands unfold.

Thus, as initial self-presentations and their qualifications start to diverge, often becoming frankly discordant, we begin to hear in each voice a polar counterpart. Tones of conviction give way to self-doubt; modest self-restraint becomes open accusation; outward condemnation becomes inner recrimination. Some participants appear to have hidden their questions with answers; others to have muffled their answers with questions.

Meanwhile, the ground of these polar voices within each voice itself divides. On one side, they become traceable to wider themes and identifications in participants' life histories; for example, to what it may have meant, well before the Holocaust, to be a "prosecutor" or to be oneself unmasked; to use one's "smart head" or to hide it. On the other side, the same polar themes emerge from the destruction itself. Within the unqualified universe of killers and victims, polarities like seeing through everything or seeing nothing, assertion or silence, are reduced to only one set of "meaningful" referents.

Stretched between these two sets of memories—remnants of the most personal constellations of meaning on one side and tracings of their most impersonal enactment on the other—and further strained by the impact of listeners' expectations, many participants' voices now start to expand. Some become diffuse and distended, as though attempting to gather in a universe of death which they, as single voices, are somehow supposed to represent. Some become raised and shrill like shouts of the killers they recall and against which, individually and alone, they are expected to stand or rage as witnesses. Other voices return to their everyday range and appeal to our own voices to join in the attempt to know and to retell. Still others simply break. They die out to silence.

SINGLE VOICES

As we now turn to each of these voices, it is useful to imagine the participants in an actual gathering together. Without question, it would be the diversity among them we would notice. We would see men and women; some who strike us by their youthfulness and others by their age; some full of energy and talk and others who stay closer to the margins of the conversation. We would hear a variety of accents, rhythms, and styles, and we would hear different kinds of silences—some signaling the limits of speech, others being invitation to deepen the conversation or simply to answer with a responsive silence of our own. Whatever these voices shared, we would first attend to the distinctiveness of each. We may, therefore, go around the circle to find out who is here.

Leon

For Leon, asserting his individual perspective is itself a kind of cause and "the essential coda," as he would put it, of his self-presentation as a whole. Early on, he noted, "One has to have a definite sense of one's own being and the intensity of feeling that goes with it. *Who* I am. *What* I am. What I am standing *for*." He is proud of his reflectively critical point of view and ready to apply it: to memoirs written by other survivors ("Some are travelogues or adventure stories—may the Good Lord forgive them—either they are dishonest or their memory plays tricks on them"); to books written about survivors such as that by Des Pres ("Unusually sensitive for a Gentile"); or, as we have already heard, to his own inability to convey the essence of what he remembers ("I give an accountant's recital, sterile and antiseptic—not a poet's reaction—of which I am not capable."). Poet or not, as these examples suggest, Leon is supremely a "word man," often to the point of breathtaking eloquence, sometimes to strained convolution (he himself wonders about being an "anal type"). Either way, his self-definition centers on his ability to state his views and maintain his perspective. In this voice, confusion, illusion, or crippling ambivalence are the greatest dangers.

Leon tied the importance of such clarity to his experiences within the camps themselves. He asserted:

> One has to know the world as it is; not some idealized picture as it should be. . . . When I looked at the SS guard on the tower, I could say I know that I hate you and you hate me. And this can be a very sustaining force. Regardless of what *Reader's Digest* might think about it, hate can be a very sustaining force. . . . The love/hate relationship definitely destroys one's ability to cope under those circumstances.

In a later interview, Leon further developed the theme:

> They took away your name. They took away all other means of identifying yourself with reference to others—you are all reduced to gray anonymity—head shaved, striped uniform, defined as subhuman.
>
> So, whatever you carry, you carry within you. There is one area they cannot enter: whatever privacy you can maintain within your mind. That's the one sanctuary. And that sanctuary is who I am, what I stand for, what's dear to me, what I despise. If you permit the cruelty of the outside world to enter this final sanctuary, this last retreat, then you're going to become a zombie. Then you become a *Musulmann*. Then the grayness and uniformity—this *Gleichschaltung*, which in German is "complete leveling," which they did on the outside so successfully, also takes place internally. And you become a mere cipher. Nothing.
>
> So this is the last refuge which you must retain. Not only in these extreme circumstances, which show the need, but always in the realistic assessment of the world as it is: a center within yourself which thinks intensely, feels intensely, and contains a part of the image of who you are, who you were, and who someday you're going to become.

It is hard to imagine a stronger case than this for the maintenance of personal identity in extremity, even when—by dint of sheer insistence—a perceptible tension enters in. The case is made too often, we may begin to feel, and perhaps too well.

This strain is also constitutive of Leon's voice and defines his individuality in a deeper, if less explicit, way. In part, it reflects those times when the "inner sanctuary" was more precarious than he first seems to suggest; when the "cruelty of the outside world" *did* get inside. In a later interview he noted: "We all live, to all appearances, a very normal existence. This is a source of great surprise and wonder for me, tinged maybe, by the uneasy feeling—, whether we all have a time bomb ticking away in us . . . whether, at a certain point, the past takes the upper hand." Leon did not specify the content of the "time bomb," and we, like he, cannot say if his anxiety is warranted. But, further on, we will hear his detailed description of a traumatic memory which remains one of the most vivid evocations of the "closing in of darkness" that I have heard in twenty years of listening to survivors. It was this episode, along with his memory of returning to the liquidated Radom ghetto, which led Leon to evoke the "landscape of death" devoid of any redeeming emotion, let alone the passion of personal conviction.

Having personally lived—and perhaps personally died—within that landscape, Leon also remembered another kind of "leveling." He described a sense of "contamination" after the war, a self-doubt that he himself offered as an explicit counterpoint to the self-preservative virtues he had earlier discussed. Leon explained:

I am trying to convey something. . . . You see, you were just climbing over mountains of dead bodies, or dying people, with the most—, callousness, and indifference. You couldn't help them, and, therefore, the normal expressions of concern, of sympathy—, you just shed it. . . .

Did something die in me, in effect? I was concerned that all the basic emotions that make possible social existence, consideration, concern, [long pause] tenderness—, all the feelings—, I felt that they were irreversibly destroyed. That after what we have seen. After the images we have had before our eyes—, [pause]

I turned over with my own hands my grandfather's gravemarker, his gravestone. With my own hands, I turned it over! When we were destroying those Jewish gravestones, to use to pave the roads, that I told you about. As a matter of fact, the SS man didn't want to pull the truck too deep in the cemetery. We had to pull them out, two or three of us, these bloody heavy stones. And I remember, sort of a hangman's humor, we used to joke, we used to curse those rich Jews who had the biggest and heaviest stones. Like their sole purpose was to make our work harder! And it is factors like these that implanted in me this doubt, that I expressed outwardly after the war, that maybe we should be put somewhere on an island, given some way of life, like lepers, in effect. Because we had been, for lack of a better word, "contami - nated."

At this point, it was "social existence" itself, and not only its *Reader's Digest* version, from which Leon felt estranged. And it is hard to imagine anything in this memory that could accommodate "a center within yourself which thinks intensely, feels intensely" and carries "the image of who you are, who you were, and who someday you're going to become." Yet, as Leon emphasizes, this capacity *not* to feel, *not* to think, *not* to identify or empathize, was equally required for survival and also a result of the "realistic assessment" of the world.

Of course, it should be emphasized that the emotions and sensitivities about which Leon was concerned were *not* "irreversibly destroyed" in him. His very self-doubt about "contamination"—and his expression of that doubt after the war—are proof of all that was not "leveled." Likewise, the story of callousness that Leon retells evokes, through its recounting, exactly the kind of focused, individualized compassion that Leon says was impossible at the time. Particularly in the context of his own pain in remembering it, the story becomes tragic in an almost classic sense—evoking our pity, our regret, our empathic care—as, one must assume, Leon also feels toward himself, while recounting this memory to us.[3]

This does not mean that the deaths that Leon knew were any less. The opposite is true. As we have heard Leon emphasize, at the heart of his memories is a landscape that has nothing to do with the scale of individual tragedy. "How do you describe a nightmare?" he asks. "Something which is shapeless, amorphous, which cannot be reduced to comprehensible terms?" I have suggested that stories about feelings like "contamination"— and perhaps even the reawakened sense of contamination itself—are part of how survivors do find "comprehensible terms" for the nightmare. Further, exactly because of its particular meaningfulness to Leon, as a man of sensitivity and culture, "contamination" is quintessentially *his* term through which to suggest the greater death. That may also be why he retold the memory of the gravestones when he did. It immediately follows his evoking a wider vision of remembered horror—"after what we have seen . . . the images we have had before our eyes." Pained as he is, in turning reflexively inward and selfward, and away from the other images that began to surround him, Leon salvages a fragment that is still tellable by him and may be still hearable by us.

Meanwhile, the fact of such surviving meanings evokes another source of strain in Leon's voice when he speaks against "ambivalence" and the "love/hate relationship," now one rooted in an entirely different strand of memory than that of the destruction. In this context, the habitual civility of an "anal type" is associated, not with the loss of personal clarity and conviction, but rather with the capacity to *maintain* perspective and balanced judgment. We have heard this strand in Leon's voice as he discussed his relationship with his children—above all, his capacity to embrace his ambivalence between his wish to warn and his wish to let "nature take its course." However strained, at times, by reductive association with confusion or weakness, that balancing fully lives on—as the fastidious cadences of Leon's voice even now attest.

Reuben

Reuben's voice is no less complex than Leon's; but in tone, content, and cultural references, his words suggest a personal style that is almost the opposite. Rather than cultivated irony and self-assertion, we now hear surrender, apology, and despair. In contrast with the reflective critic defending personal integrity, Reuben presents a world in which individual identity is enmeshed in the integrity of the group. That group is traditional and Yiddish, and it has been destroyed. Reuben tells us that he is one of its parents, its children, and its ghosts.

Like the Destruction of the Temple, the Diaspora of the Jewish people—, as years went by, they felt it more and more. I mean, the same thing is with this. The generation that lived through it, I guess they're never going to forget it. It's impossible.

The same thing, even, let's put it this way: even a parent who loses a child—I mean, in normal conditions—sometimes they never forget it. Every day they go around, you know, they never forget it. That's normal conditions.

This is something terrible, something more terrible. This was not normal conditions. They cut you off completely from *shoresh*, a tree, roots, from your roots. You're uprooted—completely. You're lost. Everything.

The Jewish people, it's never going to be like it was anymore, you know. I'm just saying, they were a good people. They had their own, we had our own culture, our own writers, our own poets. A complete ethnic group, you know what I mean. It's lost. It's never going to be anymore.

I'm lost too. I'm like a *gilgul*. You know what a *gilgul* is? (HG: No—) A gilgul is, you know, the Jewish people believe, especially the Hasidim and the mystics, they believe that the *shmos*, the soul, that the soul sometimes comes back. The same way the Hindus believe, the Jewish mystics believe too. So they say, sometimes a soul doesn't have—, sometimes a soul isn't that lucky. It doesn't go back in a human being. It just wanders around. It can't

get in. So he's lost. And they call it a *gilgul*. He's lost. That's what I'm saying.
I'm a lost soul. I'm not *yinnenvelt* or *nievelt*. Not in the old world, or the new.

Reuben's death, for that is what he describes, is further confirmed by an
even more intimate dissolution than the loss of his roots. The "inner
sanctuary" that Leon defends with such passion is, for Reuben, no more
resistant to obliteration than the "whole life" of the group. Each death, in
fact, reinforces the other, in a spiraling totality of loss.

> It's very hard, you know what I mean. 'Till this day, I don't know—, I'm just
> saying, you see, they got you down. First you're weak, you were half-dead.
> You didn't have no, no strength anymore. No desire to fight. Even to live
> anymore, you know what I mean. . . . You lost everything.
>
> It's very hard. Like someone who has a terminal illness, who is sick, who
> is dying. Nobody knows how that person feels. And usually a person who has
> a certain disease, who is dying, he gets ready almost. He doesn't care anymore,
> you known what I mean. It's not a big shock for him. He's not afraid anymore,
> you know what I mean. The same thing is with this, you know.

This vision of an inner and outer death pervades Reuben's reflections and
echoes in his voice. Like a parent who has lost a child (which did not
actually happen to him) or as a victim of terminal illness, he speaks as a
soul in permanent mourning and exile.

At the same time, it must be said that Reuben is *not* a disembodied spirit
without substance or locale. Even if so much has been lost in unfinished
sentences—in "I'm just saying" and "you know what I mean"—the culture
he grieves continues to provide a vocabulary of meanings and images
through which he gives form to his despair: *as a gilgul*; one without *shoresh*;
or one who knows a greater destruction than that of the Second Temple.
Likewise, whatever his inner isolation, he is not outwardly alone. More
often than during my meetings with any other participant, my conversations with Reuben were interrupted by phone calls from his friends—often
people whom he had known since before the destruction. There was a
constant buzz of background activity in the house (as audiotapes document
so well): televisions going on and off, cars arriving and departing, the
chatter of Reuben's five children who were all at home at the time. More
than once, a huge and affectionate sheepdog also came through the
kitchen, followed by a parade of six or seven pups to which she had recently
given birth.

Around us, in short, moved a "whole life." Its variety and activity
suggested a miniature version of the community that Reuben mourned and

which, as we heard earlier, he had once hoped to re-create in a novel. He himself spoke of his children as a "mixed bunch," referring to their different temperaments, religious convictions, and vocational interests. The ongoing death that Reuben describes, therefore, should not blind us to the substance of his ongoing life. The point is not that one balances or compensates for the other. Rather, it is that only both together can reveal the individualized, human complexity when death *is* lived—when it is not, in fact, "ghosts" or similar caricatures that we are talking about.

There is further complexity as well; for there are times when Reuben expresses quite other feelings than surrender and helplessness. As much as Leon, Reuben also associated his personal survival with wishes for revenge, with hate pitted against hate, and those wishes remain. Reuben recalled:

> I just wanted to survive. Just to live through. Mostly, maybe it was a revenging or something. I don't know what it was. But, uh, it kept me going. I'm just saying, because of that, mostly.
>
> (HG: Was revenge an idea at the time?) Yes, it was an idea at the time. Something like this. But mostly, if the Jewish people took revenge, it was on the guilty ones, the hundred percent guilty. . . . I'm just saying, you can see a difference between the Jewish morals and the other morals. Even after the war, you found very few Jewish survivors where they go into a German home and just kill people. I mean, almost nil. As a whole, they could have gotten away with it. But they didn't do it. It's a different morality. A different upbringing maybe.

The different moralities, however, did not prevent Reuben from seeing a new place for Jewish revenge and retaliation after the Holocaust. He noted:

> You see, until the Holocaust, it was a different story. The Jewish people used to be like a tree, you know. Not a strong tree. If the wind was blowing, the tree bends in the wind, it doesn't break. If it was standing erect, and doesn't bend, the tree broke. And a broken tree doesn't grow again.
>
> So, before the Holocaust, they used to bend, to go along with it. As long as the whole life was not in danger. They would give them all the money they had. They would give them everything. That was OK. That was the history until the Holocaust.
>
> So that's why the Holocaust put another perspective on it. The bending, it didn't help anymore. I mean, even if we would have stayed erect, it wouldn't have helped either. But at least they would pay for it. They didn't care. They didn't account to nobody.

As for many of the other participants, Israel represented the new perspective and the new agent of potential accounting:

It's a moral right to use any power under such circumstances, another mass genocide. Any power, the bomb, the atomic bomb. Even if a great power tries to get Israel, Israel will most probably use the last resort. Like Samson did. They will use everything they have, not to go down by themselves anymore. So they don't push Israel too much. They're afraid to push it too much.

Like Leon, then, Reuben also has an alternative to bending and qualification. "Standing erect," like knowing "where one stands" and what one "stands for," was the lesson.

Indeed, the polarity between images of deathly surrender and world-destructive retaliation lends the same kind of strain to Reuben's voice that we heard in Leon's. Likewise, when the two voices are juxtaposed, they become far more complementary than they first appear. Each is tinged by the echoes of the extremity endured: totalities of "leveling" or "broken trees" that will not grow again; unambivalent counterresponse to the "world as it is" and certainly as they knew it was—for Reuben, images of Samson bringing down the Temple, Israeli atomic bombs, counterapocalypse.

Also like Leon, there is an additional, qualifying source of strain in Reuben's voice that ties it back to the world before it was reduced by extremity. And what lives on from this past leaves single-minded hatred and mutual terror no more acceptable options for Leon and Reuben than delusion or accommodation. If Leon remains "ambivalent," Reuben remains loyal to "Jewish morals" and "upbringing." As much as personal and historical experience may have suggested the futility of such a code, the alternative was worse. Recalling a conversation with a social worker in connection with restitution payments, Reuben remembered:

I was one time at the Jewish Social Services. And the social worker there, who handles a lot of these cases, she said to me, a lot of the survivors, they act irrational, you know what I mean. She talked to me and she says to me, "You, you're a little different. You're very rational." I say to her, "I don't know. I have my own problems, different problems. I'm moody." Maybe these people are not moody. But I guess it has left a certain mark. On everybody. Maybe the ones who are not moody, maybe they don't act rational.

(HG: They express it some other way?) Some other way. They're irrational. They get too hot on the handle. They get angry all the time, you know what I mean. They get angry at every little thing. You know, angry at the whole world. They blame everything, on everybody, you know what I mean. The other way around. . . .

Anger, anger sometimes hurts you more than somebody else. More than the other person. It's not a healthy thing. It's not a good thing.

To be "angry at the whole world" is clearly a potential Reuben feels within himself, and it is one strand in his voice. But it is also clear that, for him, chronic rage leads to still another dissolution of the life that was and, most essentially, remains his own. And so he resists.

Reuben's resistance remains precarious, and to be "the other way around" is no escape from pain. The remnants of the "different morality" could also be disfigured—reduced, once again, to the self-punishing wanderings of a lost soul. It was immediately after his reflections about the unhealthiness of anger that Reuben first spoke about his daily visits to the other "ghetto" he has known. He continued:

> Sometimes, you know, I feel, you know, I'm in a bad, my store is in a bad section of the city. Sometimes, maybe, if I would have wanted, I could have moved out, years back. But sometimes, I feel—, it reminds me, sometimes like, the buildings, all boarded-up. You know, sometimes it reminds me like, like the ghetto.
>
> Sometimes, I don't know. Sometimes, I was thinking to myself, maybe I didn't want to move out. I could have moved out. . . . It reminds me sometimes of the ghetto. Everything was boarded-up. And ruined. You know what I mean. Maybe, maybe I'm punishing myself. I don't know. It could be. I don't know.

I have suggested that even this enactment and the story it retells remain analogic. The self-punishment Reuben voices and the ruins that he cannot leave are his particular "human terms" for the nightmare. Likewise, we should keep in mind that Reuben does not live in this second ghetto, but works there—I would say, recounts there. His actual legacy, his "mixed bunch," he protects at home, where he does not recount at all.

Still, no such thought prevented me from jotting down a terrible question when I first heard Reuben describe his daily returns. This was in early 1978, and Reuben happened to be the first survivor whom I interviewed several times and in depth. "Could it be," I wrote, "that no one survived?"

It would be a couple of years before I realized that the answer was yes and no—simultaneously, irreducibly.

Natalie

No such question would be raised in response to Natalie, although she has suffered one of Reuben's analogic "normal" tragedies in addition to the Holocaust: the death of an adolescent son whose loss she called a "second

Holocaust" for herself and her family. Vivacious, ambitious, and proud—with a refined sense of the dramatic—Natalie is a public person and describes herself as such. To maintain her dignity under all circumstances, to be someone on whom others rely, to be "incredibly busy with three million things" yet still have the resources for more, are her ideals—all without appearing too compromised or frenetic. Her model for living as such a dynamo is a maternal grandmother with whom Natalie closely identifies. The heroine of her youth, Natalie describes her grandmother Miriam as a virtual archetype of generative power:

> She was incredible! And my biggest compliment is for people to say, "Oh, you're just like your grandmother Miriam!" She was an incredible person, an unbelievable person! She was highly educated, very bright, but she could go into a village and completely mix with the peasants. They all adored her. She never flaunted her knowledge. But she was so incredibly beautiful. And she always had a parable, a quotation, something or other, for whatever came up.
>
> She was a Russophile. And she would tell me stories as a child. . . . I didn't know what she was telling me was Russian literature! Biographies of Pushkin, Tchaikovksy, and everyone else. Not until I was a teenager and started reading it, I said, "How come I know this? I know this!" Because it was from her. Spoon-fed.
>
> She was very vivacious, down to earth, funny. Adored by young and old. We knew people in Israel who used to say, "Oh, your grandmother—without her I wouldn't have had an education! . . ."
>
> I'm really very much like her. I'm not trying to compliment myself. . . . She was so incredible! So unbelievable! I could always go to her with a problem. And now kids come here. It's nice. When children want to be with you. It's very nice.

With all her own stories, energy, and charm, Natalie *is* very much like this image of her grandmother. Still, such a standard would not be easy for anyone to meet, even a willful and talented woman like Natalie who does not easily accept any limitations on her capacities—generative or otherwise. (Referring to her grandparents' generation as a whole, she noted: "The men were quiet and sweet and gentle, and the women were powerhouses—incredible women!") It would be an even harder model for the same woman looking back at herself as a seventeen-year-old girl, just beginning to realize her potential. She then knew Russia, not from Miriam's stories, but through a journey of humiliation and flight from occupied Poland, where the rest of her family remained behind. And it would perhaps be hardest for the same woman, now a parent herself, who could not protect one of her own children from a different tragedy. Her son, Michael, died of a sudden illness during a trip away from home.

Given this combination of character and experience, Natalie's activity does become frenetic, a dynamo driven by more than her talents alone. She herself is well aware of that. Referring to both the Holocaust and Michael's death, she commented:

> People will tell you that the pain becomes less acute after a while, and maybe with some people that's true. But the only way we are surviving is by diverting our thoughts, our emotions. By distracting ourselves constantly. By not allowing ourselves to think about it.

If Leon's voice is characterized by the stands he takes and Reuben's by his ceaseless returns, Natalie's is that of one who keeps moving—distracting, diverting, never stopping for long.

At times, Natalie's techniques of distraction are quite direct. At the start of one interview, for example, she wondered if she should do some sketching during the conversation so as not to have to "really think" about what we would be discussing. More often, distraction and diversion are built into the pattern of Natalie's speech itself. There are sudden shifts in content, dropped phrases or asides suggesting some potential upsurge of feeling, then abrupt reversals in tone. Always in the background is the fear that Natalie does most directly express: that of being degradingly exposed, pitied, or humiliated—having to "unzip my wounds," as she said, "and show my painful areas." In a related context, she added: "Maybe it's pride. Maybe it's a sense of such—privacy—or I don't know. . . . But I will not *let* people, uh, sit there, and see me going to pieces." For Natalie, to be so exposed is to become a victim again. And what she wants is for *others* to experience outrage and pain in the face of the Holocaust. She continued:

> I don't want anybody to feel sorry for me. I want people to, uh, feel angry that it happened, or feel—, I want *them* to feel embarrassed that it happened. I want *them* to feel guilty that it happened. But I don't want anybody to feel sorry for me. Even though, God knows, you know, I have two million things that I can tell you, that you would say, "Good God, I feel sorry for—" But I don't want—, because whatever pride, or whatever privacy, when I talk about it, I want *them* to feel angry and incensed and appalled that it could happen.

Natalie's self-presentation is thus both shield and mirror. She deflects attention away from her personal vulnerability yet hopes her listeners will find, reflected by her, a cause from shame themselves.

Still, it must also be said that the feeling that Natalie *could*, suddenly and unpredictably, "go to pieces"—shattering herself and her audience with the revelation of the "two million things"—emerges more strongly because of her dropped and withdrawn suggestions of the possibility. The indirection of her hints adds to their portentousness. That, too, is an effect of her voice she is at least partially aware of controlling. Although she has started to speak publicly about the Holocaust quite often in recent years—"groups are always asking me to talk about it"—Natalie noted that she avoids her personal experiences almost entirely ("I talk in general about the Holocaust—the history of the Holocaust, not my own experience") and tends to avoid any outward emotion:

> I talk about it in an almost, almost a detached manner. I think it's more effective than crying, anyhow. (HG: To be detached?) To be quiet about it. You know, Stanislawski said, it's much more frightening when someone tells you, "I'll kill you," in a whisper than screaming. You know, I agree with that.

In a later interview, Natalie compared her style with the drama, *Whose Life Is It Anyway?*, a play about a sculptor who became a paraplegic in an accident and is suing a hospital for the right to end his life. Said Natalie:

> If I wrote a play, I would build it that way. You know, bring it up to a certain—, and then soften—. You can't think of a more horrible situation. A young man. But it's constantly pedaled with, funny almost, sayings.
>
> So you see, you're never, the dramatist never lets you get to a point where you're, "God, I can't stand it anymore! This tragedy!" You know, every time you reach a point where it's—, it's softened.
>
> (HG: And what effect does that have?) You're able to sit through the whole play without feeling, really, pity for that man. You admire him. You admire him for the way he handles that horrible situation. Otherwise, you might almost, uh, receive the opposite effect. Like, "Oh God, I can't stand it! I can't stand the horrors!" You know, it's too much.
>
> (HG: So not only pity but also pulling away from the whole thing, the horror of it?) Yes. Yes. And it's sad that you have to think about these things. But you do. You do. You do.
>
> (HG: It's like this when you speak yourself?) Well, yes, I don't know. I know that, so far, from the response, people, seem to suffer with me. And also have, my God, admiration is probably the wrong word. But there's something. Some awe, maybe, or something. (HG: Awe?) Yeah. And I'm not out for awe, I can assure you. Or, uh, admiration, believe me. My purpose is to make people aware.

It can be left a question whether there might be any sense in which Natalie is "out for" awe or admiration. Without compromising all her other goals and motives, it would not be surprising if such wishes also lived on in a descendant of female "powerhouses." Further, such motives would certainly be accentuated if the most likely alternatives to awe and admiration from her listeners were condescending pity or complete withdrawal. This, in turn, leads to the question of how well Natalie reads her audience: how ready they might be to respond to her, as a survivor, with celebratory adulation, with victimizing pity, or with silent, and silencing, isolation.

Whatever the interplay between the chosen tellable and the anticipated hearable, the important point here is that, when Natalie does decide to give voice to the realities of her life, there seem to be so few possibilities of expression that are not, in some way, theatric. Meanwhile, the immediate drama that we witness—and which she retells—is the struggle itself between heroic stage-management on one side and the totality of shock or shame she anticipates when she thinks about ripping down the curtain. Of course, both Natalie's pride and her privacy are rooted in her personal heritage and style. But they also evoke a world in which exposure meant degradation far more deadly than pity and in which manipulating the responses of others was infinitely more chilling than any understatement by Stanislawski.

Lydia

If Natalie's voice tends to draw us into the role of audience, Lydia's pushes us toward a stage on which we must find our own "lines" and "method"—or confront an uneasy speechlessness. Only five years old when she and her parents were enclosed within the ghetto, she is the youngest of the participants in this study. Because her family remained in Poland for almost two decades after the war, her voice also retains a bit more of its original accent. That may be also because, as we have heard, Lydia's first language was her second language as well.

Her style is frank and to the point, and she notes that such directness is essential to her intentions:

I've heard from many people that they feel very badly when they talk about it. I don't. As a matter of fact, with my children—perhaps they weren't quite old enough when I did tell them almost everything I had seen—but I think it *should* shock them a little bit. It shouldn't be something that—, I never did cater to my children in any of life's problems. I always tried to shock them a little bit and show them. Like stopping by an accident on the highway and showing them what the accident looked like. To be sure they remembered. That they were careful. And this was, I treated this problem the same way. I think only by shocking somebody will they remember. Will it really stay on their mind.

What Lydia hopes her children do remember are not only the dangers of life, particularly of Jewish life, but also the importance of unhesitatingly acting against them. The shock she hopes to instill is partly the shock of recognition. She comments:

> I do feel that it could happen here also. And if we do not stand up and believe in something, then we're just going to be wiped out. I can understand the American Jews. They never felt what it's like to be threatened every day, and they just don't care. It's more convenient to pretend they are Protestant. They don't think anybody could stand up and say, "Let's do away with the Jews!"
>
> So I try to give my children the horror of it. And that it really happened in a civilized world. . . . Now we know this can happen. They can be on guard. They wouldn't go willingly. They'll fight. You can see it in Israel. That's a different generation. And they're good fighters too!

As we have heard, convictions such as these are expressed by several other participants—as they are by survivors in general and by many others. What makes Lydia's voice distinctive—a measured assertion against a stark counterforce—is that her present freedom of expression was born literally from screams and silences. Of her years in hiding, both inside and outside the ghetto, Lydia recalled:

> We couldn't speak. I had to be quiet. I lost my voice during the war. . . . I remember in the ghetto, I had seen many dead people. I had seen *Aktions*. They surrounded the ghetto and came in and killed many people.
>
> There was a family living not far from us in the ghetto. I remember coming out one day, and there were the kids. They had a lot of kids. They were all in pools of blood. All over the, the, the—, all around the house. On the outside. I guess I knew that if I didn't keep quiet, do whatever I was supposed to, I would look the same. I had seen enough to shock me into being quiet.
>
> After the war, the doctor told me to go out, in the open, and run a lot and try to get the voice back. And try to scream. And the voice came back. But I also used to scream at night, wake up screaming from sleep.
>
> I don't remember what my dreams were. My parents would try to comfort me. Now my dreams are not related to the war at all. But the screaming in sleep was before I got my voice back.

Lydia's voice was thus retrieved directly from a scream, itself salvaged from a silencing nightmare.

She knows, therefore, that shock, at least when experienced firsthand, can lead to silence and terrified obedience as well as to a readiness to fight or speak out. Even with her children, her descriptions of their response to her recounting suggest a thin line between the two kinds of outcome. Regarding Hannah, her daughter who had always seemed most interested in her experiences, Lydia remarked:

> The other children are, I guess maybe they are sometimes afraid to ask about it. Hannah is more open. She would come and want to know about personal things that happened.
>
> (HG: To you or about how you felt?) I really can't remember any specific thing she asked. It would just come back into our conversations. Say she has read something and she says, "I can't believe that anybody would just kill a child." I would tell her how they took little babies and swung them against the walls. She just couldn't believe it. So then I would tell her what happened, what I saw, and that really was true. And this is how things would come up.
>
> (HG: Where would it go from there?) It probably would be me who would pursue it. I don't think she would ask any more than that. I think it's—, for her, any time I would tell her anything, it would be shocking enough that she wouldn't ask anymore. But *I* would always try to make a point.

Lydia explained that "making a point" meant relating her experiences to current political dangers or events. However, she also noted that sometimes memory would come back "on its own," outside any wider narrative or didactic context. She continued:

> I think I most often repeated stories from the early years of the war. Because we were more in the open. . . . And because I was young. I was a child then, and my children love kids. I felt that they will feel it more, I think, if they hear the experiences of a young child. . . . I think they could understand the horror of the story.
>
> It would usually be in relation to something we would hear about happening now. At least, most of the time. The only story that I remember telling them that I don't remember telling them in connection with anything else was the sight that shocked me: when, after one of the *Aktions*, I came out from hiding in the ghetto and—, and the yard of the house was covered with little kids, little babies, actually, bodies, lying in blood.
>
> And I think this was probably the only thing that I would go back to and just tell them on its own.

When Lydia made her remark about her children responding more to the experiences of a young child, before recalling again the landscape of murdered children that had silenced her as a child, her outward expression did not change. Nor was there any perceptible alteration in the tone or cadence of her voice. I was, therefore, surprised when I noticed that she was crying. Tears rolled down from her eyes as though they, too, had a mind and a memory of their own.

There were similar tears in one other of our conversations. They came when Lydia reflected:

> I think it is probably more difficult for an older person to survive and not be upset, psychologically upset, about it. I, for example, feel, that my parents went through more than I did, because they had a child to worry about. Now I know how they must have felt.
>
> I, for example, don't think I could live through war looking at it now. I don't think I could go through it now. I've seen it. I know what it takes to survive. I don't think that I could take it. Now that I have children. I would see my children in the war. Not just myself. I think the worry about the children most—, I think that's what makes it so bad.

Lydia is not alone in feeling that she would not be able to survive another Holocaust or in relating her ongoing dread specifically to fears for her children. Every other participant spoke similarly. But in its very directness and clarity, punctuated by the nightmare that periodically returns "on its own," Lydia's voice may best illustrate how even the firmest parental warning remains only provisionally salvaged from a scream, itself salvaged from the silenced child she had been. Lydia's tears are analogies for the silence, and the children, between her words.

Manny

Manny's voice also emerges from a scream, but one that he usually appears to have firmly under his control. Rather than pulling against his words, his memories seem to pour into his voice in a rush of energy and outrage. To "speak out" and "not to suppress it"—"*oyzereden*" as Manny says in Yiddish—are, in fact, the hallmarks of his style and self-presentation. "Somehow I gotta' have a say on any damn thing that is going around," he notes, "I gotta' put in my two cents." The more punch and irony Manny can bring to his "two cents" the better. Typical is his account of a recent visit to what remains of Dachau. Said Manny:

I went there and I made a lot of noise. I told them, I said, "You made this place look like a beautiful park." I said, "It looked like Hell! Like Hell! You can't conceive of the Hell that was over here!"

There was a lady from Oregon in our group. She had some designer jeans on her. And she had some gold rings. I said, "You know where you are, Lady? Right now? You are in *Hell*! You can't *conceive* of how this looked once upon a time!"

I said, "Look at those nice flowers. You know what they are growing on? A lot of Jewish kids are under those nice flowers! Little, innocent kids are under those flowers!"

I wasn't bashful! Ask my wife. I wasn't bashful.

When Manny speaks like this, he is indeed not bashful. His face reddens and he rises slightly off his chair. His voice takes on the full range of lilts and tones of his earlier life—part Yiddish, part Transylvanian—and he seems to be searching for even more subtle intonations through which to convey his intensity. At times, it is as if he would like to *become* his words—to enter into their vitality like a larger, stronger body, warm enough to guard against the chill he remembers. Speaking of the first time the Hungarian Nazis invaded his home, Manny recalled:

I was sitting, standing up in my long nightgown in bed. And that sonofabitch was deliberately—the windows were open because they made sure the windows were open—there were guards all around. The windows were open. The wind was blowing. It was chilly.

And this big shot! Big, powerful guy, six feet tall, with a bayonet in his hand. Dressed up, like, like Dracula! With all the grenades and the feathers in his hat. And there is a little boy. A little Jewish kid, with the bayonet on him. What is the little kid going to do? How *ironic* the whole thing is!

So you see, these things exist. They're not made up, like some people say today. I know you know! I'm saying it for myself! Because I want to say it out, you know, to speak out. It exists! It's vivid! It's lived! It's alive!

Clearly, Manny's testimony here is an affirmation of his own ongoing existence—*his* being "vivid" and "alive"—at the same moment it affirms what he remembers. His voice enlarges with the magnitude of what he recalls. Its surviving strength is further verification of his own.

Relatedly, the "little Jewish kid's" survival against such odds is itself evidence of a unique kind of power. Having been eye-to-eye with so many Goliaths, and outlived them, David also rises in stature. Manny comments:

Look at it this way: Here was the German army—the best equipped, most disciplined army in the world at that time. In fact, the so-called "Superman" had the elite of his troops guarding helpless, weak, demoralized people.

So we must be some kind of very strong people! Even when we are down to skin and bones, I need the strongest person to guard me so I can't run away! Well, so it makes me feel very strong. . . . I experienced it as a Jew. And it makes me a much firmer Jew. That I am stronger than steel! I survived! I survived better than the so-called "Superman." Maybe this is something we have that other people don't have!

Here, too, Manny is not "bashful." His survival as a Jew is a source of pride to him, and he does not hesitate to say so.

Still, a certain tension enters in. Is it personal survival or the survival of the Jewish people as a whole that he is describing? If the former, what can be said about those who did not survive? In a later interview, Manny came to the question himself, and the tension emerges more clearly. Discussing the pervasive belief in omens and superstition that was part of his childhood, he noted:

The same hold the Catholic church had in the early days, by giving more superstition than education, that's exactly what we were fed with. And yet, it's difficult to explain. Is this what kept us surviving? Yes? No?

Let's put it this way: Nature functions in such a way, that, in other words, we're all certain spokes in the universe. All right, this particular spoke had to survive. I was still part, I still have to contribute certain things to the world. I'm here. You're here. The others were, I suppose, were so-called, what? Deficient or something like that. They couldn't—, not "deficient." I shouldn't use that word. Others were—, it's very—, these are things that are very difficult to discuss.

Here Manny is hesitant to follow his teleology of survival to its conclusion. The reduction of the world to those destined to survive and those who are "deficient" sounds too much like other theories of iron destiny.

Further, even when Manny limits himself to his own survival, a growing uncertainty emerges. On one side, there is no doubt that his personal survival reinforced a belief in his own special fate. Even before the war, he had developed a strong sense of himself as a kind of "survivor." As his prewar memories express, by his adolescence he already viewed himself as a "rebel" whose gambles were somehow destined to pay off, someone who was used to confronting "big shots" and, most of the time, emerging successful and unscathed. Likewise, many of his stories from the camps themselves—even given the odds against *anyone* surviving—have a particularly miraculous quality. Such a history, already conditioned by the kind of superstition he describes, gave him good reason to continue to believe in his own "special magic."

Such a history, however, also gave Manny good reasons for exactly the opposite belief. Even under normal developmental circumstances, a sense of chosenness like Manny's always contains the possibility of abrupt reversal. The eye that blesses may suddenly curse. "Big shots," even if outflanked, remain big enough to return to fight another day. What maintains one's faith is exactly the fact that any status *is* only provisional. Too up or too down, luck can change. Future events promise a potential balancing or some revised interpretation of the past. Manny tells us that at Auschwitz that future died. All comparisons between his own fate and that of others, or between one interpretation and the other, were reduced to a single, irremediable doom. Manny recounts:

> You were thrown into, what I would call, an open solitary confinement. Usually, when someone is not doing so well, like in business, you are consoled a little if you are not doing so well. There you had individuals in the same situation, the same destiny, predicament, but you were not consoled. You found no consolation in seeing your friend in the same situation. . . .
>
> Every minute—no, it was not precious. Because you were thinking of the next minute. Whether you will be around. And you were so absorbed in staying alive that anything that was going on around you—, didn't matter. It was just a curse. And, and, and you were part of it.
>
> (HG: Part of it?) Usually, when there's a curse, some believe, some don't. But the trouble was this: You *believed* in the damn curse! You were *living* it! And, it was just—, *there was no hope!* Usually, there is some. There's a ray of hope that *something*, something good—. No. That wasn't there. That was absolutely not there.

If survival reinforced one pole of Manny's sense of destiny, then, what he had to survive irrevocably confirmed the other. Indeed, the whole idea of destiny was itself consumed by a curse unqualified by comparison, time, or hope. That curse was believed because it was lived; one was inextricably "part of it" in a way that dissolved any other conjectures or possible interpretations.

It is, therefore, not surprising that the sense of special destiny we hear in Manny's voice—and, finally, all his speculations about good fortune or bad—are set against the echo of an all-consuming end. When he speaks of the latter, he describes days of paralyzing dread, visions of his own death and that of his family, panics in which he imagines "the worst conceivable disease" or the collapse of his business. Speaking of the last, he confided:

> I'll tell you, in spite of what I possess, I know I will always be a little bit insecure in this country. Financially, I think I'm all right. I think I'm all right. With the investments I have. Yet when I have a slow day in business—and, believe you me, I can always make a living—but that is a business that I've built with my own hands, you see that. But, oh, yes, God forbid, if something would happen to me and I would lose it, I would be very unhappy. I would be—, I probably wouldn't be able to survive it. I mean that. Not the business. The business I'm not concerned about. But my investments. If I were to lose my investments.

In the context of the other losses Manny fears, it is clear that "investments" has a general as well as a particular meaning for him. Ultimately, the word stands for any future on which it is still rational to gamble.

Manny can usually shake off such thoughts, at least temporarily. He may suddenly recall one of his past risks that succeeded irrespective of experience or reason. And sensitive to his listeners' rising interest, particularly in response to his own infectious enthusiasm, he knows how to stretch the glow. Remembering one especially miraculous escape, he exclaimed:

> I'm very impulsive! I do a lot of things by impulse. I don't think. But apparently it was a gamble. And it worked! . . .
>
> Now that we're talking, I'm thinking: Am I doing it to show what kind of hero I was?! That I am such a hero—stronger than the other guy? *That*, I can't imagine! A little recognition? Well, let's be honest! Sure! Why not?! A little recognition!
>
> Did I ever tell you about the time when I played an epileptic? Because of what happened there. I worked on it three or four times . . .

Thus Manny's voice and his stories continue, irresistible to modern listeners in search of survivor-heroes and celebrants of life. Such stories are, indeed, remnants of an ancient magic, salvaged from a cursed universe of modern fact.

Paula

Paula's voice is already familiar to us. Along with some of her particular reflections, a number of her images have been central in our general discussion—"unfinished sentences" and the dead and living tree. Although I had not initially realized it, the notion of "frames" also came from Paula. It appeared in our first conversation, within a series of reflections in which she most explicitly defined her style and her struggle:

> I don't like to argue with people. I have my own convictions, but I have no right to convince you otherwise. Maybe I'm the crazy one! And I think this goes back to the time I was taken to Auschwitz. I said, "Well, O.K., so I'm alive. God selected me because I'm not normal, not human. And if I'm not human, this is my fate."
>
> (HG: You wouldn't argue with God about it?) No, because how else would I be able to endure the things I saw with my own eyes. The shock of being separated from my mother, from my brother. And seeing the crematorium day and night, as close as a few feet: that was a constant frame.
>
> And I said: "No. That's *not* my mother! That's *not* my family!" Even being right at it. You try to use some shield, what I call the shade. I think this was my own training, my own psychological training. I still use that an awful lot. I don't hear. I know it's there. If you want to hurt me, I know you want to. But I'm not going to see it. I refuse. With open eyes. But with a haze. Because otherwise you cannot endure.

Both the crematorium and Paula's sense of her humanity were thus put behind the "shade" simultaneously. Still, within a more constricted sphere, she asserted what she also denied. Just as her dream of her mother's protection continued to return, even though it was recurrently destroyed, so Paula salvaged small enactments of care within the nightmare. Like many in Birkenau, she formed a "camp family" with three other women— in Paula's case, a mother and her two daughters whom Paula had known before the war.[4] Within that circle, compromised as it often was, a remnant of nurture and belonging persisted. Paula described other such instances:

> I decided I am not human. Because only animals would endure things like that. So I decided I was like one. Though I still tried to push away the thought that I am.
>
> Little incidents—I would see an old lady that was nearly at her death, that was toward the end, and I would comfort her before she died. Or I would close her eyes to die. And, uh, I did these things, for you know—, I was trying to prove, yes, I would do this for my mother if she would be with me. I wanted to be a little child again and hold on to something. And this helped me stay human. Or stay, you know, not lose my sanity altogether.

The "constant frame" of the killing was thus precariously countered by another frame: that of small acts of care between a "little child" and her mother.

It is as a kind of "little child," still unsure of herself and still somewhat lost within the "haze," that Paula first presents herself. She is "no expert" and has "no credential," she repeatedly asserts, and has "no one thing" on which to ground her identity. Within her limited domain, she does what she can, but makes no wider claim. "I can't fight the crowd," she reflects, "but if my thought did generate anything in one person, it will be a satisfaction. It's not enough, but I will accept it."

As we have heard, Paula ties her reticence to the fact of the "shade" itself. Not only does it shield her from realities she might not be able to endure, but its continued presence also blocks out other memories and perceptions that might give her more certain grounding. "The overall picture overlaps the good too," she said about the childhood she cannot remember, and her sense of getting few defining (and self-defining) details continues into Paula's present life. Discussing a recent vacation, she commented:

> I came back, and I don't know where I ate, what was the name of the hotel. . . . I have the feeling, a certain outline of the situation, but no definite thing. That's why I say, I always need help. Someone else has to start it. And I'll say, "Oh, I remember." The overall story—no dates, and no names . . .
>
> So I'm really a very little person. I mean, there's no one thing I can relate to clearly. It's so many little things, but nothing is good enough.

Thus speaking as a "little person" with "so many little things," Paula waits for someone else to help her through the fog. But she will not attempt to "fight the crowd" if they do not arrive.

Of course, Paula is anything but a "little child." She is a woman of pride and extraordinary insight, as her contributions to these pages attest. Even in the excerpts cited above, we hear echoes of a different stance. She does not hesitate to say (to the psychologist) that she, too, has had her "psychological training." Likewise, throughout our conversations, she recalled a variety of episodes in which, in her own "little way," she proved the "experts" to have far less expertise than their titles might suggest. And while Paula may have wanted to be "a little child and hold on to something" in the midst of the destruction, it was she who did most of the mothering and protecting in the instances she recalls. That continues to be her style and her drive. As often as she may yearn to reach out to others, she remains, in her chosen activities, as much an independent "power-house" as Natalie and as directed in her purposes as Leon. Likewise, when she *has* chosen to "fight the crowd," she is no less outspoken than Manny and her vision of reality is no less clear than Lydia's.

As Paula herself came to suggest, the "modest little girl" strain in her voice is essentially strategic. The "shade" and the "haze" protect her from experiencing an outrage and, ultimately, a helplessness that are far less bearable than her own self-restraint. Further, like the other themes of voice that we have heard—Manny's chosenness, for example, or Natalie's pride—Paula's stance can also be traced to memories earlier than the destruction. Thus she recalls her role as a young girl in her family and community: "I was, like they say, a tiny *pisher*, a tiny kid. And a tiny kid does not exist. Because in Europe, when a child spoke, it was like they say, 'a child is to be seen and not heard.' " Waiting modestly to be "heard," therefore, was a virtue Paula learned long ago. At the same time, it is significant that one of the few distinct memories Paula does recall from childhood concerns an episode in which the "tiny kid" did *not* wait to be called upon. Speaking of her school days, Paula noted:

> You know, I have just an over-picture. My teacher—, I remember one incident, but I don't remember what subject he taught me. But I remember him reprimanding me once when I said something funny, and the whole class started laughing, and I was giggling. And he said, "If Miss Marcus will allow me, now I will continue."
>
> *This* I remember. Now isn't that stupid!

"Stupid" it may be in the context of other memories that Paula carries. Yet the incident is certainly not without importance as a remembered fragment of a bright young girl's fully normal struggles between submission and self-assertion toward the normal authorities of her life.

Within the grasp of the authorities of Auschwitz, "to be seen and not heard" and to be treated as nonexistent took on an entirely different set of referents. Paula tells us that within that reduction, terminal and unqualified, she accepted the verdict that was not "normal" nor "human." And while her efforts to prove otherwise persisted behind the "shade," they offered no escape. For, in the end, no "little dream," like no "inner sanctuary," could withstand recurrent dissolution. Waking from an Auschwitz nightmare a year after liberation, Paula wrote in her journal:

> We are the prisoners doomed to death. And I can only call us stupid, ignorant, crazy. Because to live like this—denied everyone and everything, kicked and shoved underfoot, degraded and humiliated, doped and numb— only people who would just as soon be dead could live through this. Having lived it, we are no longer among the living. The living could not survive it.

At some level, Paula did not survive it. The "hollowness" remained along with the remaining "curves" and "shapes." It could not be filled.

Of course, this did not leave Paula "stupid, ignorant, crazy." These are her particular ways of giving voice to a more encompassing destruction, just as Leon's "contamination" or Reuben's "self-punishment" are theirs. Through such terms, images of a whole landscape of death are transposed into more intimate stains of the mind or of the heart.

As we have heard, Paula drew increasingly on this vocabulary of personal deficiency in the years after liberation. Initially, she *did* argue with God. She challenged *His* sanity and the clarity of *His* vision, even if she also tried to allow for His simple absence. Paula wrote in her journal:

> God, you took my mother away. And my little brother. Where did You take them? To the fire?
>
> I'm looking into the fire. And I think I would go completely crazy if I thought that You, God in Heaven, You are looking on all of this. And You have not gone crazy.
>
> You looked upon us while the innocent children, and my dear ones, were taken away. To us You granted the gift of having to suffer, of having to see all of this, and of having to continue to exist. To them [the Germans] You gave Your mercy. . . .

Paula also debated those immediately around her during these years. Far from being quiet and self-effacing, she noted in her journal: "Every day is a fight, because I'm trying to make myself understood. My rights, my principles, and somebody else's." And when she didn't fight outwardly, she confided more bitterly about how hard it is "with a smart head, to live as though ignorant."

Only gradually did Paula's inner debate between "anger" and "conscience," "self-awareness" and "self-criticism," yield toward the latter poles. She learned again, as she herself came to say, to remain "inconspicuous—like the child 'to be seen and not heard.' " Yet this did not resolve the struggle. For her own silence, in conjunction with the silencing imposed upon her, led finally to a terrible sense of complicity with the work of oblivion. Paula commented:

> I don't think any one of us really allows our thoughts to see that clearly. Because, in my own defense, I always pull that shade. You just want to forget everything.
>
> And now, all these years, we are debating: Whose fault is it that for the last thirty-five years we haven't talked about it? But it has been proven that

the mind just couldn't perceive it. The feeling was just too much—, it was just too deep-rooted.

Paula is correct in her conclusions. But that has not made the debate between "anger" and "conscience"—the question of "whose fault it is"— easier to bear. Even when she turns back to anger there is no solution, for anger risks still another reductive association with destruction. Reminiscent of Reuben, Paula explained:

> Anger, outrage—, a small match will ignite the outrage. Not even related to the same subject. And to me the worst feeling is anger. Maybe I do blame somebody else, but I can't always bring it out. And I'm just hurting myself. You know, I feel my anger. Not you.
> And again, anger can be destructive, yes? It can cause war. In one sense, anger can only cause war. And you cannot solve a chaotic situation. In a chaotic mood, you only create more hysteria. So you have to wait for the chance, until it quiets down. Because, from camp experience, hysteria just brought death and beating and animosity and inhuman behavior. And inhuman behavior, to me, is the lowest instinct that exists. In my own world, that was my strength—to hold on to being a human being.

Associating her anger with the murderous chaos she remembers, Paula bides her time. In biding her time, she also avoids a more definitive defeat. Speaking specifically about the way she has not pushed her own role as recounter, Paula noted:

> Not without encouragement, I would have gone out and talked about the Holocaust. I didn't go out and volunteer, "O.K., people, now I'm going to tell you stories!" I was just brought into it. . . . But I don't reach out. And these things play a big role in my moods, in my depressions, and so forth.

In a related context, she added:

> You see what it is: I don't want to accept defeat. This way, in my own mind, I can say, "Well, if they had known." But what if they refuse? I don't want to get angry. And I will. I'll get over it, but why give it a chance to get to that point? So I don't even give it a chance. I don't want to get to the point of the refusal. I'd rather face it alone, than the defeat.

"Defeat," for Paula, means to remember a hollowness in which even outrage is consumed. Now, as then, she would rather provisionally accept her isolation than have it reconfirmed.

These, then, are the turns of Paula's voice and of her world. When she feels she can, she launches herself into projects that affirm her strength and her capacity to provide strength to others: organizing fund drives, making contacts for new immigrants, handling the crises of friends and families. In the midst of these commitments, as she describes it, she is "wound up, day and night, everything has to wait, till later." Yet, for all her actual successes, which are many, they are never enough. Something always remains unfinished. Days of feverish activity are punctuated by days of hollowness and depression. Of those days, Paula says:

> It's an emptiness. A total lack of soul. Nothing. Just an empty, empty, you know—, you just don't care about anything. Your own family—, "Well, let 'em—," you know. In other words, I don't assert myself to their well-being or otherwise. You know, just let it go. . . . It's just, just not my interest at that point.

Of course, Paula does care. But, partly in anger, partly in expectation, she is now exhausted and waiting. "I don't *want* to be that independent the way I'm showing it," she confided in a late interview. "This is just a show. This is just a show." She is waiting—not actually to be a "little child" again—but to retrieve, one more time, at least the remnants of a dream. Immediately following the passage in her diary in which she wrote about no longer being "among the living," Paula continued:

> Now, suddenly, I realize I have tears in my eyes. They are streaming down my face. Suddenly, I feel like I am home again with my family. I am with those who were everything to me. It feels like a long time ago, that we were all together. But the fire, the cursed flames, still don't let me think. They wake me up from my dreams, and my dreams hold the only hope for going on. Their hissing and crackling have awakened me again.

THE OUTLINE OF A WORLD

Here, then, are six individual voices; six particular people. Their self-presentations remain distinct: a reflective critic, a lost soul, a proud dramatist, a young witness, an outspoken challenger, a modest diarist. Some give voice to sentences full of considered explanation, haunting suggestion, or building irony and exclamation. Others measure out their words against more evident pulls toward restraint, silence, or a preoccupying pain. Some point most directly toward fears for the future. Others seem more chronically immersed in the losses of the past. Some question God, society, or fate. Others are more likely to question themselves.

Yet with these and many other differences between them, these voices increasingly complement each other as their individuality unfolds. Those who are initially most outraged or assertive also speak eventually of self-doubt, terror, or despair. Those who first seem bound up by self-questioning, restraint, or grief also give voice to fully outward accusations or reveal thoughts of an awesome retaliation. Those who would break through all illusion suggest the depth of shock or silence that such unmasking can entail. Those who would hold back from such directness reveal the immensity of effort required to maintain the shades and curtains.[5]

Each participant emphasizes different sides of these polar themes, and each does so in ways that reflect his or her particular life history and experience. But as their individual perspectives are juxtaposed, a picture of a world emerges, a closed world of killers and victims, with the terminal versions of such polarities as its reductive axes. Within that world, ambivalence means paralysis, while certainty finds its base in hatred or leads to confirmed nonexistence. Depression and self-recrimination signal death, while outrage signals war or a chaos of destruction. Vulnerability or exposure become a totality of shock or degradation, while protection becomes indifference, deception, or delusion. Bad luck means the certain doom of the deficient, while good luck means the iron destiny of supermen.

We shall hear more of this world as the conversation deepens. Its ongoing presence in memory pulls at survivors' voices and provides their characteristic ring of extremity—of the "worst conceivable" in Manny's phrase. Somehow, they must struggle to speak of that world *without* "embodying" it or being consumed by it. Meanwhile, they speak to a world all too ready to view them exactly as such embodiments, which only adds to their aloneness. Within that extended isolation, some voices become even more strained by the immensity of what they must transmit—more awesome, portentous, ghostly, or pained. But however strained they become, they remain only echoes of the screams and silences from which all such voices are salvaged, and by which they are still sometimes consumed.

Thus there are times, in the midst of all apparent clarity and strength, when participants may suddenly give voice to the most overwhelming fears and guilts that continue to haunt them, which haunt them at that very moment, and for which "fears" and "guilts" are never the right words; the feeling of insecurity is too pervasive, the doubt is too profound. At these times, it is the dissolution of meaning that seems most real. Even the most searing expressions of that dissolution—contamination, damnation, degradation, ignorance, craziness, tears, silence itself—only point to something more.

But there are other times as well, more frequent in later conversations than in early ones, more likely when one knows the recounter well. Now, from out of a depth of terror or despair that is itself background, there emerge memories of particular loves and hates, felt commitments and perceived betrayals, for which fear and guilt, or hope and desire, are precisely the right words. Rooted in another part of the participants' pasts than the destruction, these memories carry the remnants of all those everyday conflicts of loyalty and rivalry, esteem and insult, before becoming reductively transformed by extremity. And the struggles now expressed between clarity and doubt, or between assertion and anxiety, are familiar to all of us. They are certainly not without pain and intensity. All the normal conflicts of development are present. But in the images of power and dependency now recalled, time, hope, and the modulating balance of ambivalence continue to play a mediating role. The "worst conceivable" (as well as the best) are, once again, the stuff of fantasy and dreams.

In survivors' recounting, these kinds of memories frame the others, just as they are framed *by* the others. The nightmare recurrently breaks into the dream; yet the dream somehow "re-forms" and "goes on." To see only the destruction is to condemn survivors to only one of the worlds that they know and to keep that world—and its truest legacy of legacies' terrible fragility—from impinging on our own.

It is particularly important to keep this duality in mind as we now listen intensively to Victor. The eldest of the participants and, in his own view, close to death, he perhaps more than any other struggles to weave the different strands of his life together into a comprehensible and communicable whole. Dreams and nightmares, different sets of memories, battle with each other in his voice, his stories, and enactments made of his ongoing life itself. Once again, it is tempting to view these as "symptoms" and thereby end the conversation. Here, the object is to listen differently: to hear Victor's voices, stories, and enactments all as part of his recounting—acts of creation and re-creation though which one more single voice strives to tell us the fate of his world and, by implication, our own.

Chapter 4

The Stories of the Prosecutor I

If I have searched my mind properly, it is not a matter of revenge, nor one of atonement. The experience of persecution was, at the very bottom, that of an extreme *loneliness*. At stake for me is the release from the abandonment that has persisted from that time until today.

Jean Amery, *Resentments*

THE VOICES OF THE PROSECUTOR

Every voice implies a wider story: the story of that voice and of the life in which it is grounded and which it articulates. And, in fact, it is impossible to listen to survivors' voices without also beginning to hear the stories they simultaneously retell. Thus Leon's voice as a man of words and convictions already suggests the story of a "word man" in a world in which the promise of culture has been irrevocably betrayed. Reuben's voice as a "lost soul" already begins the story of one who must remember the life that was destroyed even at the risk of himself becoming one of its ghosts. Natalie's voice as a self-conscious dramatist initiates the story of a recounter who would both communicate her memories and guard them—all without losing her audience, her dignity, or the truth. For these and the other participants, presenting who they are means also presenting how they have become who they are and how they continue to live.

In the presentation of Victor that now begins, the evolution of story out of voice is traced more directly and in considerably greater detail. It is as though we raise the level of magnification here, entering more fully into the process of retelling. Later on, I shall return to the recounting of the other participants in light of what we have learned through sustained immersion in Victor's words and in the stories of his life.

It will be noted that voices and stories—even of a single participant—are now described in the plural. This is to suggest the interweaving of polarities, of meanings and reductions of meanings, and of different worlds of memory out of which survivors' voices and stories take form. Using an analogy of "concentric circles" that he has also applied to his own writing, Wiesel wrote of a Hasidic master:

> His tales? Each contains many others. Imagine a series of concentric circles whose fixed centers are buried in man's innermost being: The I inside the I, conscience become silence and peace, memory inside memory. [1]

In entering into survivors' voices and stories—here those of Victor in particular—we also find "I's" inside of "I's," memories inside memories, with "I's" and memories interchanging, interweaving, but attaining no final integration. We also find conscience becoming silence and peace. But the silence and peace that Victor knows are not those of redemption. And the conscience on which he must finally rely, at the end of his stories, is not his own.

The Prosecutor

Few of the participants speak about the destruction of a world, and of its memory, more persistently than Victor. The echoes of that destruction resound at the heart of his voice, and its visions shape much of what he continues to see. Like Reuben, Victor constantly returns to images of failed inheritance, generations cut off from both the past and the future, peoples erased not only from ongoing history but from memory itself. Unlike Reuben, however, Victor does not speak as a ghostly remnant of the past but rather as its interrogator. He tells us he is a "hindseer": not one "who looks forward with the eyes of progress," but one "who looks back to what is behind." In looking back, he questions. In questioning, he prosecutes.

> Some Jews went ahead. They continue it, to marry again. And they were lucky that they were saved. I said, "No, I am *not* that lucky." I am not satisfied with this. *They!* The six million that was killed. Because of this, I am not satisfied that I survived. I don't call it a miracle. When six million Jews paid with their lives for my survival. Or for the resurrection of the Jewish state. I am not satisfied. And this is the thing that I became a prosecutor when I was

reading the Bible. If there was *something*. So I became the prosecutor. And I am still the prosecutor.

To be "the prosecutor," then, is first of all an act of loyalty. Contrasting himself with those who, he feels, more comfortably "went ahead" to "continue it," Victor takes the role of the six million left behind. He looks back and prosecutes *for them*.

To prosecute is also to search. Echoing Manny's exclamation of the unqualified curse—"usually, there is *something*"—Victor reads the Bible to see "if there *was* something": something that might explain what he experienced and salvage faith. In fact, as we have heard, Victor's reading the Bible had become an obsession. Beginning seven years earlier, at the time of his semiretirement, he had started to bring the Bible with him to his job and studied it during free hours. By the time of our interviews, he had reread it several times. He explained:

> I feel that when I sit down at the Bible I am a prosecutor. And the Bible is the material that I am trying to find something to criticize it. . . . I say, "God, where are you? Are you dumb? Are you deaf? You don't see nothing! Are you blind? Or are you *not at all?*"
>
> So why does these people fool me? Why so many thousands of generations want to put down the knowledge of religion, the authority of God. . . . Why was this bluffing going on? I want to search. I want to search. (HG: And what do you want to find?) I want to find the truth.

Like Paula's questioning God in her diary, Victor's prosecution is thus also an interrogation. Ultimately, it is a search for evidence—damning evidence. And within the tribunal that Victor initiates, it is no longer his own survival that is on the line, but that of God and religion and inherited tradition as such.

What happens when the "bluffing" is unmasked? What is left when the prosecutor succeeds? Victor tells us that what remains are remains: old bones under old tombs.

> I went to Israel. I went to the cave of the graves of the Patriarchs. There was, according to the Five Books of Moses . . . a double basement. And the bodies are down there. When you look through the chain, you see inside, two candlesticks, copper-made. But those two candlesticks, they was too polished to be made by the time of Abraham. This was later.
>
> This is everything that religion is. Religion is built one way. It was put away rough. But the words was polished up, and the means was polished up,

like those two candlesticks. Polished up, to suit better the sanctity and the purpose.

King Solomon says, "Keep off your feet from God's house?" Why? I read Maimonides, *The Guide for the Perplexed*. And Maimonides says, "Keep off your feet in order to give it more reverence." Where one can touch it, where one can go in, it loses the flavor of sanctity. It isn't much at all. But if the Jews have to stay *outside*, they hear only the crying from the calves, from the sheep, and from the High Priest. They give it more reverence.

Victor wants to go inside God's house—to see the High Priest and the sacrificial rites directly: "In their time, people was blind. They worshipped something far away. . . . Everything far away . . . *I* want to see it closer." The closer Victor looks, the less there is to find—"It isn't that much at all." And when the words and mystery are removed, the prosecutor can only look back upon himself. The reduced image of God is joined by a reduced image of humanity. Said Victor:

This what I find leads me back to where I began. I come to an end. I cannot go forward. That man is just an animal like any other animal. Like the ant, like the rat, like the cow, like the horse. . . . We are just another animal like they are.

Such conclusions offer Victor no consolation. In a related context, he continues:

Now, forty years later, I see a lot of races that are destroyed. It's the law of the jungle. The weaker has to give under. He has to be destroyed. And the stronger survives. . . .

It's the law of the jungle, even by man. Some people are in business. They are fortunate and everything goes straight. The other one, he has to go out of business. Why? It's also the law of the jungle. . . . You got to be strong. You got to try to survive. It's all circumstances. This is a world of circumstances. Birth, marriage, reproduction: The whole world is a world of circumstances. The ant, the rat, the cow, the horse, and the man—a world of circumstances.

Whether by strength or fortune, some survive and others perish. Victor's conclusion that some "are fortunate and everything goes straight" reminds us of those other survivors who "went ahead" feeling "lucky that they survived." But if he accepts the "law of the jungle"—an arbitrary world of struggle and "circumstances"— what now can be the grounds of his dissatisfaction? Having won his case, the prosecutor appears to have lost it.

These comments, drawn mainly from my first interview with Victor, present his thoughts in their most general form. Yet even here, he gives voice to a circle of themes that will close in around him as the conversation deepens. The initial "hindseer" who prosecutes for those who were destroyed gradually finds himself drawn into unwilling complicity with that destruction. The more he unmasks, the more tombs and Patriarchs are robbed of sanctity, the less claim they have on our care and attention. Great or small, the dead are simply dead: a heap of bones exposed and unprotected once all the words and the mystery have been stripped away.

Victor has seen such a charnel pit before: the obliteration of reverence he witnessed on the edge of the rubbish pit at Treblinka. He has learned how easily human beings could be equated with ants and rats and their cries reduced to the calls of slaughtered lambs and sheep—all justified by other high priests and other theories about "the law of the jungle." Thus, in his fight against turning into stone—joining in the indifference he associates with "going ahead"—Victor discovers within himself a terrifying complement to the process by which people are turned into garbage and into ash. Partly as a result, just as the prosecution of God became a prosecution of man, so it also becomes a prosecution of the prosecutor himself. That tribunal is provisionally framed, and its story is enacted, within a more intimate circle of creatures and creators, fathers and sons.

The Old Man

Even without the particular problems associated with being a prosecutor, Victor has other—in some ways opposite—reasons for self-recrimination. For if we take the simplest meaning of being a "hindseer"—*not* being one who "went ahead" to "continue it"—we come to the other major theme in Victor's self-presentation. Well before he attempted to unmask his legacy, Victor tells us that he forsook it. Although he continues privately to identify as a Jew, he usually keeps his Jewishness a secret from a potentially hateful world. His wife is Catholic and their children were raised in neither religion. They are, as Victor put it, "not now nothing."

Thus Victor also "went ahead," but in a way that left much of his past behind. Now, aware of his advancing age, he speaks of feeling little connection with either the past or the future. Like Reuben, Victor tends to describe himself as cut off from the cycle of generations, and, also like Reuben, he sometimes expresses resigned acceptance of that fate. Speaking of the isolation he feels within his own family, Victor commented: "I will go my way; they will go theirs. And death will take care of everything."

Contrasting, as he often does, the perspectives of an old man and a young man, he added:

> When a man feels closer to death, what's the difference how a man ends? This way or that way . . . An old man, full of wrinkles on his face, the feet do not work anymore, the hands do not work anymore, everything stops to work in him. When it comes to this, he is something surplus. Even to his closest, he is something surplus. He is useless. He starts to become a burden. To his closest. That's life. That's part of life.

In this mood, at least, Victor is reconciled to his "circumstances." "Death will take care of everything," and the "surplus" have no claim on their survivors.

But Victor has other moods as well. And it was exactly his sense of being close to death that had initially caused him to look back on his life and to question. In the beginning, he questioned himself. In the course of our conversations, he went back several times to one particular incident he had witnessed during the destruction. Two young Jews, both highly religious, had been caught by the Germans and were awaiting execution. Victor remembered how they turned away from their heritage in a last gesture of outrage and despair:

> While they was waiting for the Germans to come out and shoot them, the two boys, they scratched their faces, they scratched out some of their beards. Now this is a sign. For scratching the face, for a Jew, is forbidden to inflict themselves like that. This was a sign that, at the last moment, they came to regret their ancestry. They regretted what they are and what they were made.

In a later conversation, Victor also remembered an older man who made a different choice under similar circumstances. At the moment of inescapable death, he affirmed his Jewishness and chose, said Victor, "to remain what he was":

> As you grow older, it gets more important. You want to remain what you was. And to procreate what you was. As you are young, it is not important. You still have a span of life in front of you. But the old one said, "No, I am not going to do it. I am going to remain what I am. You can kill me. I will remain what I am."

Victor related the story of this old man to his own aging and his regrets about what he had left behind and incomplete. Now no thoughts of death's inevitability provided solace. Of the old man's fidelity, Victor reflected:

This is a power in life. It has a power. It makes a difference when he is old. He dies easier. He thinks he has accomplished everything. I feel I have not accomplished everything. I failed. It's harder to die. . . .

When the strength leaves the man, he starts to reflect on things. He looks back. That's why we have in the prayer: "Don't send me away empty-handed when I am old. When my power will be diminished. *You*, don't forsake me! Don't forsake me when my power will diminish!" This is to God, you understand? All true, I question God. But I take the merit of the words. . . .

Those who wrote this wasn't young. A young one doesn't weigh these words. But an old one reflects on those words. [2]

These words are not "polish" for Victor but speak directly to him. They are his words, the prayer of an old man looking back and trying to salvage the hope that God and the generations will not abandon him as he feels he has abandoned them. Both his hope and his guilt survive *in spite of* what he has witnessed; they are retrieved from memories *other* than those of the world reduced to survival, death, and "circumstances." Both are remnants of a legacy that Victor cannot leave behind.

The Young Man

As the incident retold by Victor suggests, at a moment of complete despair, a young man may also look back at his heritage, tearing away its last mask of hope as he tears away his beard, itself now only a mask of allegiance. If somehow he survives, he may continue to look back—not to reflect or to prosecute—but simply overcome by horror in the wake of his own and his people's fate.

This is how Victor discusses his choices immediately after the war. Regarding his no longer practicing Judaism, his words remind us of Paula's memory of her father's voice. Recalling that the round-up that brought him to Treblinka occurred a few days after Rosh Hashanah, 1942, Victor reflected:

It's kind of an unfinished thing. To continue it, I cannot. I left it like it is. . . . To go to the temple to pray, I have no heart. Because of this what I have seen. And every time the season comes, I think of the season. And I leave it like it is.

I remember, before, in my hometown. I went with my father to the *schul*. And they called him up to officiate. They invited somebody who *knows*. I went with him, and sing with him, and know everything. I couldn't do it now. Not because my father is not alive anymore. Because of what happened.

There are occasional exceptions when Victor does go to the temple. In a later conversation, he further clarified his way of continuing as a Jew, now emphasizing fear and the need for secrecy as much as emptiness of heart.

> I will tell you something. I am an agnostic. But I do sometimes go on Yom Kippur to the temple. And I cry sometimes. I hide my eyes, my face, from people.
>
> I can't get away. I am always a Jew. But I get away in the sense of not showing off that I am Jewish. So that others, who are not Jews, do not know. I learned—conspiracy is the biggest weapon you can possess. When one doesn't know what you are, you can find out secrets, what he really thinks. Even in America, when he doesn't know you are a Jew, he will talk to you against Jews.

Conspiring to find out secrets, rather than more directly unmasking them, is Victor's method here. He became a secret Jew in order to learn the secret hatreds of others—and be prepared for them.

Victor discussed his choice of work similarly. Although, he emphasized, he came from a "business family," he has worked in a factory most of the years he has been in the United States:

> I wasn't in business. I went to work in a factory. Do you know for what reason? Because I was sick and tired of Polish people saying that Jews are always in business. "The Jews are always in business." They hate the Jew regardless. But this pierce my heart. I was one Jew in a factory of a thousand people.

As we shall hear, Victor will amend this first explanation of his choice of factory work in a later conversation. But that will not change the fact that at work, too, he was a secret Jew, at least until the day he began to bring the Bible.

Victor also explained his marrying a Christian in terms of his wish for anonymity: to get away from the hatred he had known and to help his children get away as well. Most directly tied to the issue of abandoning his heritage, this decision evokes Victor's most severe self-questioning:

> I sinned. Despite that I am not religious. I sinned against my father and my mother. Because they didn't do it and I should do it. I married a Gentile. . . .
>
> It has nothing to do with Deity. It has to do with letting things go the way they are. Don't change them. But, at that time, there was the feeling to get away from all this that happened. And, in the future, to keep it away from those who come after me. Because there was the feeling that no one can stop another wave of that. If it comes, we will not be here, like the six million are not here anymore. I was horrified by what happened and ready to go out of the line. And I did.

These reflections are also qualified as the conversation deepens. Still, Victor's essential predicament remains: trying to protect those who "come after," he went "out of the line" of those who came before. In so doing, he condemns himself to escalating isolation from both past and future.

Although Victor is the only participant who did not marry another Jew, most of the others also recall a period after liberation when "getting away from it"—through continued flight, disguise, or anonymity—was uppermost in their minds. This is true even for those, like Manny, Lydia, or Leon, who now speak most forcefully about asserting Jewish identity and awareness. With or without such assertion, the possibility of the curse returning on themselves or their children remains a shadow for all. What makes Victor unique is the starkness with which he puts, and has lived, the impossible choices. To save his life and his line, Victor must let himself and his line die out. To "continue it" risks allowing both to be murdered again. Within these axioms, Victor, in his own way, "went ahead."

The eldest of the participants, Victor is also the only one who had married and had had an adult life before the destruction. His first wife, who was a Jewish woman, was taken to Treblinka on the same transport as Victor. Married in their twenties, and both active in the Zionist movement, they had looked forward to having a family and one day living in Palestine. But this was 1940, and both Victor and his wife realized that it was not a time to start a family. Victor recalled their conversation:

> A pregnant woman cannot run as fast as a man. Without that, she could run as fast as I could. I was married twenty months to her and then come Treblinka. She always told me: "We will have to run away. Like this, I can run with you. But, when I have a belly, you will run away, and have to leave me behind. You want this?" I said, "No."
>
> This was not the time to have children. This was a time to have sex, but go out before the station—you understand? Pull out. As we say in Poland: "He has sex, but he goes out before the station. He runs out of the train before the station."

Victor finally did have to leave his wife behind: when she was taken to the gas chamber from the station at Treblinka and, three days later, when Victor escaped from the death camp by concealing himself in an outgoing train. The images burst in the horrible juxtaposition, which was also the way they emerged in our conversation. The themes of running away and broken covenants and fruitless seed go on.

It was thus not surprising when Victor later introduced his own theory about survivors' procreation. Having met in Israel the children of two survivors whom he had known before the war, he was shocked by the damage he thought he perceived:

> One has a boy who has the voice of a girl. Another one, who was hidden with me, he has a Mongoloid child. I say it's consequences of this what happened. It affects their seeds. The mental stress. Everything has a limit in this world. And it comes to a situation where it affects the seeds.   •

Thus Victor provides his own starkest interpretation of the legacies that survivors, as fathers, have to bestow.

The Father

In spite of Victor's theory, he finds no such damage in his own children. In fact, Victor expresses great pride over his son's strength and good looks. Recurrently he notes that girls turn their heads when they go to the supermarket together, a tribute from which Victor takes his rightful paternal share. He comments that he "was also very good-looking" when he was his son's age. Likewise, Victor is proud of his daughter's independence and high academic achievement. He points out that in spite of holding down a part-time job, she finished high school among the top ten students in her class. He only wishes he had made enough money to help her go to a better university than the city college she now attends.

If anything, within his own family, Victor experiences *himself* as disabled and superfluous—a "surplus, even to his closest." As suggested, in one voice he accepts that status as an inevitable result of his life's circumstances: his age when he started a family, his factory wages, and especially his having not continued to live as a Jew.

Regarding his age, Victor noted that he was already in his late thirties at the time of his first-born, his son, and already in his forties when his daughter was born. He reflected:

> When you bring up children, the father should not be more than thirty years old. When he is forty, there is not time anymore; he skipped over one generation. He should be a grandfather. I am in my sixties and my son is forty years younger. He still looks at the front of life. I don't anymore.

The young man and the old man look through different eyes. Likewise, once again a generation has been lost, and Victor accepts his going with it. He continued:

Forty years is still a nice looking father. Otherwise, your children are already ashamed of you. My daughter is only twenty. I take her to college and she says, "Daddy, don't get out from the car. Just stay in the car." Why? She's ashamed. I could be her grandfather.

Whether or not Victor has correctly interpreted his daughter's feelings, the important thing is the role to which he has relegated himself.

With regard to finances, Victor is more clearly conflicted. On one side, he speaks again of accepting his choices, as much as he would have liked to have provided more.

I did what I want. And what I wanted was because of the past in Poland. The antisemitism. . . . My wife sometimes says, "Look at him! Look at him! You are the only Jew who works in a factory! How come you wind up like this?" My daughter too. She has far-seeing eyes. She also says, "You are better than him. How come he can afford a house for a quarter-million dollars?"

But this is not my talking. This is their talking. When I talk materialism, it is their talking.

Of course, I would be happier if things wind up different. . . . But on the deathbed, a man doesn't think about the money he left or didn't. I assign myself to be what I am. This is what happens to the man who didn't look with the eyes of progress, straight with the eyes of progress. He lived with regret, not progress. He looked in the back, behind.

Victor acknowledges some shame for not being able to provide more amply. But, once again, death and fate "take care of everything."

Still, as Victor's quoting his wife and daughter suggest, he is not always so able to fend off the sting of their comments. With evident sarcasm, he noted that his son usually addresses him as "Vic" and only calls him "Daddy" when he "needs to borrow twenty dollars." He was particularly preoccupied with his son's current love affair—and the money it was costing in phone bills—and came to discuss it in terms that suggested everyone's imminent betrayal:

He's in love with a girl. He calls her long-distance from my house, twice a day. He does not listen to me. I told him I would disconnect the phone. . . . If one is in love, he is crazy. He's going to spend my money and everything on it. It's a materialistic life in this country. The women will like him as long as he spends. After that, she will say, "Get out of my life."

(HG: That's love?) That's love in a materialistic system. That's how it is. The wife stays with the husband, though when she has a younger one, when the husband gets old, she makes with him a pact. She applies for a divorce. She gets half of everything, and she makes richer the other one.

We shall hear that Victor has far more sympathy with the "craziness" of love (even in a materialistic system) than these comments suggest. But the conflict between the old man and the young man continues, here drawn most clearly as a struggle between the one who is "surplus" and another ready to take what he can get and quickly get away.

All of these issues of fidelity and betrayal converge in Victor's thoughts about not having maintained his Jewish heritage. Here, there is no doubt about the conflict Victor experiences, a struggle that grew in intensity as our conversations progressed. Speaking of his son specifically, he went back and forth between each side of the question:

> If my son wants to get away from it, from one side, it makes me happy. History can repeat itself. I don't want that my children should suffer the way I did. But, if there should be peace, it would be different. As long as a man is alive, he wants to continue what he is. But I don't want to have on my conscience that I lead them to another Holocaust. Just like I don't want to have on my conscience that I led them to destroy the continuation.

In later interviews, the conflict between the two anticipated destructions escalated. Victor reiterated that in old age continuation becomes essential. At the same time, he cannot forget the young man's perspective—his own young man's perspective—that he also imagines in his children:

> It gets important. As it gets closer to the grave, it gets important. Now I look around. I have a life *after* the Holocaust. . . . I feel guilty because, after my generation, my family dies out as Jews. My son marries a non-Jew. My daughter marries a non-Jew. I didn't procreate Jews.
>
> But the reason I didn't was because of the past. Because I didn't want *them* to accuse *me* at the last moment: "If my father wouldn't be a Jew, this wouldn't have happened to me."

And yet, back again, if his children do not continue the line, Victor imagines his heirs becoming "prosecutors" in a different and more terrible way.

> If my children marry Jews, it would be a relief of an obligation. That would take up the line again. With the procreation. Otherwise, they will have children, and those children may be Christians. And those Christians are liable to harm, to do harm, to Jews again.

Thus the circle of reductions inexorably telescopes down to the worst conceivable possibility: the one that actually happened. All prosecution ultimately signals *that* prosecution; all abandonments and betrayals become *those* abandonments and betrayals. The still ambivalent relationship between a man and his God moves through that between young and old, heirs and ancestors, Christians and Jews, and finally to the confrontation, once more, between killers and victims. Roles and identities change with different choices in Victor's dilemma, but the overall scheme and its reductive vortex remain the same. In Victor's voices and stories, as in those of the other participants, we hear its echoes many times.

For the moment, it is enough to say that, unable to accept any of the futures he imagines, Victor's solution is to approach death without a sense of future. His solution, he says, is to "keep quiet."

> I cannot see the future in generations. I can only see my own life. After that I don't know. . . . I would like them to retake again where I cut off. But without me to show them the way. Without me to talk them into it. . . . Let things settle themselves, not that I should help settle them. . .
>
> So I keep quiet. Let their destiny work out by themselves. Because I am not sure. I am not sure that my way was right. With the religion. And everything. I am not sure.

On one level, Victor's generative silence is reminiscent of both Paula's and Leon's realization that, in the end, their children will create their own legacy, based on their own needs and circumstances. Likewise, we are reminded again of the irony that survivors, who know better than anyone the limits of one generation's capacity to anticipate for the next, should be celebrated as "bestowers of legacies." Still, Victor goes an additional step. He questions the relevance of *any* intergenerational memory. In response to my asking him what he hoped his children might remember from him, he answered:

> I don't think, by them, I want anything to be remembered. I don't think this would do any good. My life is short. Their life is short. How long can a man remember one who was living and who is not alive anymore? I don't think this is the case.
>
> When we go, we go with all the history. And if it goes with all the history, you just divide between the living and the dead. And when one is dead, if he will be remembered, or if he will not be remembered, is just the same.

Chilled myself by this vision of a world reduced to survivors and the dead, I reminded Victor of how much history he himself remembers: all the people and stories of Jewish tradition that, in fact, he had brought into our conversation. How did this fit into his vision? Victor replied:

> What good does it do for them? To me, it's a part of history. I remember it. But what good does it do *for them*? It's one-sided. It works on only one side. I remember because I read them, I study them, I dwell in them. I remember. But what good does it do for them?

Victor had, in fact, answered the question earlier when he summarized one of the results of his study of the Bible. It complemented his sense of a personal existence uninformed by the future. While the Bible remained a source of history, he said, "the prophecy is taken out."

A Failed Business

Thus locked within the circle of his private remembrance, and caring for no other, Victor's conscience does attain a certain "silence and peace." In that voice, he once again juxtaposed the forward-looking businessman and the hindseer.

> When you are a businessman, your character is—, you put things behind you which are not important to your business. You go ahead only with this which is important to you, for the business. If you don't want to be a businessman, it makes you a different character. It makes you a man who lives with the past. You are happy with what you have. You have limited. But you think of the past. You are a hindseer. You cannot go with brains like this into business. There, you look at nothing from your past. Just the future.

Still, reviewing his own past and hopes and their termination without connection with the future, Victor also summarized his feelings in a very different way. In that voice, he drew again on an analogy from finance.

> It's something—, the feeling is like you start off a business, and you didn't have a success. You have failed, in short words. You start off a business, and you accumulate all you have, and you are a failure in the business.
> (HG: You end up feeling—?) Very bitter.

MAKING A STORY

When Victor's bitterness finally erupted, he became "the prosecutor," and it is in that role that he gives voice to his final rebellion and final appeal. No longer able to reflect passively on his circumstances, past and present, Victor finds in prosecuting a way to reverse what had become unbearable. Within Victor's court of inquiry, it is God who is guilty of turning away from His line—and Whose faithfulness was only a "bluff" in the first place. Now it is God who has grown shamefully powerless, an old man with failing hands and failing eyes, while Creation is His failed business, a war of the jungle with neither profit nor prophecy. Thus reduced, it is now the Creator who must wait to know if His words and deeds will be remembered. Or whether He, too, will be abandoned to face a lonely, unrecounted death.

In effecting such a reversal, Victor is aware of his motives. He commented:

> I am trying to justify myself. In order not to let the sorrow grow higher. To keep down the pain . . . With this, I can go ahead. I calm my pain. When I say, "It's Him! He is guilty!" Not I am guilty.
>
> It's up to us what kind of conclusion we take of things that happened. It's up to the individual. You can let the blues get so high that you can get a heart attack. Or you can keep them down. It's up to your own philosophy.

Prosecuting God is Victor's philosophical conclusion: a way of shielding himself from a sorrow and pain that, he says, could be fatal to experience directly.

It is vital that we listen closely to Victor here. The role of prosecutor is his creation: a voice and a story he has constructed, quite literally, in order to survive. Within that role, he is able to continue: "With this, I can go ahead." So understood, although the task of the prosecutor is to strip away "added words" and "polish," becoming the prosecutor is itself an act of *adding* words and polish. It is a way of framing "the things that happened" in a more bearable, and perhaps also more tellable and hearable, way.

What is the source of "pain" and "sorrow" that being the prosecutor alleviates? Victor speaks most directly about his guilt for not having "continued the line," and there is no doubt that his self-recrimination about what he has left behind is agonizing to him. So also are his feelings of declining power and relevance, of being left behind himself, particularly within his own family. Still, it must be said that Victor has known far worse betrayals than either a man's abandonment of his ancestry (whom he continues to recall with love and sadness) or the abandonment of a people by their God (whom they continue to beseech, if only to question). The apostate's desertion is qualified by remorse and remembrance. The God he prosecutes remains a God for whom he searches within the dialogue of study. Compared with the absolute obliterations of reverence that Victor has known, reductions completely *unqualified* by regret or remembrance, Victor's struggles with God, his ancestry, or his heirs are like wayward dreams, remnants from a time *before* nightmares became actual and unqualified. And although such dreams may be reduced and disfigured by the pull of the nightmare—sometimes terribly so, as we shall hear—they also persist independently. They persist to give form *to* extremity.

There is, therefore, a deeper sense in which becoming the prosecutor allows Victor to "go ahead." Along with reversing his self-recrimination and providing a context for his rage, the whole drama of prosecuting God (including the guilt that is its underside) is itself an organizing frame—like a dream or an allegory. Compared with the arbitrary landscapes of destruction he remembers, Victor's struggle with God "makes sense." All the enemies and opponents are now condensed into a single One. Victor's relationship with that One is characterized by an ambivalence—a depth of relationship itself—totally absent from the atrocity he remembers. And because God does remain a mystery—even after the prosecutor's most determined efforts to "see it closer"—the possibility of some eventual reconciliation, of finding "something," is still imaginable. Here the curse is *not* terminal; really, here the curse cannot be terminal.

Becoming the prosecutor also "makes sense" because it really *is* a kind of allegory—a story that is precedented and familiar. As noted, it draws on the long tradition of those who have questioned God's power and existence; for Victor, especially the tradition of Maimonides. As we shall hear, it also draws on more personal antecedents, a whole other set of contexts in which Victor questioned the reverence due to "creators." There are memories inside his memories—other stories about betrayal and loyalty, about "going ahead" and being "left behind"—which have nothing to do with either God or extremity. The story of the prosecutor also organizes, and is organized by, these.

In becoming the prosecutor, then, Victor not only "makes a story" of what is "not a story" but also makes a single story out of what are many stories. In reviewing his life as a whole, this is the story he retells:

> Some Jews went ahead. They continue it, to marry again. . . . I am not satisfied. And this is the thing that I became the prosecutor when I was reading the Bible. If there was something. So I became the prosecutor. And I am still the prosecutor.

"I became the prosecutor / I am still the prosecutor." As we proceed, we shall see how encompassing the story is: how much of Victor's life can be contained within his account of not being one who "went ahead" but who became "the prosecutor" instead. We will also see how much of his life cannot be contained within that story, how burdened and how precarious it remains.

STORIES ABOUT THE PROSECUTION OF STORIES

Victor has his own love for stories and for the senses of mastery and continuity that telling stories conveys. Occasionally, when remembering an incident (both from the destruction and from other times), he would rise from his chair and re-enact it for me, making sure I understood the details of setting and situation. Victor became most involved, however, not in the stories from his own experience but in those he remembered from the Bible. These, too, he retold with care. And beyond any single tale, what he spoke about with greatest appreciation was the unity of the Bible as a whole. He explained:

> I am not religious, but I respect the Torah, the Books of Moses. I respect it because you seldom find a man in our generation who can put up a book, and have everything under control in his book, like Moses.

In a later conversation, he related the integrity of Scripture to his own failing health and growing isolation. He again recalled the prayer of the old man, while associating the strength he sought with the central image in Judaism for the power of the text, the Torah as a "living tree."

> I have not given up, but I feel like it. Because, when your power is leaving, you want to make yourself lighter. That is why we pray to God, "Don't send me away when I am old. When my power leaves me. You, don't leave me." Stay with me. To help me out.
>
> The Scripture, it says, is "a living tree for those who hold onto it." That means, the one who goes by it, who dwells in it. I value it. I value it. Because it is a living tree for those who dwell in it. It's a way of life of a people, who belong to it.

Even as he prosecutes, Victor reaches out for the living tree. He would like to still dwell in the text and feel again that he belonged to its life.

Yet Victor does not still belong to it, at least not as he once did. And from out of the text that he has made his own—the voice and story of the prosecutor—he begins to demonstrate how much has been lost and how that injury came to be. For what Victor does as a prosecutor is to take the biblical narrative apart. Indeed, the story of the prosecutor becomes, most essentially, a story of the prosecution of stories: unmasking them, undoing them, making war on them.

In performing this unmasking, Victor's primary method is to juxtapose his own experience, both during the destruction and after, with the section of Scripture he has chosen to criticize. Sometimes the juxtaposition is self-conscious; sometimes it is not. But, either way, the results are the same: Evidence is produced to prove that someone, sometimes whole peoples, have been left out of the biblical narrative, left out and left behind. What appears as prophetic foresight Victor reinterprets to prove that the end of the story was added later, tacked on to create the *illusion* of a knowable future and the appearance of continuity with the past. Commandments that were supposed to be inviolate Victor shows to have allowed exceptions: Sometimes lambs were slaughtered on the Sabbath, there was killing even on the holiest of days. As Victor's criticism mounts, the tension between narrative and memory also increases. Analogies become literal. Stories decompose into a field of disparate elements. In the opposite of any redemptive sense, words become flesh.[3]

Words and Flesh

More precisely, in Victor's prosecution of the text, words become corpses. For the central theme of Victor's prosecution is that there are bodies buried beneath the stories: bodies that need to be dug up, properly identified, and recorded. We have already heard him speak metaphorically of religion being like the "polished up" candlesticks over the tombs of the Patriarchs. But Victor would like to do more than make analogies. As a prosecutor, he would like to go inside, unearth the double-basement, examine the remains. He comments:

> Something was . . . Something is there. Like the tomb of Abraham. We go to Israel and know there is a double-cellar where the bodies rest. There must be some secrets because they don't let nobody go in and see how long the body is, how tall he was. The bones are there. There is no flesh, but there are bones. There must be some secrets, because nobody was there to look inside.

Victor does not specify what secrets the bones might reveal. The important thing is the documentation itself. The facts themselves provide a ground of truth without which it is simply too easy to add later words or theories. It is to underline the prosecutor's documentary obligations that Victor cites Maimonides:

When Maimonides wrote his books, he revealed a lot of things that ones before didn't reveal it. He also said something you cannot see you revere more. You give it more reverence. Like we cannot go deeply into the tombs. We stay outside, and the bodies are in a second basement, a basement beneath the basement. This is for reverence. Otherwise, I think scientists would be interested to measure the age of the bones. To see how old they are. They are not allowed to come down. Why? For reverence.

In the tradition of Maimonides, Victor is ready to reveal the secrets. The secrets are the bodies themselves: *that* they are and *what* they are—measurable, countable, datable Jewish corpses.

There is no question what other Jewish corpses are at the back of Victor's reflections. He has told us that he became the prosecutor because of "the six million that was killed," and their reality and identity are what fuels the prosecutor's work. Still, as in his focus on the tombs of the Patriarchs, the connection is often implicit, and sometimes strikingly so. Moments after recounting a direct memory of the Holocaust, for example, Victor spoke about the "holocaust" in its original meaning: the ancient ritual of providing burnt offerings. This was in the context of citing an inconsistency between biblical practice and traditional Jewish law—evidence in *Isaiah* that ritual sacrifices were sometimes carried out on the Sabbath.

There was not much critics in the Old Testament. Very few. For example, the holocaust, where they bring the sheep to the slaughter . . . On Saturday they was also killing lambs, and killing was a job. So why slaughter lambs on Saturday? Now, in the Diaspora, it is not allowed. A butcher is not allowed to kill a chicken on Saturday. But the priest then was allowed to kill rams and bulls. This is a criticism. Why then allowed and not now? The Sabbath is the Sabbath.

It was on a Sabbath, in 1942, that Victor became aware of the full extent of the slaughter at Treblinka, which he compared to the slaughter of lambs and sheep. Just before the reflection above, he had used the term "Holocaust" to refer to that destruction. Yet he never made an explicit connection between his thoughts about one Sabbath and those about the other. It remains for his listener to experience the chill of "revelation" when the different lambs, different Saturdays, and different "offerings" are juxtaposed.

Victor's use of the Bible often strikes us as analogic in this way. His strategy is reminiscent of the Holocaust writers whom Alvin Rosenfeld described who introduce analogies "only to reveal their inadequacies" as the narrative unfolds. In the case of Victor, the strategy is not intentionally literary—certainly he is not trying to be ironic—but an effect that follows naturally from the way he has constructed his role and methodology as prosecutor. Within the frame of that voice and the frame of the text that is his object, his scope is inherently limited. Focusing on what God and religion have not accomplished—as opposed to what the killers did—he fights a highly circumscribed battle: a contradiction discovered here, an omission noticed there, all within the Bible's own terms. There is never any doubt that the Holocaust is the background, but it remains the background. If only provisionally, it is mediated by all that being the prosecutor entails: the role itself and its antecedents, the given narrative of the Bible, the nature of evidence and accused, and the room for "speculation" that both allow.

As the prosecutor, then, Victor actively re-creates and qualifies a destruction that was traumatic and unqualified. In telling and enacting stories about the inadequacy of stories, Victor is able to reconstruct that failure as an *unfolding* revelation, as a story itself. And now it is a story that is gradual enough that we, too, can enter in and follow.

In the course of prosecuting, Victor also re-creates his life since the destruction, and here also he finds a biblical story to serve as analogy and allegory. Likewise, here, too, there are bodies that the revered text excludes. Now, however, they are living bodies: the bodies of survivors.

The Generations of Cain

It is often said that Noah was the "first survivor," but for Victor the title belongs to Cain. Compared with the hero of the Flood, untarnished in his righteousness, Cain is a far more ambiguous figure. Having had the fruits of his labor unaccountably rejected by God in favor of those of his younger brother—his "fruits of the ground" in contrast to Abel's "firstlings of the flock"—Cain turns on Abel in his humiliation and kills him. When God discovers the crime, Cain remains resentful, even sarcastic. "Am I my brother's keeper?" as though saying, "Do you *still* want me to be the shepherd, rather than the farmer that I am?" God does not answer. Instead, Cain is banished from both the land and his family. He is condemned to be a "wanderer and a fugitive" to whom the earth will never again "yield her strength" to his attempts at cultivation. Only at this point—terrified at being totally cut off from God, the earth, his fellows—does Cain appeal. Driven from the land and from God, he anticipates certain death. God yields at least a bit. He "sets a sign for Cain"—a sign of God's protection—

and Cain survives. Although still shorn of his trade, his people, and his homeland, he is able to go on. He makes his way to the land of Nod, east of Eden, and there he and his generations continue—at least in name—until they disappear from the Bible's main line of names and narrative like shadows of an ancient misunderstanding.

In his own interpretation of the story of Cain, Victor would clear up some of the shadows. Or, more accurately, he would take Cain and his generations *out* of the shadows. For Victor's purpose is not to absolve Cain's crime (which remains in the background of his discussion) but to restore his history. Whatever happened in Eden, there was also much that happened in Nod. Marriages were made, children came, generations of this branch of Adam's tree also continued. In Victor's view, these are the facts that need to be recorded. Even if Cain went "out of the line," he should not be left out of The Book.

It was with the story of Cain that Victor first began his search and his prosecution. It was also the story he first discussed with me when he initially described his rereading the Bible.

Saturday, we were working five hours overtime. Three and a half hours I was reading the Bible. I would do my job and then sit down at the desk to read....

I search about everything. Like, to search how many years it is from Adam to Noah. The Bible only says generations, it doesn't say years. From Adam to Noah is ten generations.

And the Bible doesn't take account of Cain and Abel. Because Abel got killed. And Cain went over to the city of Nod and he married over there. Now, but, for Cain's ten generations it is only written the names of them. It is not written how old they was when they had a procreation. But for Adam, for his *other* children, what got born after Cain and Abel, it *is* written. And based on this, when it says he married after so many years, I figure out how many years to Noah.

I also ask a question. I ask a question: If Cain killed Abel, and Cain run away to Nod and married over there, and had a son, and built a city, and called it in the name of his son—if there was *only* Cain, what for did he need a city? The Bible says a city? And who did he marry? Who did he marry?

The Bible tells you, Moses tells you. Not directly. But on the next page, he says, "And there was people, giants, at that time and thereafter."

So if, in the time of Cain, there was supposed to be four—Mama, Papa, Cain, and Abel—and he run away to a city, he must have met over there a giant. He married a giant. And they was not considered, they was considered half-animals. And they, the Bible says, people and giants intermarried. And they come out a different race. After they intermarried. So, already, by that time, there was giants.

Thus Victor asserts that Cain, too, found someone to marry—although it was an intermarriage. Cain also had children, and they had children—however old he or they were at the time of procreation. Cain also was part of a line of generations—even if that line came out a different race than the line Cain had left behind. Given all of this, the uniqueness of Adam's more direct descendants—the ones to whom the Bible pays so much more attention—should not be overstated. Victor concludes:

> Science brings men to the idea that everything in this world is made through procreation, through evolution. Adam was not the first man. There was giants. There was already two factions. Then come other factions. . . . They dig out bones now which are millions of years old. That means there was people before. Adam was not the first man.

Once again, the evidence of bones raises questions about the reverence due to traditional texts and patriarchs. And here Victor would dig deeper than the Patriarchs' "double-basement," now itself a kind of "cover."

At this point, Moses is still an ally of the prosecutor. He supplied Victor's textual evidence that there were people before: the giants with whom Cain intermarried. But it soon becomes clear that Moses also could be indicted for denying Cain his history. Discussing again the fact that Cain's generations were not given a dated genealogy, Victor comments:

> The other one was marked how old they was, how old they was when they had a child, how old the child was when it had its own child. But this is not the fact by the generations of Cain. You don't have such a bothering. I say this is because they come out from a race that was not worth to mention in the Bible. It was not worth it. They was not from the fair race. They was animals like.
>
> And also they was doomed to be destroyed, the Cain side. They was doomed to be destroyed in the generation of the Flood. So this was also why Moses didn't bother with them.
>
> Moses was from Adam's side.

Victor's reference to the "fair race" concerns a passage from Maimonides that interprets the Bible's descriptions of Adam's later children in these terms. But even without that addition, the sense of Victor's Cain condensing into the symbols of a dream, itself pulled toward a nightmare, emerges throughout these reflections. A race, considered subhuman, has been doomed to be destroyed. Their successors do not view them as even "worth to mention"—they "go ahead" and leave the "surplus" behind. Cain, already exiled, becomes the failed progenitor of this forgotten people. Even Moses, with other loyalties, turns away. Victor continues:

> The generations of Cain, after he married, he went over to the City of Nod and he married over there. They are not now nothing. . . . There was nobody to bother with it. Even Moses didn't bother with it.
>
> By Moses it was given over, it was written down, from generation to generation. From Cain, nobody give it over from generation to generation. From Adam, after he married, there was a Scripture. And they give it over. And Moses put everything on paper. Everything.

Clearly, Moses did *not* put everything on paper. Some peoples and generations "even Moses didn't bother with." Charging Moses with that omission, Cain, through Victor, rises as prosecutor. The beloved "living tree" is attacked at its roots. And even the greatest of storytellers is unmasked as much more a "businessman" than a "hindseer."

Living Trees

Victor agreed that Cain's story was a recounting of his own: his regret over his own "age at procreation," his intermarriage and his description of his own children as "not now nothing," his struggle over what he "left behind" and his outrage about others—including himself—being left behind in turn. Our discussion of these parallels was the context in which he also mentioned his bleakest theory of survivors' procreation: damaged seed leading to damaged generations.

This was additionally the context, however, in which he first used the word "love" in our conversations, striking by its appearance because of its complete absence to that point. Here also, the topic was generativity and continuity, although not of human seeds and generations. Recalling the years he spent in Italy immediately after liberation—it was there he met his wife—Victor confided:

> I will tell you something. I will tell you what I won't tell my wife. If I would have the money, even at my age now, I would still take a chance and farm. Not in America. Here it is too expensive. In Italy. In Italy you can still farm.
>
> (HG: So this is—?) This is my dream! I am in love with it. I love it! I love it!
>
> (HG: Farming in Italy was a happy time?) Yeah. Yeah. Not in Italy so much. My wife was sick then. She had tuberculosis. But in the youth, yes, it was happiest when I was eighteen. When I was on the first farm in Poland,

the Zionist farm, for going to Israel. All true, I wasn't yet married. I was still a youth. But I had my best power. My best power. I didn't feel tired then.

Victor went on to say that he imagined having a farm every night before going to sleep. In those reveries, he pictured how many acres he would have, how he would prepare the soil, what he would plant. Like the figurative "living tree" of Scripture, he spoke of these dreams as thoughts that totally absorbed him: "This is something that interests you. You dwell in it. You dwell in it." With the same enthusiasm, he began to describe the planting he actually does in the small yard behind his house.

> I have trees. I planted trees when I bought the house. I have peach trees. I am still planting trees. I plant this year an apple. I didn't have an apple. I had peaches and plums. And I read for apples, you should have two different kinds of apples, for pollination. They do better. And I plant a pear. I need to make this better. I need to plant another pear tree. One peach tree, I don't remember if I put it in or if this tree put itself out from another one. I don't remember this. In Autumn, when it's colder, I will have to dig down to the roots to see if it is connected with the roots to the other peach. Or if it is for itself.
>
> I like to do things like this. I might not eat it, but I like to do it. I like to see how it grows. I like to go to that tree and see if next year it will bear a fruit. You can see it. When you work with it, year by year, you can see.

Here, at least, Victor finds a generative future of seeds and good fruit. Apples and pears do better when they are "intermarried," and here there is progress when a peach tree establishes independent roots. Within his dream, his memory, and the attentiveness of his cultivation, Victor salvages at least this much of Eden.

Still, as though to tell us how fragile such remnants are, even these reflections come to an agonizing conclusion. The fate of Cain, that other tiller of the ground, returns to haunt Victor's own fruitful offerings. Victor continued:

> Unfortunately, I plant two plums. And when I was cutting the lawn, I cut in on a flower. And my wife got mad. She go out and broke the tree. She brought me a branch of the tree. And then she went out with a saw and cut off a tree which I would have plums already this year, the second time.

We need not decide the subtleties with which accident, a wife's spitefulness, and Victor's provocation may have conspired together to create this exchange. Whatever the balance of motives and circumstance, the story is undone again. Here, the crime of severed branches is retold through an enactment: one more re-creation of the death of creation.

The Ends of Stories

Even without another's destructive collaboration, the restoration Victor seeks would not have come from any existing "living trees"—actual or scriptural. There are too many corpses buried beneath the garden and the text for that sort of resolution. And, in fact, the final thrust of Victor's prosecution of stories is an attack on the very attempt to end stories prematurely, analogically, and falsely.

This is the essence of Victor's criticism of prophecy in the Bible. He tells us that establishing continuity between events foretold and those that came to be is one more "polishing over" the actual facts of the past. For example, regarding what some have taken, in *Isaiah*, as a prophecy of Christ, Victor comments:

> They say Isaiah foretold there will come a Jesus. There will be a birth of a child, and he will be wonderful, excellent, and everybody will listen to him. But they don't see what Isaiah writes next, which is about another child. The church reads only one line, not the second line. . . .
>
> So they need only the Old Testament to justify their means. The New Testament say, "The old things are forgotten." So that means they have no obligation to the old things.

Now loyal to Moses and his specific line, Victor says it is a still younger generation who takes what it needs and does not "bother with" the rest. Indeed, he continues by speaking in generational terms: "They don't stay loyal to what came before. They are not interested. They are like children who don't care, who aren't interested in the past." Instead, such "children" are interested only in what furthers their own stories and survival, which includes "finishing" the stories of others.

Victor does not restrict his criticisms of this sort to Christians. Speaking of religion in general, he asserts: "It's all a put-up: ours is just a longer put-up." The prosecutor then speaks most directly of the facts that prophetic readings ignore:

> All the miracles happened when *we* was not. When we *are*, it doesn't happen miracles. So where *is* He? Did He weaken? Has He lost his power?
>
> Ezekiel says in his prophecy that God says that two-thirds of His people, He will burn them in fire and crystallize them like gold. And one-third, the

one-third will remain. He will lead them to the Promised Land. I will show them the way. They will not thirst. There will be rivers, fruits, and they will walk back each on his own. Now, Ezekiel was living in the time of Babylon. He was prophesying about Babylon. . . . This was not to us. This was for Babylon, not for us.

A part of Victor is clearly taken by the poetic resonance of Ezekiel's prophecy in the modern destruction. But it is exactly such compelling coherences, and the going forward they may legitimate, that arouse the prosecutor's suspicions. Meanwhile, Victor says that the best that any prophet can do is size up his own generation's circumstances.

I say, every generation, every generation has *its* prophet. He could be a dreamer, a politician, someone who sees what is going on. It is not the future. It is judging the current situation and the circumstances of the people.

Knowing how little the circumstances of his own life were predicted, Victor opts for a future without prophetic assurance. "I cannot see the future in generations," he says. "I can only see my own life." Life goes on, but "the prophesy is taken out."

If there can be any acceptable ending to Victor's story, it would have to be an actual and not a symbolic restoration: his children choosing, on their own, to "take up again" what he, and history, have "cut off." This is the small margin of hope, still qualified by the terror of renewed destruction, to which Victor holds. There is, however, at least one biblical precedent for such a return and, after the story of Cain, it is the chapter to which Victor most often returns himself. Recalling his trips to Israel, he noted that he always visits the tomb of Rachel, the second wife of the Patriarch, Jacob. Inside the tomb there is a velvet curtain carrying a gold inscription—in Victor's view, two inscriptions. He said he had made several photographs of it, as though trying to fix and hold its image against other images he carries. Victor explained the significance:

It is written in gold letters on velvet, "High in the Heaven, Rachel cries for her children." And then, underneath, it is written, "There is a recompense for your prayer. Your children will return to their borders." Now I say the two wasn't written at the same time. The first was written when the Jews go into exile. When they went by here, they cried. Then, when they came back, after sixty-six or sixty-seven years, they put on the second line. "There is a recompense for your prayer." They put that on when they came back. When they return.

In this instance of "added words," there is justification, according to Victor, in historical fact. Rachel's children did return; they added the words themselves. For that brief moment, the exile is over, and the remnants of a story are gathered in.[4]

Exile

Victor's personal exile is not over, and his own stories reach no satisfactory conclusion. Even as he re-creates his history through the voice and stories of the prosecutor—including the prosecutor's prosecution of stories—the Holocaust's obliteration of voices and stories continues to pull at his words and the enactments of his life. They are repeatedly reduced to scenes of mowed-down flowers, cut-down plum trees, and, as we shall hear, worse.

Still, even at their most agonized, such stories remain only tellable beginnings. They are individual "human terms" for a much greater destruction. In order to enter further into their creation and their dissolution, we turn, in the next chapter, to a deeper exploration of the two worlds of memory—the memories inside memories—from which they arise.

Chapter 5

The Stories of the Prosecutor II

His tales? Each contains many others. Imagine a series of concentric
circles. . . . The I inside the I . . . memory inside memory.
                                        Elie Wiesel, *Souls on Fire*

MEMORIES INSIDE MEMORIES

Shorn of all its particularizing details, the story Victor repeatedly recounts
is a simple one:

A man is shamefully betrayed and left behind by another in whom he
had believed. Occupied with his own purposes, the betrayer does not look
back but simply goes ahead to continue whatever he and his fellows have
begun. Meanwhile, bereft and alone, the abandoned one also goes ahead
as best he can. He survives, he finds his place, and, in his own way, he too
puts the past behind him. But then, many years later, he again meets his
betrayer, who by this time has become well established. The abandoned
one rises up. He vows to reveal the secret history of perfidy and, by this
means, bring the betrayer to his own shame and ruin. He starts to do exactly
that: accuse, prosecute, unmask. Yet face-to-face with his enemy—feeling
the intensity of his rage at the same moment as recalling the fidelity that
once bound them—the would-be avenger is haunted by a terrible question:
Has he been, and is he now, the betrayer or the betrayed?

The story is familiar. It is the stuff of our own fantasies and dreams,
especially those of childhood, as it is of Victor's. It is also the stuff of
memories—not traumatic memories usually, but certainly ones that carry

their own kind of pain. These are memories of rejection, exclusion, humiliation, or simply loss: recollections of all the ways others do "go ahead" and
leave us behind. They are also recollections of all the ways we, in our turn,
leave others behind.

In themselves, such memories have nothing to do with extremity. They
are rooted in a world that has *not* been reduced to "survivors" and "surplus,"
one in which the "worst possible" manifestation remains the stuff of
fantasies and dreams. For Victor, they are "memories inside memories,"
remnants from a time when exclusions and departures—as well as regrets
and remembrance—had the same meanings to him as they do to all of us.

The End of Childhood

Victor recalls more than his experiences during the Holocaust and
during the years that followed. He also remembers his life before the
destruction and, in thinking back, captured one memory from the beginning of memory itself. It was the sole instance he gave of a memory
predating adolescence, and he recalled it with evident pride:

> I can remember when I was still running on the street barefoot, in a shirt
> only, and some manager of a farm come to us and tie up his horse with a
> saddle. My brother who was older than me, eleven years older, he took the
> horse and he ride down the street. And then he turn to the left, to a friend
> of his. And you know how a boy rides on a horse! And I try to run after him.
> I was afraid to turn around. That I would not find my way home, back home.
> And I remember I wore a white shirt, no underpants, no nothing, and
> barefoot. How old could I be then? Three years? Four years?

The scene is idyllic enough. Yet it is not difficult to imagine that the
incident entailed more intense feeling than emerges in its retelling so many
years later. The little boy chases after an admired older brother who,
oblivious to his follower, disappears around the corner. The child is torn
between continuing pursuit, increasingly futile, and giving up the chase. If
he stops, he will be completely on his own, stranded in the city with
nothing but his white shirt, and unable to find either his brother or the
way back home. Of course, one way or another, things worked out. The
little boy did find the way back home—well enough, more than sixty years
later, to recount this earliest story of being left behind by one who "went
ahead" and did not look back.

The youngest of seven children—five brothers and a sister—Victor
often watched his siblings fade into the distance. The oldest were already

married with families of their own when Victor was born, and they made only infrequent visits to the household. Four left Europe before the war, leaving Victor and two brothers (who did not survive) still in Poland in 1939. Some of these departures do seem to be genuine instances of abandonment. Victor spoke of one brother who, in 1931, left his wife and four children in order to go off and "have a good time" in Belgium. By the time of his return, six years later, his wife and both his parents had died of illnesses. The four children, raised by Victor's parents, were then abandoned again when, after a year back in Poland, this brother left for the United States without them. They were eventually killed in Treblinka. Victor reflected:

> He didn't feel bad about her [the brother's wife], but he feel bad about the children, for they wind up in Treblinka. And when he come back in '37, his wife wasn't alive anymore, his father and mother wasn't alive anymore. And then he leave again.
>
> (HG: Were you angry at him for this?) No. I was not. But when I come over here I realize what a heaviness he put on my mother and father, for they was in old age. They had four children, plus his four. Those children wind up to be surplus in our family. . . . I come to the conclusion it was not right.
>
> For this reason, probably, he told me, he made papers that he wants to be cremated when he dies. I say, "Cremated? Why? Why is that?" He told me, "Well, if God could agree that my children wind up killed in Treblinka, I can agree to be burned, after death."

Victor is thus not alone in feeling both abandoning and abandoned. For this brother, too, guilt and protest are intertwined, and ashes are the final reduction of all who have become "surplus."

Victor's conclusion about his brother's misconduct is not typical. Rather than directly blaming his siblings, he more often spoke of his own obligation to make up for whatever they left undone. Regarding the fact that his surviving brothers also did not raise their children in Judaism, he commented: "My brothers did not do it. So the responsibility falls on me, the youngest, to continue what my father give over. And I fail to do so. And they also fail. So what will be the end?"

Victor's taking on the "responsibility of the youngest" is also a theme in his memories of earlier times when his parents were still alive. Because he was one of the few children still living at home during their last years, he had particular reasons to feel specially relied upon. Still, he lets us know that his sense of responsibility was not without ambivalence. Then, too, he was torn between his obligations to those who "came before" and his wishes to move forward with his own life and plans.

This conflict emerges most clearly in Victor's memories of the last years of his father's life, between 1934 and 1936, and this is the period before the war that Victor recalls in greatest detail. Having lost his mother as he turned twenty, and his father less than two years later, Victor says of this time:

> During those twenty months, I realize more the facts of life. I was older already and thinking about the death of my mother. And here my father die twenty months later. . . . A man grows up, and he starts to understand some things.

As Victor suggests, the facts he was beginning to understand concerned loss itself and the imminent change-over of generations. Along with his siblings, it would soon be up to him to carry on "the line," yet establish his independent roots as well.

Victor's father had different tasks. A highly successful trader in lumber and grain, he had long ago established his life and his way. Now approaching seventy, he was an old man concerned with his own "continuation." And while two of his sons had already followed him into the family business, none besides Victor was then at home. Victor himself was working elsewhere. But given his father's needs, here again the responsibility fell on the youngest.

> I was working nights. In the morning I come home, and my father—there was waiting a team of horses—and my father said, "Come, dress, come with me." Two of my brothers were in the military service, the ones who usually go with him. I say, "What for do you need me?" He was going out to the Polish dukes, the nobility, to buy grain. So he say, "I need somebody to talk to while I am on the way there."
>
> It takes an hour to travel, maybe more. So I wash and rest and went with my father. We come home in the afternoon. And I went to sleep to be ready to go to work again, at night.

Victor easily acknowledged that such a schedule was not to his liking. He chose, however, to go with his father.

> I will tell you, pleasant or not pleasant, it was for the respect. For the father. I wanted to satisfy him, so I did a little sacrifice. Sometimes I fell asleep on the buggy. Sometimes he pushed me, with the elbow, and says, "Don't sleep. Maybe I need to talk to you about something. This is important."

(HG: How did you feel about that?) I realize he wanted to talk to me, so I listened. I didn't rebel. There was no sense of rebellion against the parents at that time.

Besides respect, Victor more particularly tied his obligation to a recognition of his father's age and stage of life. Clearly drawing on his own experience of aging, he again contrasted the different perspectives of an old man and a young man.

He was already close to seventy. . . . And maybe, when one is old, maybe he thinks he'll have a heart attack or something. And my mother was gone. So maybe he want to talk to somebody who survive who will know where something is. Maybe also he want to talk, by talking, he will sharpen his own mind and remember. So he will know where it is when he needs something.

When a man talk of his age, there is some reason why. He doesn't talk without reason. A young man talk without reason. Because it's talking, not from the heart. It's talking just from the mind.

An old man doesn't talk for nothing. He talks from experience. Or he talks to his children, he wants them to know how to operate the business. Or he talks to his children that they know where things are. How much he has paid, how much he owes. One should know about this. He doesn't talk for nothing.

At least in retrospect, Victor views his responsibilty in terms of his father's need, at that time, to relieve his obligations and have his thoughts remembered. As long as someone is minding the business, it—and more—can go on.

At this point, then, it was Victor who might have done the leaving behind. He tells us, however, that he never felt the kind of disrespect toward his father that he experiences from his own children. Even the age difference between them—his father was fifty when Victor was born—did not figure then as he described it in his own family.

My father was eleven years older than I was when my own son was born. But this was a different time. I wasn't ashamed of my father. And there were lots like me at that time. Lots of families then, they make children and make children and people didn't think about it. My father was my father. There was respect for an older man at that time.

Victor is no doubt accurate here, personally and culturally. He describes his father, in fact, as a patriarch in the fullest sense of the term. Strong and active until his last days, he ruled and supported his family, including the "surplus." Likewise, as Victor's description of the morning trips suggest, little kept his father from pursuing his trade and pursuing those whose assistance and audience he wanted.

At the same time, Victor was pursuing some of his own aims during this period, and not always to his father's pleasure. In recalling the business trips, Victor revealed an additional reason why his father may have wanted to speak with him. It concerned the other work Victor was doing, a job in a local factory.

> Maybe he want to talk and refresh his own mind. Or maybe I will gain from his words something. Because my father didn't want me to work in a factory. He wanted me to be a businessman. To do the same thing *he* does.
>
> (HG: He said that's what he wanted?) Yeah. He criticized me. He criticized me. That nobody in the family should work in a factory. And I work in a factory. He wasn't happy. The same thing I am not happy with my boy. In some respects, he was not happy with me. . . .
>
> I tried to satisfy him and satisfy me. Maybe for this reason I worked nights. Then I have the whole day in front, and if he wants to talk, I am here. . . . The other boy was in the service, who usually go with him. So maybe he wanted me to stop working in the factory and get over to the business. To do the same thing he does. I was the last, the youngest.

During these years, then—before the war and all that was to follow—there was a quite different context in which Victor was made to be concerned about not continuing what his father had begun and wished to pass on "the same."

Whatever was to come, however, here there were no implications of ultimacy and no closed circles of betrayal and recrimination. Victor continued to work at the factory. Based on the double-shift compromise, and perhaps a mutual acceptance of the differences between them, he was able to satisfy himself and satisfy his father without either of them falling into the fixed dissatisfaction of the prosecutor. Although not without intensity, this was a fully normal conflict between father and son—retrieved from a time before "going ahead" became reductively associated with betrayal and being left behind with oblivion.

Ardent Lovers

Victor's memory of the conflict with his father also reveals another kind of reduction that may occur in the wake of extremity. For certainly the story of the factory job suggests that Victor's later choice of factory work over business might be more complicated than he first described. Along with whatever contribution made by Polish antisemitism, Victor may simply have preferred to work in a factory.

When I raised the question, that was what Victor confirmed. "I liked work in the factory. I liked it. My father didn't like it. But I did like it." He also noted that he actually had been in business when he first came to this country and could have continued. Again, however, he chose otherwise.

> I did go into business. I was working for a few months with my brother in the jewelry business. He come over in 1920 and made a success. I was a salesman for him. And another man, one of the customers, offered to set me up in business for myself. But I never like it, the business. I said, "No. No business." I didn't like it. And I didn't want to go home, and just think about how I owe this one, or that one owes me. . . . I just made up my mind I didn't want to go into business.

Although going into business might have relieved Victor of one set of debts, it would have enmeshed him in a network of others. It was clear that this, too, was a family tradition he wanted to leave behind—largely because he recognized he had a different kind of desire.

As our conversation deepened, it emerged that desire also figured more centrally in another one of Victor's postwar choices that he had initially explained in terms of horror. While his readiness to "go out of the line" and marry a Christian was undoubtedly conditioned by his experience of the destruction, there were also more affirmative reasons why he wanted to be with the particular woman he married. Recalling again his not staying in the jewelry business with his brother, Victor remembered another potential opportunity he had turned down:

> I started with my brother in the business. But then I went back to Italy after three months because I left my heart over there. I started to travel. I lost three or four years.
>
> (HG: You "left your heart"?) I fall in love in Rome. So I make three trips there and back. I was already here three months, and then I go back to Italy. Where I stayed six months with my wife.
>
> I even read, every month there is a Jewish newspaper. And in it they write about some woman, her husband die, and they are looking for someone to marry her and take him into the business. This was Jewish people. I read it. I pay no attention. I was in love with *her*. You understand?

Here Victor was a "hindseer" rather than a "businessman" in a different sense than he had explained before, now looking back with loyalty but certainly not with sorrow. He further noted that such loyalty, and its priority over more traditional obligations, was fully shared by his bride.

> I didn't marry in the church. We married in the court of Rome. She cannot have communion because she married a Jew and she didn't ask the Holy Father.
>
> The priest asked her. When she went in the last time to have communion, he asked her. I kneel down too. I was listening to what she says and what the priest says. I am on the other side. Her kneeling was for the confession. My kneeling was to listen through the hole, to put my ear on it, to hear what is going on.
>
> So he ask, "Did you ask the Holy Father for permission to marry a Jew?" She say no. He say, "Why not?" She say, "Because I marry him just the same. Because I love him." So he told her, "You will go to Hell. You will never get out of Hell."
>
> She was also in love. She say, "I didn't ask, because if he will say no, I am in love, I will have to break his rule. So I will go ahead and marry tomorrow." She went on Sunday morning and on Monday we married.

While not precisely in the spirit of Maimonides, it is clear that ferreting out the reality behind the sanctity was also a part of Victor's early relationship with his wife. Here, of course, uncovering the secrets of the "fathers"— and keeping secrets from the "fathers"—had more to do with the bravado of young lovers than the rage of a prosecutor.

In fact, it appears that Victor did a fair amount of "investigating" during this period. Of a trip he made to France around the same time, he recalled:

> So I was also in Paris. I walk out at night. What do you see? You see a boy and a girl, and they kiss. And the girl hold her foot up. This is the culmination point. She raises her foot and hangs on, and they can stay like this for half an hour. His tongue in her mouth and her tongue in his mouth. And sometimes I went behind a tree. And looked and looked and looked. To see how long does it take?

However long it took, Victor was also pushing the boundaries of privacy in his own love life. He continued:

> You see this only in Paris. In France. Because in Italy, when you kiss in public, they take you to jail. The Pope is over there. I once went with my wife to Villa Borghese. It's an entertainment place, lots of trees, and you can rent a horse, which I did. I brought my boots and breeches.

I was there with my wife. And two policeman come up and say, "You're under arrest." Why? Because it's not allowed in public parks to kiss. That's what they say.

I say, "I'm a foreigner. What do I know?" Finally, my wife pull out her identification card. It says she works for the city of Rome, which pays these park watchmen. So they soften up. They say, "Forget about it." They give her back her card and say, "Don't do it in public. You can do it in lots of places. Just not in the public again."

Thus another version of the story of the horseman and his pursuing prosecutor—certainly the lightest and most forgiving.

In the thrall of these memories, Victor himself grew lighter and more forgiving. In spite of his concerns over his own son's current love affair, and the irresponsibility that Victor thought went with it, he also found a significant bond of identification. Thinking about what he had just recounted of his own romance with his wife, Victor noted:

I was the same. When I was in love, I was the same. Ardent. An ardent lover. I see me in him. I see, when I look back, I see where I was. Three times, three times I went back over to Italy! . . . I was also in love. I was also crazy.

As further confirmation of how "crazy" he was, Victor shared an aphorism coined, appropriately enough, by the first of his brothers to have left home and "gone ahead."

My oldest brother, whom I met here because he left Poland before I was born, he said: "A hair from a pussy is the strongest thing in the world. Why? Because a hair from a pussy can pull a boat of twenty-five thousand tons over the ocean from one side, from New York, to the other side, to Italy, with you on the boat too! This is its strength," he said. This is its strength. Because I was in love.

Here, then, is another instance of the legacies survivors receive and transmit—as prosaic as our own. Recalling his brother's affirmation of human desire, Victor can pass it on to his son. Seeing himself in his son, Victor can reconfirm his own rightful place in the tradition of "ardent lovers."

Just as such legacies may be passed forward, they can also be passed backward—to those who came before. Thus Victor revealed another "fact of life" he had learned during the twenty months after his mother's death. It concerned his father's capacity to leave the past behind without betraying it. Victor recalled:

I remember, when I come home, my mother had passed away and there was living across the street a woman who was a widow for some years. And she happen to come see my father. So when I come home, I think maybe she is inside, maybe there happen something between them. So I move the doorknob on the outside door. I move it to let him hear that somebody is coming. And then I move slowly to the other door. There was a corridor, and the other door, I didn't open right away. To give them time to sit comfortably, you understand. Not to make my father think I broke in and caught him in a hot moment. To give him time to hear that I am coming.

It should be said that Victor expressed considerable discomfort after having shared this recollection, just as he was careful about not letting too much be revealed at the time. His concern, however, stemmed from respect for his father's privacy and memory rather than from any judgment about whatever "hot moments" may have occurred. "In his respect," he affirmed, "in this respect, I am very modern." He related the same modern views to his judgment of his children's behavior.

For example, this week my daughter invited a girlfriend to supper, and they were going out, and she say, "Oh boy, there will be boys!" In our time, the girl didn't show off that willingness for boys at that age—even an older girl, between twenty and thirty, she would not say that. This is the promiscuous generation! They are more sincere now.

(HG: "Sincere" meaning?) I approve of this more. I am a modern man as far as this is concerned. I go along with it. This thing, I go along. (HG: Which is like what you were saying about your father too?) The world doesn't regress. The world goes to progress, it goes ahead. And with a world that goes ahead, one cannot stay behind.

In this context, at least, Victor places himself squarely among those who "go ahead," now a group that includes both those who came before him and those who come after. And here the secrets to be found behind double-doors are secrets of love rather than betrayal. They can, therefore, be revealed without betrayal and without that revelation leading to endless searches of double-basements: investigations involving other bodies, other memories, completely other reductions of reverence.

These memories, and the life they retell, are salvaged from another part of Victor's past. As we listen to him recount them, we almost forget the rest of what he has told us, which is now far in the background, almost unreal. Meanwhile, this retelling shows the persistence of dreams as well as nightmares, stories that may be drawn upon to re-create the dissolution of stories but that also "go ahead" on their own. Within their unfolding, a world emerges that we easily recognize: *our* world of parents and children and conflicts of desire, all still informed by an essential loyalty and an essential faith in the reconciliations that time and maturation bring. In this world, seeds still grow to fruition. The fruits of one's labor, too, may still be found acceptable. Neither a "ghost and human wreck" nor a "celebrant of life," Victor simply lives and harvests what he can.

His cultivation, however, is bounded by other memories we do not share, and sooner or later the "deepness" returns. Even while developing the salvaged meanings of one world, Victor reveals the ongoing presence of the other and of its ongoing capacity to reduce all meaning back to its own. There are "memories inside memories." And, inside those, further memories still.

Midnight

Sometimes, as in the story of the severed plum tree, the reduction of meaning is recounted through an enactment: stories that are lived as well as retold. Victor described such a time at the end of the same conversation in which he had remembered his coming of age and the early years of his marriage. The episode took place just a week before that interview. Noting that he usually takes a nap during the day and thus sleeps lightly at night, he said that on this day he had been working throughout the afternoon and fell into an unusually deep sleep just after midnight. He also mentioned an ongoing concern about his home being broken into, as had recently happened to a number of households in his neighborhood. He continued:

> When I go to sleep, I put my revolver, I put it beneath the carpet where I can put the hand down to get it. Because maybe at night there will come a thief, and he would start to plunder, and he would come in my room, and I would wake up. I sleep downstairs, and I put my clothes on a chair and the chair beneath the knob. So, if one wants to break in, he has to maneuver, and I will wake up.
>
> This week my boy comes home from work one night. And for some reason, he pushed the door, and I got scared. And I got up and hit the gun and was ready to shoot. . . . He didn't say nothing. He just push and push the door. And I got up and took my gun and was waiting.
>
> And he come in the door. He wasn't in yet, the door was open. So he reach in and adjust the chair so he can push open the door. And I see him, because he comes from the light. My room is dark. I learn this from the war. If it is a thief, he doesn't see me in the darkness. I have time to shoot. So I

didn't pull the trigger. . . . When he comes in from the light, and I am in the dark, in that split second, I hold it up. I don't shoot. I don't fire.

(HG: But that was a very close call—) I was shocked! I was shocked! I was sick an hour before I came back to myself! Because I could shoot him. I was sick.

"You break into my room. You know I have a gun. I could use it. I could pull the trigger. You was dumb that you didn't give a word. Before you move the door. Before you move the door."

I didn't sleep during the day. Otherwise, I don't sleep so hard. I hear when he put in the key and I know it's him. But again, this happened because I didn't sleep during the day, and I was—, and that pushing the door—, I hit the gun. Who is there? Because I didn't sleep.

Victor clearly had been shocked by what he had almost done, and he remained upset as he told me about it. Yet even then, as at the time, he oscillated between blaming his own loss of clarity and blaming his son for not having been more caring and careful himself. With unusual bitterness, Victor went on to speak about his son's lack of consideration almost as though he were, in fact, the plunderer whom Victor had been anticipating. He exclaimed:

They are always in a hurry, the youth! They are just walking dummies. Just walking dummies. They are thinking only of their interest. That's all. That's all they live for. To have a good time. That is all.

And so it seems, in a terrible but lingering moment between waking and sleep, both of Victor's pasts started again to collapse together. In a single confrontation, the old man at home meets the young man coming in from his nightly labor; the one left vulnerable and alone meets the one who cares only for himself; an aging patriarch, rising from the darkness to catch his despoiler in the unmasking light, meets an intruder who himself respects no bounds to his invasions of secrets and sanctity. Once again, the possible roles for the protagonists have been reduced to only two—the betrayer and the betrayed—and the combat between them is absolute and deadly. The future belongs to only one, but they are both impossible choices for the survivor who wishes "to remain what he is and to continue what he is."

In this way, compressed within the story of an already strained conflict between father and son, and almost silencing that story forever, are echoes of a tragedy never dramatized by the Greeks nor prophesied by the blind seer, Tiresias.

HUMAN TERMS

The story of a man prosecuting God, taken by itself, is poignant and heroic. The story of a man consumed by remorse over his felt betrayal of his ancestry is more profoundly sad. The story of a man feeling victimized and abandoned by his own family, and sometimes seeming to collude in that abandonment, is more disturbing still. The story of a man nearly shooting the son he loves—just as he reasserts a sense of generative strength and goodness reflected in their bond—is excruciating. With each story, the pain and outrage escalate. We approach the limits of our capacity to empathize.

If we do have such a response, it is relevant to note that, to this point, we have heard Victor speak only in general about the destruction. He has recounted particular "facts" hardly at all. And certainly one could approach this history in an entirely different way than through the kinds of stories we have heard Victor retell. For example:

Obliterations of reverence? At Treblinka, the facade of the building containing the gas chambers bore a large Star of David and was built to resemble a traditional synagogue. Hung in the entrance was a curtain, plundered from a real synagogue, which bore the Hebrew inscription: "This is the gate through which the righteous shall enter."

Severed roots? At Treblinka the assistant commandant's dog was trained to bite off the genitals of male prisoners. The shepherd attacked on the command: "Man, bite that dog."

Secrets and unmaskings? Treblinka was nothing but secrets and unmaskings: from the railway station with its fake ticket window; to the "infirmary" that was a garbage pit for people; to the "barbers" and "bath attendants" on the way to the gas; to the mass graves where the "resettled" were laid out, dug up, burned on pyres, "resettled" again.

Dissolutions of stories? Each of the 900,000 people murdered at Treblinka carried a universe of stories, as complex as the stories of prosecutor, his memories, and his fate.[1]

These facts, however, are not stories and do not lend themselves to stories. There are no characters; no action and reaction; no trajectory of plot through beginning, middle, and end. There are only scattered images, like a pack of snapshots returned without a traveler whose journey they record.

There may be good reasons, therefore, not to get ahead of ourselves and speak of the "facts" of the Holocaust too soon. While approaching those facts through the lives and stories of individual recounters might risk "psychologizing" them, not doing so risks bypassing human response altogether. And, indeed, if stories like Victor's already test our empathy, how much less will we be able to enter into accounts of which Victor's stories are only the palest shadows. The truth is that while such images may momentarily shock or terrify us, we are left strangely untouched compared with our responses to Victor's struggle. His pain and the closing circles of his guilt and rage are feelings we can share, at least to some degree. Those events, recounted as discrete data, are beyond the capacity of our responsive empathy—almost as though they did not really happen to anyone.

So the events can also seem even to those who lived them. "Even to us, our mind couldn't grasp it," said Paula. "So how could I make you understand something that my own mind doesn't grasp?" "Even when I was in Auschwitz," said Reuben, "I still didn't believe it. I saw smoke and everything, and I didn't believe it. I didn't believe nothing." "Sometimes I wonder if it touched me at all," said Leon. "I become almost clinical about it. Sometimes I don't believe, I can hardly believe, it really happened." Here again, he recalls a "landscape of death" seemingly untouched by "human emotion."

When, in recounting, survivors attempt to retell that landscape, they tend to put "human emotion" back. "You have to see the individuals before they became victims," Paula insisted. "We weren't always a group, and they weren't always a group, without a soul, without feelings." Speaking, as he so often does, of his own struggle to convey it, Leon exclaimed: "I *cannot* convey it! And to say something and come down with all the impact of a laundry list—facts, dates, places—it denies the whole essence of my memory of the Holocaust!" Once again, Leon compromises. Memory is described in "human terms" and retold through "the experiences of individuals." Stories are made for what is "not a story." A completely impersonal destruction is framed by a perspective that *is* personal: one still grounded in the life and voice of the recounter.

In these ways, recounters also "psychologize." Within their re-creations, there *are* identifiable characters, communicable emotion, and coherent trajectories of action and response. Although certainly agonizing, their stories present a mediated *unfolding* of pain or horror—a revelation of death rather than an invasion by it. At the same time, there is usually something about such accounts, the way they abruptly end or the way they insistently repeat, that conveys that they are, in fact, compromises—still not "grasping" it; still struggling with "the whole essence."

Thus far, we have heard Victor's re-creations of the destruction as a whole: his stories about the end of stories, and about the ends of generations, remembrance, and fidelity as well. We turn now to some of Victor's more particular memories of the nightmare. We may be surprised by the sense that, even here, Victor's stories are not completely unfamiliar.

The Rubbish Pit

Early in these pages, I suggested that even Victor's memory of the *Lazaret* is not a "pure engram, engraved into his consciousness and later recalled completely without mediation." Now that we have become familiar with the other stories Victor retells, and with the general concept of "making stories" of a "not-story," it is relevant to present Victor's recounting of this memory in full. The time is Friday, the week after Rosh Hashana, 1942, Victor's second day in Treblinka. He recalls:

> The next day we was working on the clothes—to look in the pockets, to sort out money to money, gold to gold. And I have seen one Jew fill up a suitcase with money. And he was carrying the suitcase. They have a place, they call it a "Lazaret," that means "infirmary." It was behind the trees so nobody should see it. And everybody takes a suitcase of rubbish there and put in the rubbish.
>
> So he takes a suitcase of money. It was nicely packed and tied with a belt. And the German, the *Hauptmann*—"*Hauptmann*" is usually a German captain—he was suspicious of what is in the suitcase. So he went up to him and he said, "Halt! Open this up!" And he opened it. And it was full of money, English pounds and American dollars. So right away he call a Ukrainian. The Ukrainians was under the Germans. He call a Ukrainian with the bayonet fixed, and he led him to the *Lazaret*, on the other side.
>
> This I have seen because I have rubbish. I understand what's going on because I have seen them far away. And he opened the suitcase. It was maybe a hundred feet away or less. He opened the suitcase, and I could see the things packed in there, like hundred bills and things.
>
> So he went behind those trees. And the way they shot—, this I find out from a friend of mine who was a militia man. They had them open the mouth, and they shoot him in here, to cut the esophagus.
>
> So here was fire. And here was always burning rubbish. And there were some dead bodies burning over there, with the skin folded and the bone showing, that I could see. So they shot him. He fall down.
>
> And when they left, I went over there to put in my rubbish. I put in my rubbish on this side. He is burning over there on the other side. So I say, if he burns, I don't want to put more rubbish on him to help out the Germans. So I put the stuff here, and I went back to work. This was Friday. And Saturday come wagons to pick up the clothes.

Victor thus tells a complete story, clearly situated in time and space, and structured by a number of narrative strategies. First, there is the amount of particularizing detail that Victor includes. It is Friday. There was a specific "crime" (attempting to destroy the money before it fell into German hands) and a specific punishment. The perpetrator, the executioner, and the witness are all identified. As the narrative develops, additional information is sketched in: the significance of the *Lazaret* in the background, the relationship between *Hauptmann* and Ukrainian, and the mode of execution. These are the terms within which Victor's story moves, as he himself re-creates his movement from the sorting square to the rubbish pit.

As he does so, we move along with him, for Victor does not get ahead of himself. Throughout he reminds us of *his* perspective—what he could see and what he could not see—as he progresses toward increasing revelation. He saw the Jew fill up the suitcase; he even remembers what the suitcase looked like. He witnessed the confrontation between the German and the Jew. He was close enough, "a hundred feet away or less," to hear the *Hauptmann's* words and to see the "hundred bills and things" that had been discovered. By contrast, the *Lazaret* is concealed; it is "behind the trees so nobody should see it." Likewise, although Victor "understands what's going on," he does not witness the actual execution and did not learn until later how such shootings were carried out. He arrives at the rubbish pit only after the killing. There he presents the scene that his eyes took in, as though still taking it in: "Here was fire" and "always burning rubbish" and bodies burning "with the skin folded and the bone showing, that I could see." His gaze narrows to the particular, identifiable body of the man who was shot. His corpse is burning on one side. Victor puts his rubbish in on the other side and goes back to work. It is still Friday.

Within the personal perspective and bounded context that Victor establishes, his story retains its integrity. Also within those bounds, another kind of integrity is preserved. The Jew's attempt to destroy the money was an act of resistance, as Victor states more clearly in another recounting of the same episode: "They find him taking a suitcase of money, bills. He tied it up with a string and took it over there. And they caught him on the way to the *Lazaret*. . . . He was taking it so it doesn't go to the Germans." Victor goes on to tell us that he, also, found room for a small act of resistance, even with the full terror of the pit closing in. He kept his own rubbish away from the burning corpse so as not to "help out the Germans." A distinction between people and rubbish is salvaged, even when everything conspires to obliterate it.

Finally, the structure of Victor's story, and its significance to him as *his* story, may also be related to the ongoing themes of his life. Here again, there are secrets and unmaskings, prosecutors and damning evidence. Here also, the images are doubled. Both the Jew and the German have something to hide: one within a neatly packed suitcase; the other behind a wall of trees. Both the Jew and the German would protect the interests of their "business": one the financial yield of his people's labor; the other the financial needs of the Reich. Each would resist and unmask the other: the Jew by burning the money; the German by burning the Jew. Within their opposition, only one can go ahead with his secrets and business intact.

Of course, the opponents in Victor's story are not equal, nor is the scale of the secrets they hide and the unmaskings they intend. Although provisionally balanced within the narrative of a single victim and a single execution and executioner, the balance does not last. And as the Jew and his secret are consumed, the organizing frame of Victor's story also starts to fail. In the pit are other burning bodies, anonymous bodies, with no recounter who will ever tell their story or speak of how they got there and of what they were accused. Further, in the pits of Treblinka there were usually enough such bodies that the rubbish had to burn near someone; if not one than the other, if not now than later. For there was "always burning rubbish" and always burning bodies, whether on Friday or any other day.

Victor, therefore, focuses on the corpse whose story *can* be told. In order to save his story, he has to put some of the "mystery" back. He, therefore, does not linger over the other corpses and the truth they revealed—that all were rubbish here, and all were doomed to die. Later, Victor recalled the terror closing in:

> There is no way out! I am trapped! I am in a trap! I am closed in, within a concrete wall, tall up to the Heaven. I cannot get out. There will come an end to me too.

In a related memory, Victor described being near the darkest center of the slaughter, the gas chambers and burial trenches:

> I heard the motor. At the time, I didn't realize—, I was thinking that the motor was digging the graves, not producing carbon monoxide. I was thinking that the motor was digging the graves. . . .
>
> I was feeling like a sheep that's tied up in the slaughterhouse. And an animal knows. When they let them loose, behind the fence in the stockyard, they feel the death. They feel the blood inside. They hear the moaning. They know. . . . The animal has more knowledge, feels more the death than man. Man doesn't know that here is a danger. If he doesn't see nothing, he doesn't know.

After, I hear the cries of the people: "AHHHHHHH!"—and finished. "AHHHHHHH!"—and finished. And all the Ukrainians with the guns guarding, one next to the other. I see this is combat-readiness, with the bayonet on the rifle. Every ten feet. And here people undress.

I say, "What is this?" I asked once. I was working close to the gas chamber. So I looked down, and I asked somebody, "What do they do with those people over there?" He answered me. "They send them to Heaven."

So I was sure. They was killed. I didn't want to believe. I didn't want to believe it. I wanted to believe only what I and my eyes see.

(HG: How did you feel at that moment?) Helpless! Helpless! I got to do what they want. If they want my life, to take my life, they are the lords.

Confronted directly with the extermination, Victor does *not* want to "see it closer." Even knowing, he does not want to believe, and here he is grateful for the limits of human vision. Hearing the cries from these sacrificed "lambs and calves," Victor would restore the "secrets."

Only later, when Victor becomes the prosecutor, would he choose to unmask. And, even then, his revelations are indirect and gradual. They are framed and limited by the ways he constructs the role of prosecutor and chooses his texts and his accused. At the time, Victor had far more immediate concerns. There was the threat of being consumed by the revelations of *these* "lords" and their own boundlessly penetrating eyes.

What Is Also True

Despite efforts like Victor's to shade it out, the lethal vision does get inside. It gets inside in the sense of "inner time bombs" and recurring anticipation of "the worst conceivable." It is evident in "unfinished sentences" and in tears that seem to have a memory of their own. It is expressed in horror of the past and terror for the future; in both the inability to stay and the inability to leave.

For Victor, it gets inside with the force and permanence of a bullet shot down one's throat. This is the image included within, yet most alien to, the rest of his story of the rubbish pit. It is the one thing that Victor did not witness personally but learned afterward, another "memory inside memory" and not one of his own. Yet it is this fragment of atrocity to which Victor most fixedly returns in his later retellings of the rubbish pit, as though standing for all that his personal story does *not* recount. Victor speaks of the image in exactly that way. Recalling a recent conversation with his daughter, he noted:

Human nature is not to believe in this. In the worst that can come, nobody believes. With time, everything gets polished up. And people who read about the Holocaust today—, like my daughter, she was born here, and she ask: "Daddy, is all this true what they did with the people?" I tell her: "This is true. And what you are not told, what you don't know, is also true." She asked me, "How what I am not told can I know? What I am not told, how can it be true?"

I say, because the Germans try to hide everything, and there is no survivor to tell. There is always something more that is not written in any book. Like this what I find out from my friend. . . . The Gestapo arrested one who has a false passport. He say, "Open the mouth." And he pull out the gun and shoot him in the mouth. I hadn't known this until this time.

He had seen this. There are lots of atrocities that no one will ever know. So I answer my daughter, I say: "This is true, and what you don't know, what is not told, is also true." I tell her this. I didn't know they shot people in the mouth, to cut the esophagus. Therefore, I told her, "This is true, and this, what you are not told, is also true. What is not in the book is also true."[2]

Victor's assertion that "there is always something more that is not written in any book" refers most specifically to the fact of absent witnesses. But he begins his reflections with a more general point: that "in the worst that can come, nobody believes" and "with time, everything gets polished up." Victor's recurrent phrase about all that is "also true"—almost a chant in its repetition—suggests the infinity of not-told truth beyond the books and behind the polish. Through his inclusion of the other man's memory within his own story, a fragment of that infinity enters in—like the bullet itself.

Survival

Having endured three days in Treblinka, Victor was one of the few in the history of the death camp to escape and one of the much fewer, among those who did escape, to survive the war. By hiding under bundles of the victims' clothes in an outgoing train, he gained provisional freedom from the killers' grasp. But the life he thereby salvaged did not exclude the death in which he had been immersed, a death reiterated during two more years of terror and hiding within occupied Poland. Treblinka would remain inside his other memories, as though Victor was now living along two tracks of time: one leading outward to escape and ongoing life; one forever circling back to an inescapable, irrevocable ending.

Still, even his description of his escape initially appears to be structured by memories other than those of the horror he had just departed. Even on the train, Victor tells us, there were forward-looking "businessmen" and a "hindseer" haunted by the past. Describing his meeting other escapees in the boxcar after the train was away, Victor recalled:

> They were counting the money they had taken. I come over to them. They ask me, "Why don't you count your money? Are you afraid to show that you have money?"
>
> So I say, "I have no money. I was only there three days." Well, three days, they understand. One who was only three days there, he didn't eat human flesh, and he didn't take money. He was still too much in himself, destroyed mentally. Of this what he has seen that has happened. But one who was there three weeks, he was turned into an animal. . . .
>
> One give me five dollars, one of them. "You was only in three days and you come to the idea to run away?" And they believed me. The one who give me the five dollars, he say, "Maybe you will need this to buy out your life.". . .
>
> I myself am still broken. I hadn't reached the state of mind to think about taking money. That so many people—, in my mind, I was still more strongly thinking of the back, what happened yesterday. Their mind was already stronger to get out. In my mind, I wasn't thinking about money, the will to get money wasn't there.

Reminiscent of other stories he tells, here, too, Victor's division between those who look forward and those who look back is a distinction *between* himself and the others. The memory to which he turned next, a later meeting with another escapee, is similarly structured. Now, however, the line between those who "went ahead" and those "left behind" is also drawn between surviving husbands and forgotten wives.

> One who run away from Treblinka, after three weeks, he was joking already. He took me to a woman, maybe five months later. I didn't go for five months to a woman. Because I loved my wife dearly, my first wife. And no woman could have the power to make me step out. And I have more pain about this what happened, in Treblinka, remembering her alive, and then she perished, than from anybody else who was killed. . . .
>
> When he come back, he went right away to a woman. Because he was three weeks over there. He lost a wife and child. I lost my wife only. We didn't have no children.
>
> I say, he should have more pain. He say, "A wife is nothing. A wife is just like a whore. A child, that is what hurts more," he told me.
>
> But he went. He joked the whole day. He took lots of money, gold from in Treblinka, when he run away. He was more used to it. He has longer experience. One week experience in Treblinka, three weeks experience in

Treblinka, was making a man a butcher. After what he has seen, how they killed so many people.

Once again, Victor describes himself as the one who looks back to the past and to those who were lost. The other man, he says, has had too much recent past: so much that the rest of his memory and his capacity for pain were lost.

Undoubtedly, these episodes occurred as Victor recounts them. At the same time, structured as they are, they are strikingly continuous with other stories he retells. Some go ahead. They become money-takers, pleasure-seekers, even "animals" and "butchers." Others are left behind—"surplus" or "whores" in the eyes of their betrayers. Still, it also becomes clear that Victor is not simply making a prosecutor's point. For one thing, the distinction he makes between himself and the other escapees involves far less judgment than at first appears. Of the transformations of character he witnessed, Victor noted:

> It could have happened to me too. Because this is stronger than a man's character. He might have the best character. But he would do everything. Like the man who took money over there. He wasn't there one day. Hardship makes the man change his character. It could happen to me, too, if I would be there longer.
>
> I don't make such a difference between myself and the other one who took the money. He opened his eyes. My eyes were still toward my heart. His eyes were maybe on the outside. . . . There is a fraction of a difference between one survivor and the other. Everybody went through just the same over that time.

Victor is thus not emphasizing the differences he initially suggested, at least not with the same vehemence we have heard in similar polarizations of his. Such distinctions become only fractional within the destruction that all survivors know. Within that nightmare, all were reduced to the potential of "doing everything."

But were they so reduced? That is, do words like "butchers" and "animals" apply at all, or are these also borrowed moral terms from a borrowed moral tale? The limits of such epithets appear to emerge in Victor's own account. However callous or selfish their weeks in Treblinka had made them, the men whom Victor meets in the boxcar understand his situation and share some of their money to aid Victor's own survival. Although only minutes from the death camp, their capacity for sympathy and solidarity has clearly not been destroyed. Conversely, notwithstanding the ways

Victor was consumed by what he had seen and what he had lost, he did, in fact, escape and "went ahead" himself. Eventually, he also "goes to a woman," even if he did not feel compelled to degrade the memory of the woman he had lost forever.

In view of this, Victor is right not to "make such a difference" between himself and the others. After Treblinka, *all* would somehow contend with going ahead and remaining forever behind, with *both* an ongoing life and an ongoing death. After Treblinka, in other words, the two kinds of survivors—the "businessman" and the "hindseer"—are really one. And Victor's recurring story about leaving and being left becomes, in this context, a way of giving form to the irreducible contradiction of survival itself.

THE EXTENDED SILENCE

To remain alive and yet know the presence of an all-consuming death is an awesome, sometimes overwhelming, task. Nonetheless, most survivors' lives have gone on, and they are based on much more than memories of the destruction. Thus, in contrast with Victor's first accounts and probably our own initial expectations, we come to learn that Victor's second marriage began as one of love and passionate fidelity. It was certainly not motivated solely by flight from the horror he had known. Likewise, his choice of factory work had a more intimate history than the history of Polish antisemitism. Victor eventually tells us that it reflected his own preference as much as the prejudice of others. Although containing their own sources of conflict, neither such "going ahead" had to evoke the debilitating spiral of inner and outer prosecution that we have followed. And, in fact, for many years, they did not. As a younger man, even after the war, Victor had pursued his chosen trade and chosen partner with the same "crazy" determination that, at the best times, he recalls in his father and can still affirm in his son.

Still, the deaths and their memory also go on. "What is not told in any book" increasingly demands expression, and especially so when survivors must attend to the task of remembrance in isolation. For some, their ongoing lives themselves become part of the media of recounting. Thus texts that are reclaimed are also prosecuted; trees that are planted are also cut down; sons that are raised are nearly destroyed—as is the prosecutor, the farmer, and the father himself. Such re-creations are agonized and agonizing, and yet even they only point to something more. "What is not told is also true." In this context, what is not told is also worse.

Victor, like all the participants, accepts that much of the destruction will never be retold. But that resignation has not reduced his or the other participants' impulse to recount *something*, however compromised and unfinished. Nor did such resignation prepare the participants for the degree of indifference or active avoidance with which even their incomplete recounting would be met. The struggle to find "human terms" for all-pervasive death required painstaking, sometimes disfiguring, effort. The struggle to find listeners could become one additional death that had to be confronted.

An Unrecognized Past

When Victor speaks of forward-looking "businessmen" and those who are left behind and discarded, there is one further context to which he refers. These themes are grounded in his life before the destruction, and they were made indelible by their worst possible enactment during. But they were also confirmed by the world he entered *after* liberation. That world, too, had its "materialists" and broken covenants. Postwar Europe and the United States provided stories and storytellers fully as open to critical unmasking as those that would later absorb Victor in his analyses of Babylon and Eden.

In spite of this, most of Victor's prosecuting, when it finally emerges, is directed toward issues that are ancient and biblical rather than modern and political. Yet there are at least a few instances when his indictments reach out to secular justice rather than to God's. Referring most specifically to the case of Archbishop Trifa, whose deportation for war crimes had been dragging on for years, Victor commented:

> I am not satisfied. I am not satisfied with everything which took shape after the destruction of the six million people. I am not satisfied with American law, with Trifa. It makes of justice a mockery.
> So they play with my past. They do not recognize my past. They don't recognize the six million who were murdered. They deny me. What I say, they deny. And they deny them, who was killed.

Victor's dissatisfaction goes beyond the frustration of his desire for revenge and even beyond the denial of his own history and that of the murdered. Carrying an unrecognized past was painful enough, but especially so because the failure to punish the perpetrators made another Holocaust that much more likely. Victor commented:

I was thinking when I was in the hiding, during the Holocaust, I was thinking with my brother who they killed later. He asked me, "What do you think they will do to the Germans after the war?" I said, "Well, the Russians will come and probably take all the Germans to Siberia." It didn't happen. They start to send them out to Siberia, but then Truman sent a telegram to stop it. . . .

This was because America had another interest in it. To rebuild Germany and to get German scientists over here, Von Braun and the other ones. . . . So it didn't happen. Again, materialism took place over it. Materialism took place over the bodies of our dead brothers. . . .

It would not have gotten them back. But I have to continue to live. And the longer I live, the longer the pain, the longer misgivings about this. Not misgivings, but heartbite. That nothing was done. . . .

It's not just the revenge. Once the world knows, and they are punished for it, it is less likely to happen. Leaders would be afraid. "If I do this again, how about if I lose the war? They will punish me, and I don't want that." It didn't happen. It went with half-punishment.

Why did so many years go by? They should have been punished. It should have been known. It would have been easier for the pain of those who were hurt by them. It would have been easier for the hearts, the pain, of the survivor. What he lost because of them.

These are Victor's most direct statements against a "polishing up" far removed from God or His prophets. Likewise, the "materialists" with whom he is here concerned have nothing to do with fathers and sons, husbands and wives, or the "going ahead" that is part of survival itself. That may be why the reverberations of guilt that so often follow Victor's prosecutions are absent here. Not "misgivings," he corrects himself, but "pain" and "heartbite" in response to what business continued to be transacted "over the bodies of our dead brothers." In this context, Victor can indict those who "went ahead" without evoking a spiral of self-recrimination as well.

Still, the moment remains a fragile one. As we have heard, survivors have had good reasons to suppress their more direct expressions of outrage, and most soon learned to keep their dissatisfactions to themselves. They learned to "survive again" and "fend for themselves" and be "an American, too."

Victor also learned to "fend for himself." Whatever his unspoken memories and embittered hopes, he had more than enough experience keeping his "secret" thoughts to himself. He, too, went ahead. He remarried and followed the trade he had chosen. Within the extended silence, Victor was also silent.

Death and Remembrance

Only in his later years, as Victor began to anticipate his death, did the demands of memory fully return. As he told us, a young man, "with a span of life in front of him," needs little beyond the evidence of his personal survival and his generative potential to sustain faith. But an old man needs more. "When the strength leaves the man, he starts to reflect on things." He looks back to those who made him and forward to what he has made. He asks what he has received from those who came before and what he has created and maintained that can be passed on to those who come after.

The old man also looks out to the world in which he has lived his life. Here, too, he needs to find some acceptable balance between making and being made, between choice and fate. If he surrenders fully to "circumstances," he can rid himself of regret or protest, but he simultaneously denies his own freedom and accomplishment. He becomes *only* a "victim" or an "instrument," and his sense of worth will depend on the worth he finds in the Creator or Creation whose instrument he has been. Conversely, if he cannot accept his fate at all—being unable even to imagine some possible reconciliation—he faces another risk: that of an eternity of separation and rage. Either way, for the old man, his personal survival is not enough. Whatever he has made or failed to make in his individual life must now be situated within some common life which he has inherited, to which he has contributed (just by living), and by which he may be remembered or betrayed.

These are the dimensions of Victor's final struggle with remembrance, and we hear him attempt to resolve it in more than one way. In one voice, he does surrender to fate and circumstances, and he expresses acceptance. That the Creation he accepts is one reduced to war, death, and oblivion—with himself as one of its agents—does not change the fact that it is reconciliation nonetheless. Thus we have heard Victor speak, *without* apparent bitterness, of having seen "a lot of races that are destroyed" during the years since the Holocaust.

> The weaker has to give under. He has to be destroyed, and the stronger survives. . . . It's the law of the jungle even by man. . . . This is a world of circumstances. . . . The ant, the rat, the cow, the horse, and the man—a world of circumstances.

The "law of the jungle" characterizes the family as much as any other set of relations. There, too, the strong survive and prosper.

> When a man feels closer to death, what's the difference how a man ends? . . .
> An old man, full of wrinkles on his face . . . he is something surplus. Even to
> his closest, he is something surplus. He is useless. He starts to become a
> burden. To his closest. That's life. That's part of life.

As "part of life," becoming useless surplus gives the old man no grounds for
complaint. Indeed, he might as well already be dead. For the dead, too,
have no claim on those who continue, nor any way of feeling injury if they
did. They are simply gone.

> When we go, we go with all the history. And if it goes with all the history,
> you just divide between the living and the dead. And when one is dead, if
> he will be remembered, or if he will not be remembered, is just the same.

Meanwhile, the claim of the living is not much more. Having to continue
in a world of war and circumstances, they are simply one more generation
trying to survive, without precedents or prophecy.

> I don't think that, by them, I want anything to be remembered. I don't think
> this would do any good. My life is short. Their life is short. . . . I will go my
> way. They will go theirs. And death will take care of everything.

Survivors, killers, and the dead thus find each other again at the end of
Victor's life. They are co-equal partners in a Creation outside of memory,
blame, or care. In the mood of these passages, Victor accepts such a universe
as his—and our—rightful inheritance and home.

    That Victor also speaks otherwise has less to do with revulsion than with
truth: the truth that he did not die or become a killer and the truth that
he can still salvage memories in which moral outrage and human fidelity
have *not* been reduced to meaningless "polish." This does not mean that
these remnants stand intact. Victor knows, with more evidence than he
knows the contrary, that what was destroyed once can be destroyed again.
And if his reconciliation with death and oblivion is a false one, his appeals
for remembrance, and his prosecution on behalf of those forgotten, could
prove equally misguided. The very act of awakening such cries also awakens
the power of the nightmare to silence them again. And confronting the
nightmare in isolation adds even more to its reductive force. To scream into
deaf ears—for all the escalating "heartbite" of watching and remembering
in silence—finally risks an eternity of estrangement: "pain in its pure state,"
as Primo Levi described, without hope of awakening.

For these reasons, Victor's appeals and prosecutions remain indirect. Directed toward God or his family, they are framed by meanings and memories that qualify the terror and give it "human terms." For all that his re-creations are reduced and disfigured by the destruction they evoke, they are still only analogies, tellable by Victor and, potentially, hearable by us. And within the stories of the prosecutor, at least one conversation between recounter and listener *is* preserved. Victor still can exclaim:

> God, where are You? Are You dumb? Are You deaf? You don't see nothing! Are You blind? Or are You not at all?!

Following the old man's prayer, he still can repeat:

> "Don't send me away empty-handed when I am old. When my power will be diminished. You, don't forsake me! Don't forsake me when my power will diminish!"

Victor knows that there are far more chilling silences to be borne, and within which to be consumed, than the still somewhere expectant ones that follow these words between creature and Creator, or parent and child.

The Last Re-creation

Victor's final re-creation is a story that he leaves for his own survivors to complete. It is constructed, not out of the media of his individual life, but through the medium of his foreseen individual death. Toward the end of our last conversation, he told me that he did not plan to leave any instructions about his burial. Although he had definite fears and preferences, it would be the task of those who live on to decide how his remains should be known and accounted. He reflected:

> What will be will be. I cannot change things. I cannot change events. If I would be the only one in the world, it would be different. But there are lots of people. Everybody has his idea. Everybody do the way he wants.
>
> After death, it will take care to itself. As long as I am alive, I have certain lines. But I am not going to tell my son, "Bury me here or bury me there." Or my wife. They know. My wife knows that I am Jewish. My son knows. If not religious, I still say that I am Jewish. My daughter knows.
>
> (HG: You feel comfortable that they will know what to do?) Whatever they will do, when I am not here—, the only thing I wouldn't like—that a cross should be above my tomb. That's the only thing. That I feel uncomfortable about that cross. . . .

(HG: And you would say that?) No. I believe in their conscience. (HG: You still want to leave it to them?) I believe in their conscience. (HG: You still wouldn't say it directly?) No. No. No. I believe in their conscience.

Thus, refusing both to test or disbelieve in the future, one more Jew will be buried. His tomb will not be among the Patriarchs in Israel nor in the cemetery near Kielce that is gone. It will not be in the rubbish dumps of Treblinka nor in Eden nor in Nod. Rightfully accounted for or not, the corpse of this dead Jew will lie, like a strange seed, somewhere near the heart of the American heartland.

Chapter 6

On Having a Story to Tell

Tragedy is manifest in the individual, in his well-defined personal suffering. The dimensions of our suffering could not be fully expressed in an individual soul.

Aharon Appelfeld, *Beyond Despair*

HUMANIZING FATE

A story from lived experience marks the boundaries of a journey. However large or small the area of experience gathered in, every story moves, as the classical definition says, from some beginning through a middle to an end. In retelling experience as stories, narrators affirm both their mastery over the memories to be recounted and their faith that their listeners will be able to follow their retelling to its conclusion. That is, in recounting a memory as a story, narrators affirm that what they have to convey is both tellable and hearable. Neither the recounter nor the listeners will become lost in circumstances irrelevant to the main line of narrative. While there may be hesitancies and backtracking, a story does not wander endlessly. Neither the recounter nor the listeners will be fully overcome by terror or by grief. While storytellers may evoke horror or loss, they do not stop recounting. Neither narrator nor listeners will succumb to guilt or despair in the realization of how much—or how many—the story leaves unrecounted. In Victor's terms, stories "go ahead"—whatever they may have to leave out or leave behind.

Stories and Survival

For these reasons, every story—just by virtue of being a story—is implicitly a narrative of survival. Whatever was experienced *can* now be told with coherence and perspective. Whatever transpired, it was somehow gotten through. The storyteller can look back on the past and, from a point in the present which is different, tell its tale.

Because all stories are narratives of survival, stories and storytelling have also been closely linked with the concept of legacy. Although the connection holds most clearly for traditional societies—and may now be invoked more in sentimentality than lived actuality—there are important truths in the association between narrative and intergenerational continuities that remain essential in development throughout the life cycle. Thus, along with representing the normative experiences belonging to a particular way of life, recounting stories expresses the more basic conviction that there *is* a "way of life": a body of relevant precedents confirming that life does, in fact, go on. It goes on both for recounters (as evidenced by their ability to tell the tale) and, indirectly, for those who have not shared the experience but someday may. If the ones who have "been there" have a story to tell, listeners can hope that, faced with similar circumstances, they, too, would emerge with voice and meaning intact.

Such assumptions apply both to individual and collective experience. Regarding the former, every individual life is punctuated by periods of radical disruption and loss, by pasts that have to be abandoned and futures not foreseen. However such "life crises" or "stage transitions" are described, they are part of even the most ideal developmental circumstances (although, as with physical pain, we tend to forget the pains of development when we are not immediately in their grasp). What gets us through such periods is the faith—conditioned by past experience and the attitudes of significant guides—that we *can* get through. And as we begin to reaffirm our own endurance and duration, our sense of *having* an ongoing story, we tend to seek out and make use of the stories of others. The faith we confirm in ourselves is further confirmed by the recounting of others who have "gone through it." Their words, in turn, mediate the whole body of available stories about maturation that we may now assimilate as our own. In this way, narrative legacies are made immediate and actual. In a fully mundane sense, we re-enter the "world of the living" through our participation in life's retelling. A people's stories—both their particular content and the institution of storytelling itself—become part of the story of a single person.

So, too, do a people's stories about themselves *as* a people: their collective history. Like the narratives of individuals, historical narratives are also implicitly stories of survival. Now, of course, it is a collective "we" who remain to retell "the things that befell us." And although the rhythms of historical narratives are different from those of individual life histories, they contain the same promise of redemption from an eternity of wandering or loss. "In every age a hero or sage came to our aid," exclaims "Mi Y'Malel." In recounting those salvations, faith is confirmed in restorations to come—if only through the continuing ability *to* remember and recount.

In their uses of stories and storytelling, survivors are not different from the rest of us. They also draw on narrative precedents to give form to their experiences and to confirm their survival itself. And if their stories begin to wander or stop completely, they also go on. As I have emphasized, it is necessary to attend both to creation and dissolution in recounting—even if acts of creation continually re-create Creation's end.

Usable Texts: The Stories of Others

Early in these pages, I suggested that the role of "storyteller," like the image of "legacy-bestower," has been part of our own expectations of survivors. These ways of portraying survivors have become particularly prevalent in recent years, a point to which I will return. It should also be said, however, that some survivors actively take on the role of storyteller as a defining aspect of their voice and self-presentation. This, for example, is true of Elie Wiesel. Throughout his work, but especially in his writing about the Hasidic masters, he describes himself as a storyteller and speaks of the "tales" and "legends" he has to convey. It is relevant to ask, therefore, what are the tales that Wiesel and other survivor-storytellers have to retell, and how do such recounters understand their purposes?

Wiesel answers both questions succinctly. "The essence of a Hasidic legend? An attempt to humanize fate." The role of the recounter? The recounter, says Wiesel, does "nothing but transmit." Yet the very act of transmitting joins storyteller and listener in a second humanization, now of the story itself. In repeating the stories, Wiesel writes, "we make them ours."

And so the story that I have tried to tell here has been told more than once, by more than one person. It is always the same, and I, in turn, do nothing but transmit.

A needless repetition? No. Repetition, in Judaism, can assume a creative role. . . . We must ask the questions and make them ours by repeating them. In Hebrew, the word, *massora*, tradition, comes from the verb *limsor*, to transmit. In our history, this need to communicate, to share, comes close to being an obsession.[1]

Stories, and the tradition they convey, are thus only truly known when they are retold. Further, Wiesel adds that each recounter will retell in his or her own way, according to individual memory and preference. There is thereby a third step of mediation. Along with being received and transmitted, stories are personalized. They are made part of the recounter's own story which they, in turn, express. Enumerating the Hasidic rabbis whose stories he has told, Wiesel continues:

> The Baal Shem, the Maggid, Levi-Yitzhak, Israel of Rizhin; now it is my turn to show them the way I saw them as a child; as I see them still. They are subjective, incomplete portraits, with their share of unavoidable repetitions, errors, gaps. They may well say more about the narrator than about his characters. . . . He [the narrator] takes what he needs and leaves the rest for another time. . . .
>
> All the more since—in his role of storyteller, and that is the essential point—he has but one motivation: to tell of himself while telling of others. He wishes neither to teach nor convince, but to close gaps and create new bonds. Nor does he try to explain what was or even what is; he only tries to wrest from death certain prayers, certain faces, by appealing to the imagination and the nostalgia that make man listen when his story is told.[2]

The circle is complete: stories humanize fate; their retelling internalizes and humanizes stories; their recounter finds and externalizes his own story in the stories of others; his own story, as a storyteller, becomes itself the story of all our efforts to humanize fate—to salvage stories, rescue prayers and faces, from fate and death.

To enter the circle of stories and storytelling, one need not be, like Wiesel, a storyteller by profession. Victor also finds and retells his own story through recounting the stories of others: other prosecutors (Maimonides), others left out and left behind (Cain), other longed-for returns (the children of Rachel), other storytellers (Moses). In so doing, he also "humanizes fate"; above all, just by finding "human terms" and stories through which to retell the "not-story" he remembers. Thus, for all his prosecution, Victor still can return to the "living tree." And, quite literally, he wrests from death certain prayers and certain faces otherwise lost and unrecounted.

Reuben, too, "tells of himself while telling of others." He finds his story most particularly in the legend of the "Dead Hasidim," looking back at their losses in loyalty and in grief. Reuben notes:

They say, if you want to go ahead to the future, you have to look back at the past. You can't go ahead, you can't have a future without a past. You can't bury the past. You might correct what you did wrong in the past.

Have you heard of Rabbi Nahman of Bratslav. . . . After Reb Nahman of Bratslav died, they never named another rabbi after him. They used to go only to the grave. . . . "Why should we worry what's going to be tomorrow? Let's worry what we did wrong yesterday." . . .

So I'm just saying, the past is very important. The past is very important. You may have a bad past, but still you may correct certain things.

As one who describes himself as having lost his past completely—his roots and more—Reuben can still find stories from that past through which to retell his own story of self-questioning and returns. Within that text and those terms, strained as they become, he also closes gaps and creates new bonds.

Other participants find and retell their stories through more modern texts and more transient situational contexts. Along with "making a point" to her children, Lydia described her recounting as contextualized by the shared retelling of others' stories of loss.

> It could be a simple meeting, but there has to be a subject in some way related. I don't think you can just pick up and start talking about it. . . . If I went to visit someone, and perhaps there was a death in the family. It would have to be a serious situation where I would—, somebody else's experience would bring out mine. And perhaps then the person could understand me better, and I would feel that I really can sympathize with that person because I know what it's like—almost. I think this would be the only situation that I can think of really. Otherwise, it just doesn't lend itself to discussion.

Leon described his recounting as similarly contextualized. Rather than being a "continuous presentation," he noted, "it usually arises in the context of, almost as a by-product of, another conversation." For him, the "other conversation" is most likely to concern the importance of identity and clarity—of "knowing who you are" and having "a realistic assessment of the world as it is"—that he emphasizes as the lessons of his own experience.

As a different kind of "word man," Manny finds other kinds of narratives in which to situate his own story. In addition to traditional legends about good and bad fortune, he has sought secular tales in which to ground his questions about chance and destiny. In the same context in which he struggled over the question of why "certain spokes in the universe" are fated to survive, he noted that he had been reading another story about fate and creation. Said Manny:

> These are things, I can't really discuss them intelligently. Maybe, what's-his-name, Carl Sagan can, because I happen to read his book right now. And I'm *very* fascinated by it. Although it takes me a long time to read it. Because he talks about the creation of the world, how the world was created, one step at a time, which is very fascinating to me. How it came to be the way it is. But he says, in all of it, when it comes to the end, he says it was a "Great Designer." And the "Great Designer" is God.

In the narrative of *Cosmos*, Manny seeks to "humanize fate" in the most fundamental sense: to find some logic connecting his ongoing personal story and that of Creation itself.

Perhaps more than any other participant, Natalie seeks to transmit as well as discover her own story in the stories of others, and thus be a storyteller in the fullest generative sense. As we have heard, she has her model: her grandmother Miriam who "always had a parable, a quote, or something or other, for whatever came up" and who "spoon-fed" the opus of Russian literature to her grandchildren. Natalie continues to draw on the Russians in retelling her own stories—on the techniques of Stanislawski, for example—but her masters have also become more varied. Any text that gives voice to the struggle between self-sufficiency and collapse in the face of overwhelming tragedy may serve as a model. The play, *Whose Life Is It Anyway?*, depicts one side of the consequences of being able to "maintain dignity," even under the most terrible circumstances. The protagonist gets through his suffering with self-respect, and others' admiration, intact. But there are other stories that Natalie reads that suggest, at least implicitly, that a person's need to protect herself from too much vulnerability may have quite different consequences, particularly if she is a mother struggling with the loss of her son. While discussing the possibility of one day writing her own memoir, Natalie pointed to the book that had been lying on the coffee table in front of us during our last two conversations—a copy of *Ordinary People*.

Paula also has sought out stories that concern mothers and vulnerability, especially at her own most vulnerable times. She recalled one such period, fifteen years after liberation, when she had to undergo a long hospitalization for a respiratory infection. Her illness reawakened the old debate between anger and guilt. On one side, alone in the hospital, she again felt excluded and "nonexistent"—an isolation exacerbated when relatives failed to send her an invitation to a nephew's Bar Mitzvah, presumably because they knew she would not be able to attend. At the same time, she blamed herself for having had to leave her own family during the hospitalization. Confronted once more with feeling both abandoning and abandoned, Paula attempted to find a solution through reading the stories of others. She recalled:

> When I had to be hospitalized, and leave two young children, I felt guilt. . . . I blamed myself for getting sick, and the children have nobody to care for them. And yet, I guess I couldn't help it. . . . That was horribly agonizing until I buried myself into reading—old novels, biographies, and psychology. And every character that I read about, I felt I was part of that character.
>
> Until one day I said, "I'm going to go cuckoo of this altogether!" You know, this has to stop too. . . . I mean, I just *lived* those books. And whatever the subject, I found myself—, I pick up one character, you know, and I just *lived* with it. . . .
>
> (HG: Can you remember any characters that were particularly important to you at that time?) Oh, well, anything to do with mothers, you know. That was *it* at that particular time. Or, or, I can't define it really. It was a confused time. One thing led back to everything else.

Paula made it clear that "everything else" stood for the much greater abandonments she had known. However, she did not dwell on these. Instead, in order to escape her escalating isolation, she again created one of her more intimate circles of connection. Reading stories led to writing letters.

> I took up one thing, then another. These characters. And then writing letters, which was wonderful. Just writing letters, it was most rewarding. See, going back, when you are locked away from the world it means that nobody cares about you. And that was like reliving history—, like nobody cared about the six million. What happened. Because nobody took them in. OK. And in spite of the fact that the world was aware of it. OK. Namely, America. OK, this is going back to history, which let's not get into. That's not my department!
>
> And here, this was like reliving history in my own little world because I was secluded. I was cut away from the world. Yet if I got a letter from my friend in England who told me exactly, word-by-word, I did such-and-such; these are the reviews I read; what is going on in the theatre—I mean, I was *with* her. In other words, she included me in her activities. In her everyday funny things and not funny things.
>
> *That's* what counted. Yet, when my family had a joyous occasion, and they didn't send me an invitation, that I cried over for a week. I'd have written a note. But because they dismissed me from the living, that bothered me. But they did it because they knew I couldn't go anyway. People don't always see—, all right, I'm oversensitive!

Whether or not we agree that Paula is "oversensitive," we know the deeper echoes of feeling "dismissed from the living"—both during the destruction and during the extended silence that followed. Even here she pulls back from her building outrage about the history that is not her "department." As is her usual tactic, she bides her time and waits for opportunities more likely to succeed.

In a later conversation, Paula mentioned another book she had been reading in which she found her own story once again. It was the memoir of a psychiatrist who, in spite of all his work with others, was never sure he had clearly expressed his own feelings. Paula commented:

> You can say things when you're not afraid of the consequences—that you might hurt yourself or somebody else. Like, in one of the passages he says, he really wishes—this is it *exactly*—when you don't have to reach out, would it happen on its own? He wishes his children, and his ex-wife, would come to his deathbed. Of course, he wouldn't ask for it. And they wouldn't think about it. He wants to reach out. But not on his own. I associate many of his thoughts with my own.

Thus Paula discovered another who wants to "reach out" but chooses instead to wait and see if it might "happen on its own." Reminiscent of Victor's final story, at the end of a life, a remnant of faith is preserved by not being put directly on the line.

Stories' Limits

Such, then, are some of the stories that the participants find and retell and in which they attempt to situate their own stories. They are a diverse collection. There are whole texts and incidental episodes; traditional legends and modern memoirs; narratives of preservation and creation (of universes, dignity, personal identity) and tales of ending and loss. Each is selected on the basis of themes relevant to its particular recounter, often at times of greatest uncertainty or aloneness. Those preoccupied with motherhood find memoirs of other mothers; those in grief find stories of other mourners; those wondering about the meaning of their own survival find narratives about the logic of a world's survival and its design.

Notwithstanding all their differences, these *are* all stories: narratives that can be entered into, recounted, and shared. There are meaningful precedents—characters and situations with which to identify. There are experiences—of individuals, peoples, even universes—that can be retold through sustained unfolding from beginning to end. Other destinies are assimilated to one's own fate, which, thus mediated, becomes itself tellable and hearable. At least to that degree, life goes on and fates *are* "humanized." Wiesel put it succinctly: "The difference between death and life is that life transmits, death stops."[3]

Still, some things—and some stories—death does stop. Whatever gaps may be closed and new bonds created through what can be transmitted, there are also gaps that persist and bonds that cannot be repaired in any story. From one point of view, Victor's entire struggle may be understood as an attempt to tell us this. For all his own love for the stories he studies and remembers, he makes war on them. Too much and too many have been left out—there are corpses beneath the stories, other stories beneath the stories. Stories, like tombs, must be excavated; the "polish" stripped away; bones disinterred. And even then there is always "something outside the book"—and beyond the bones—that will never be revealed. Ultimately, Victor's prosecution becomes an attack on all stories after the destruction. There is no "going ahead," no continuing unfolding. Even his own story as a prosecutor of stories, his continuing survival, becomes a story that excludes too much. He, too, is prosecuted—at least until Victor becomes one more corpse whose story may or may not be correctly remembered and retold.

While Victor is unique in the degree to which he lives—literally becomes—his war on the text, he is joined by all the other participants in knowing how little their stories genuinely contain and convey. "It is *not* a story," says Leon; it is not even sound. For all his willingness to compromise and re-create, he must still conclude that "no words are adequate to acquaint the people with the reality of the Holocaust . . . there will never be anything definitive about it." In spite of all the stories Natalie does retell, there remain the "two million things" not recounted, including most of what she experienced personally and which, she is convinced, would not allow either herself or her listeners to continue. For Lydia, some of her memories may return in the context of others' losses or while "making a point" to her children. But other memories—such as the one that took away her speech entirely—return "on their own," outside any narrative context. Paula, too, for all she may "pull the shade," still struggles to remember and retell. When she "sees it all again," her pen "wants to go on and on." But it goes on "by itself." It slides from her hand as her strength slides from her spirit.

Reuben tells us he lost his strength years ago. Although he may provisionally identify with the "Dead Hasidim" and tell his own story through theirs, he also tells us that they and their ways are themselves dead.

Immediately after his reflection above about the importance of "learning from the past," Reuben continued:

> You may have a bad past, but still you may correct certain things. But I'm just saying—, [long pause] you see, I don't think so. The people of Europe, the Jewish people, it's never going to be like it was. It's never going to be anymore. It's impossible. It's gone. The way it was, the way we lived, it's not here anymore. It's finished.

Learning from the past implies continuity: the capacity to "correct certain things" and move on. But in the totality of the extermination that Reuben recalls, it is exactly the connection between life before and life now that is "finished." Whatever may be learned from the past, therefore, is superceded by the fact of its destruction.

Manny, too, for all he partakes of stories of survival and purposeful destiny, cannot forget the bodies beneath the Dachau gardens or the terminal curse that put them there and that haunts him still. As we have heard, he also has his staccato images of corpses and rubbish dumps that take over when tellable and hearable stories come to an end:

> People don't want to listen to the, the—, how do I describe the—,? corpses that were lying around there, like, like, like garbage. Or the stench . . . the agony—, the, the, the, the—, the sorrow. I don't know if there is a word. For the pain. To describe—

On this ground, all the participants meet. Whether it is the truth that will not fade from Paula's memory, the truth that Victor insists is "also true," or the truth that Manny sees but cannot describe, it is not a truth for stories and unfolding.

Wiesel, who is and would be a storyteller, comes to the same conclusion. He cannot escape, as he writes, "the dilemma of the storyteller who sees himself essentially as a witness, the drama of the messenger unable to deliver his message."[4] Noting that he has told many tales unrelated to the Holocaust, he sometimes wonders if he is "speaking of other things with the sole purpose of keeping the essential—the personal experience—unspoken." Yet he also suggests there is always some link, some connection. Applying to his own writing the image of the "concentric circles," he comments: "*Night*, my first book, became the basis of my entire edifice. Afterward I tried to construct concentric circles around this testimony."[5] As I have suggested, the most characteristic arc in Wiesel's circles is the story itself of "the messenger unable to deliver his message." Stories of agonized storytellers stand for other agonies that do, in fact, remain untold.

CONCENTRIC CIRCLES

How, then, should we understand the stories that the participants find and retell? What should we make of their collection of Hasidic legends, memoirs of modern mothers and psychiatrists, tales of prosecutors and condemned? I have suggested that these stories, too, are like "concentric circles": plots and memories framing other memories, including those that cannot be told in any story form. Thus, for all its own extremity, Victor's stories of the prosecution of stories still "humanize" *that* dissolution of stories. Other participants' stories of loss, abandonment, or pain give "human terms" to pain for which, as Manny said, there are no terms. In this sense, all the participants, like Paula, "relive history in their own little worlds"—through the still recountable stories of the "normal" pains or losses of a life. "Little worlds" are burdened and sometimes fully consumed within that process. But there are also opportunities: forms through which recounting *can* go on; stories in which recounters not only tell of themselves while telling of others but also tell of others—sometimes millions of others—while telling of themselves.

As we have heard, some of the participants are particularly self-conscious about their storymaking. Natalie, for example, knows exactly what she must do to keep her narrative and her audience intact. Like the dramatist on whom she models her style, she "brings it up to a certain—, and then softens. . . . Every time you reach a point where it's—, it's softened." What remains unexpressed behind the "softening" is suggested; but, as in Natalie's description of the process, it is left unspecified. Her listeners, therefore, must actively fill in "what is not told but also true."

So likewise must listeners rely on their own imaginations in response to Natalie's retelling of her life in general: her own story *as* a survivor. That, too, becomes a story about untold and untellable stories: a personal drama held together by the themes of privacy and dignity on one side, and suggestions of an awesome revelation on the other. It is this personal drama about the reteller herself, much more than direct memories of the destruction, that Natalie most essentially recounts; and there is little doubt that this is what her listeners receive. Thus, if one of the "concentric circles" that Wiesel builds around his memories is "the drama of the messenger unable to deliver his message," and Victor's is his story of the prosecution of stories, Natalie's is the drama of the dramatist who will not fully open the curtain. That story *can* be retold.

Leon is also particularly aware of the process of re-creation in his recounting. Indeed, some of this study's most central concepts—the notions themselves of "making a story" and finding "human terms"—were originally contributed by Leon. What is of additional interest is that these concepts emerged in the context of Leon's thinking about a particular story he had told, and the retelling of that story is itself an intriguing story. As I summarized in the opening pages, Leon recounted this episode to me in each of three interviews I conducted with him over a two-month period in 1979. In a fourth interview, I specifically asked him about the story's significance, as I had also begun to do at its third retelling.

In fact, there was a lot to talk about. For, besides repeating the story itself, Leon repeatedly asserted that this horrific episode was precisely the kind of thing that he usually does not remember, let alone retell. So here we have a situation in which a recounter repetitively remembers what he says he almost never does remember yet does not remember that he keeps remembering it. What, then, makes recounting this story so compelling and, perhaps, *also* so horrifying? The story and the question are worth considering in some detail.

Leon's Story

As suggested, the first time Leon remembered this story, he was speaking more generally about the challenges of memory. He reflected:

The memory is selective, no question. And the selection is probably toward suppressing the traumatic events and concentrating on others which have some human or redeeming quality. It's funny—about fifteen years ago some - one visited who was in one of the camps with me. In this camp, we were unloading supplies for the SS. And we were talking like it was the good old days! For example, we were once in a freight car and there were broken cases of wine. The wine was still in the bottles. We drank some when the SS couldn't see us. And when a case wasn't broken, we made *sure* it was broken! And the few instances like that—we made them into the good old days!

And after a while we caught ourselves. What tricks the memory plays! It slides over all the unredeemed trauma, and suffering, and pain. And we didn't mention the time when we buried our friend who was shot. He went with us together to the Jewish cemetery to turn over the gravestones and to carry them back. Because whenever there was no other work, they took us in trucks to the cemetery. And then we broke up the stones with sledgehammers, because we were paving a road, a muddy field in the camp, with those stones. So we were always going to the cemetery to perform this work. And once they caught one of our fellows in a minor infraction. He had stolen a loaf of bread to give to his sister who was starving in another camp. Sometimes she'd be marching by our camp. First they beat him up. Lieberman was his name, Lieberman. Then they told this fellow to come along with us, to the cemetery. They shot him right there. A young fellow. And we buried him—right at the cemetery where we were taking the stones. And somehow or other while discussing this time with the other fellow who was visiting, we never mentioned it. We just mentioned those other, better times.

Leon thus situates the story of Lieberman within another story about the nature of remembering, and the point of that story is clear: Memory is selective. It selects *in* what is "human" or "redemptive," like the sabotage of the wine bottles. It selects *out* what is unredeemed and traumatic, like the story of Lieberman that Leon remembers here.

The second time Leon retold the Lieberman story, it was again framed by his more general reflection about memory, now more directly about the sharing of memories with others. He noted:

You only go into it, you only talk about it, when you feel somebody really wants to know. Somebody cares. That will prompt you to open up. Although still to a limited extent. You won't open up the floodgates. And dare to let it completely take you over. You only do it to a limited extent.

But it can just come up—I was talking with someone who was interviewing me, some years ago. And I was really trying to remember. And I remembered a scene—I was in a little camp, and one of the Jewish fellows was caught stealing a loaf of bread. Because his sister was in a starvation camp nearby. So he tried to smuggle it to her. And they caught him. And they beat him up severely. And we thought that this was the end. But then, a few days later, they were taking us out to the Jewish cemetery. Whenever there wasn't enough work in the camp, they took us out to the cemetery. To overturn the Jewish monuments, the gravemarkers, and bring them back to the camp. To break them up and pave the muddy roads. And they asked this fellow to come along. And the SS corporal, who drove the truck, he asked this fellow to walk ahead of him. And he pulled out his Luger and he shot him. And we buried him in the Jewish cemetery.

And the funny thing was, I vaguely recollected this incident. Oh, I think I mentioned it once before to somebody. But now I remembered the name of the corporal, the SS corporal, Schwetke. And I remembered the name of the Jewish boy, Lieberman. And the interesting thing was, before the war, I used to have an excellent memory. Perfect recall. But after the war, something happened. And I have no memory at all. I carry notes in every pocket. Names—it all has to be written down. Even visiting relatives. But here I came up with this memory. And I could see the scene in the cemetery. All of a sudden this lithe, young, nineteen-year-old boy, full of life—what was his first name? Paul, Paul Lieberman—he just lay there with his head shattered. And we digging the hole, wondering who is going to be next.

Perhaps confirming what he says happened to his memory, Leon thus remembered having remembered the shooting of Lieberman in an interview some years ago, but he did not remember having remembered it with me only ten days earlier (although I may be the person to whom he had "mentioned it once before"). The episode itself is still presented as traumatic—the kind of memory that can "open the floodgates" and "completely take you over." But there is the suggestion that with the right kind of listener some leeway, at least, is created. And there is also something—says this man who had to break up Jewish gravestones (including, we recall, his own grandfather's), this man with notes in every pocket (including the names of his relatives)—about being able to remember names.

There is no need to repeat Leon's third retelling. What is worth citing—because it develops the theme of names—is the beginning of his own reflection about why this incident, terrifying as it was, became one of those he remembers. Leon noted:

> This had a traumatic impact on me. Because here I was working with a fellow who was beaten up, and we thought the punishment was behind him. One moment he's living and breathing and working next to me, and the next moment we're burying him with a hole in the back of his skull. . . .
>
> This Schwetke, he was a truck driver, and not known for any special brutality. We got to know them, the SS. This was a very small camp, and we were there for over a year. We knew them by name. We knew their traits.
>
> But to see both the victim and the executioner, to have acquaintanceship with both—acquaintanceship in the sense that you knew what made them tick—it must have made an impression on me sufficient that I retained it.

At least up to the point of the shooting (Leon will say more about what happened after), both executioner and victim are known and named. Does this, in fact, provide the memory something "human," even some "redeeming quality," and therefore, despite what Leon says, actually make it *less* traumatic than his other memories of the destruction? Is that why the Lieberman story is repetitively retold? Or, on the other hand, does the acquaintanceship Leon describes only increase the horror of what unfolds? And is that why the story seems to compel repetition? Or, in some more complex way, are both assertions true?

Atrocity as Tragedy

Perhaps what is most striking about the Lieberman story is how *untypical* it is of the Holocaust more generally. Rather than the degradation and extermination of a people, here we have a single victim executed, in Leon's phrase, because of an "infraction." Indeed, Lieberman's infraction—sequestering bread for his starving sister—was an act of valor and resistance. Even when such acts were possible during the destruction, they were generally irrelevant to the fate of victims—all were doomed in any case. Equally untypical, as Leon notes, is to know the name, not only of the victim, but even of the executioner—even to feel he is a kind of "acquaintance," as he was of Lieberman's as well. And, almost bizarre, Lieberman is buried in a Jewish cemetery—the very cemetery that is itself being unearthed, pulverized, and scattered on the muddy roads.

Here, then, we have a "crime," a punishment, a named victim, and a named executioner, all held together by a coherent unfolding of context, action, and response. The Lieberman story, in other words, clearly *is* a story: within its terms, a story of a familiar kind. Reflecting on the differences between tragedy and atrocity, Lawrence Langer has suggested distinctions that also help us here.[6] Tragedy requires some controlled image of the number dead—not the pits and heaps and ravines of bodies, dead and dying, that characterize atrocity. In tragedy, even terrible events are still within some version of acceptable human fate—which is exactly what atrocity's arbitrary "wasting" of people aims to attack. In tragedy, victims are still identifiably living and human; not atrocity's doomed, defeated, or "walking dead." This is what allows us to feel sympathy for tragedy's victims, in contrast with the dread, disgust, or numbed malaise that atrocity evokes. By these criteria, then, while immersed in an ocean of atrocity, the Lieberman story more closely resembles tragedy: the failed but heroic resistance of an attractive young man—"lithe" and "full of life" as Leon remembers—cut down by his oppressors. Such stories not only allow retelling; they virtually compel it.

All this, then, on the side of what makes the Lieberman story tellable and, of course, hearable as well. In discussing it, Leon agreed that this memory did differ from many of his others, particularly his later memories of Auschwitz.

People hadn't become ciphers yet. They were still, up to that moment, human beings. With a name, with a personality. And when they were gone, their image was retained. But the mass disappearing into the gas chambers—, they're just a mass of people going—, like in a slaughterhouse. There was a difference. A qualitative and a quantitative difference.

Earlier, we heard Victor's story of a single victim's resistance and execution, and then his description of the "slaughterhouse" at Treblinka. For Victor, too, there was both a "qualitative and a quantitative difference"—a difference large enough to make even the unmasker of secrets not want to know more. We also heard the difference that Paula described between the "little incidences" in which care and human recognition could be salvaged and the "constant frame" of the crematorium behind "the shade." Within such differences, perhaps, also lies the difference between fates that a story can "humanize" and those that it cannot.

Leon, in any case, agreed that having specific names and bounded circumstances also made recounting more likely. This was precisely the context in which he first spoke about "making a story" of the "not-story."

> It's like trying to describe a nightmare. How do you describe a nightmare? Something which is shapeless, amorphous . . . It is *not* a story. It has to be *made* a story. In order to convey it. And with all the frustration that implies.

In fact, a certain amount of frustration was developing for Leon even as he spoke, and it was directly related to our discussion of the Lieberman story. This was because he absolutely did *not* agree with my suggestion that this episode, however tellable, was any less traumatic. And so he tried to convey better the nightmare from which it was retrieved.

> Yeah. Yeah. Yeah. You see a cause and effect relationship—a crime and a punishment. But, see, this is a good example of how hard it is to convey. You pose the question. I owe you an explanation. There are a few elements you couldn't have known.
>
> You see, in a perverted sort of way, the SS were proud of this camp. We had become their expert workers. They used to show us off! They used to say, in German, they never saw *Juden* work in such a fashion. Despite the killing all around us, we imagined this was a little island of security. And the Lieberman incident destroyed the whole thing.
>
> You see, this was the moment of truth. Lieberman was a favorite. Even to them, to the Germans, he was a favorite. He had black eyes, smiling eyes, with so much life in them. And all of a sudden we see that no one's life is worth a damn. The very Germans you thought took this almost paternal interest in you. They would kill you with as much thought as it takes to step on a cockroach. And so our pipe-dream was shattered right there. It was suddenly and dramatically shattered, along with Lieberman's skull.

Leon then described the "shattering" from the inside. As I noted early in these pages, his account remains one of the most vivid evocations of the "closing in of darkness" that I have heard in twenty years of listening to survivors. And it is clear that this, and not Lieberman's burial, is the real end of this story: an end but not an *ending*; a cessation of a narrative but not its conclusion. Because, as Leon said, this end really had nothing to do with the universe—narrative and otherwise—retold to that point.

> It was a feverish feeling. A feverish feeling. A terrible intensity . . . When Lieberman was shot—the moment before there was sun—, even in a cemetery you were conscious of the world around you—, but with this execution, the whole thing came to a standstill. It is like—, the only reality left over here is death. Death—and we performing—like a mystic ritual. I wasn't aware of *anything* around me.
>
> There would have been six of us. Six left. Six left. Six automatons digging the hole. . . . And even the SS man Schwetke, he ceased to be real. All of a sudden, he has left this known-to-you universe. And become something else. In one moment, the universe became—, what was real was only the turmoil within you. The rest was gone. The rest ceased to exist.

Associated with his other memories of all-consuming terror, Lieberman's killing was also part of Leon's evocation of the "landscape of death" and the silence it contained.

> Entering the ghetto in a dead silence. Those columns marching in. And the same thing with Lieberman. The silence. Following the shot. He was our friend! He was our companion!
>
> This is probably what makes it so unbelievable. This pure landscape of death . . . It appears to be devoid of the human element, of the redeeming feature of a human emotion. . . . Even sound, even sound would be out of place. There is no sound actually. There is no sound.

In the end, then, the story of Lieberman is also part analogy for a "shattering," and a silence, on a different scale.

The Drama of One Death

Leon's story of Lieberman is similar to other narratives that emerge in survivors' recounting, both written and spoken. These accounts may also be retold more than once, or their special status may be indicated by their appearing fully formed within reflections that appeared to be about something else. They likewise tend to focus on a single person—often a favorite of the prisoners and even of the guards—who undertakes an act of resistance. The act fails, the resister is executed, and the despair that follows is always more encompassing than the story initially suggests. Rather, it is as though the death that these memories retell reframes and recapitulates other losses that the recounter has known—of "pipe-dreams," of the "known-to-you universe," of tragedy and emotion and stories themselves.[7]

At the same time, it is apparent that these narratives, although leading to so much loss, are themselves a provisional restoration. They salvage a tellable story itself; in these instances, in a form more like tragedy than atrocity. They are also particularly hearable, for these stories genuinely *do* recall specific instances of the "human spirit" in resistance; "moments of reprieve" in Primo Levi's phrase, "in which the compressed identity can reacquire for a moment is lineaments."[8] Finally, for both recounters and listeners, through these stories it begins to become possible to respond emotionally to the wider destruction—most particularly, to begin to grieve. At the same moment that Leon describes the closing off of emotion, he himself exclaims about Lieberman, "He was our friend! He was our companion!" If Leon became an "automaton" then, his recounting affirms that he is not one now.

As a man who had wondered at liberation whether his capacity for care had been "irreversibly destroyed," Leon's retelling of the Lieberman story may have particular, personal significance. But the use of one death to mourn others is more general, and it appears to have been so even within the destruction. Thus many women's memoirs of Birkenau retell the story of the resistance and execution of Mala Zimetbaum—probably as close to a heroine, even a romantic heroine, as Auschwitz could allow. Mala was already well known in the camp before she succeeded in a dramatic escape with a Polish prisoner who was her lover. The two were caught, but even at her execution Mala continued to resist, cursing her killers and slashing her own wrists. Lena Berg described the significance of Mala's story and particularly of her capture and execution:

> Every community has its legend, its myth; that of Auschwitz was a romance involving Mala, a girl who worked as a messenger, and her lover, a Warsaw Pole who also had a camp job. She was proficient in several languages, and universally admired in the camp for her intelligence and beauty. One day all Auschwitz was electrified by the news that Mala and her lover had escaped, he in an SS uniform and she in that of a wardress. . . . Mala's fate became our main concern. . . .
>
> Mala's death shocked the camp to the core. She had been our golden dream, a single ray of light in our dark lives. Prisoners who might momentarily be taken to the gas chamber, who lived in the shadow of the crematoria through which millions of human beings had gone up in smoke, wept bitterly

when Mala was killed. One death moves the imagination more powerfully than millions; one death is a drama throbbing with emotion; a million, only dry-as-ashes statistics.[9]

Even within the terror, especially within it, the imagination craved tellable and hearable tales. Even then, the "drama of one death" could provide "human terms," although only at the cost of dissolving again within the terror from which such terms were salvaged.

Stories as Monuments

Recounters find and create what stories they can, but the "not-story" of not-one-death remains. Many recounters try to convey that as well, pointing to all that their retelling does not retell. In the same context as his reflection on the need for "human terms," Leon also invoked an analogy from the plastic arts to describe the struggle.

None of it captures the essence. It may be impossible. Like a piece of sculpture—it is either representational or abstract. It's either one. But here you try to do both. Because it has to be described in human terms. It cannot *be* described otherwise. Otherwise it has no meaning, unless people somehow already know. So it has to be described in terms of the experiences of individuals. But, at the same time, you have to be true to this—, to this indescribable atmosphere.

Leon's own story of Lieberman cannot be separated from the indescribable universe to which it leads back; the drama of Mala and her lover cannot be separated from a landscape of unstoried extermination. As listeners who do not "already know," however, we take what we can get. For us, it requires deliberate effort to go further.

Survivors always go further, and some try with particular persistence to recount more than single deaths. Thus, in his own efforts as a storyteller, Reuben also attempted to construct "concentric circles" around his memories of the destruction, almost literally so. His purpose, above all, was to describe a *collective* life that was destroyed, the "whole life," as he says, that used to be.

I tried to write . . . not a history, or documents. But I tried to write a novel around it, *around* it . . . a novel, not about the Holocaust, just about the whole, the *whole life*, before the Holocaust, with the Holocaust included. You know what I mean, the whole life . . . A novel around different characters. How it was.

In Reuben's novel, then, the Holocaust would be framed by the stories of individual characters but always in the context of the wider life they inhabited. He wished, in turn, to show that "whole life" in its full complexity, *its* cultural individuality and vitality. Expressing a care reminiscent of Victor's description of his fruit trees, Reuben described the branches he would wrest from destiny and death.

> How it was. The whole variety of the Jewish people. You know, we had, within the Orthodox, we had Hasidic Jews. And we also had the *Misnagedim*, who didn't believe in the Hasidic rabbis. . . .
>
> And then, even between those two groups, within them, you had some who were pro-Israel before the war. And some who were against Israel before the war. . . . There were all the different Orthodox.
>
> Then you had other Jews. They were not Orthodox. You had the Zionists, and the Bund—they were socialists, you know—and then you had the Communists—all Jews, all one hundred percent Jewish. They spoke Yiddish. They defend Jewish culture. The whole thing.
>
> And then, in those too, among the non-Orthodox, you had the intellectuals, the scholars, and you had the regular workers, who were not intellectuals.
>
> See, I'm just saying, you had a complete life. The whole thing. So many different characters. The good and the bad. The whole range. You don't see it anymore. It's all disappeared.
>
> (HG: And your novel would have been to—?) To show the variety. All the different people. I tried, for a long time, maybe ten years. A few pages. That's all I got. To me, writing the story, would be, like a monument to the—, to the Jewish people. The way they worked, and the way they lived, and the way they dealt with people. How it was—how happy they were, how sad they were, at different times.
>
> (HG: A monument . . .) Yeah. A monument. It was a type culture, and a type people—I'm not saying Jews all over the world, but *this* culture. It's never going to be again. The way they lived, for generations. It's hard for anybody, actually, to imagine. To imagine what it was like.

As he indicates, Reuben never wrote his novel. He suggests it was a dream that could *not* be salvaged.

> To write you have to concentrate. I used to sit in my store sometimes. But I decided you have to be almost—, separated completely. You have to go in a different world. To go back. Dreaming back—, to get back the pictures, the scenery, and everything else.

For Reuben, such efforts proved futile in more ways than one. Inwardly, remembrance was simply too painful. He recalled having heard Elie Wiesel speak and saw, in Wiesel's struggle, his own.

> I saw Elie Wiesel once. He looked like he suffers so much. He lives back through it, through his books. I can see it in his face, in his eyes, he suffers. It is agony for him. It can be torture. The living back through.

Even if he had been able to endure the agony, Reuben also doubted his story would find readers. He noted that the world he remembered was "completely different, a completely different life; it might even look strange to many people." Identified with that world and its destruction, Reuben anticipated that he himself might also appear strange and disturbing. "It wouldn't be a good relationship. People would feel bad, feel guilty, to see me. Or maybe the other way around. It would upset them to see me. I don't know. Who knows? Who knows what goes on in people's minds?" Reuben may not know what goes on in people's minds. But he knew enough not to risk finding out with greater certainty.

As I have suggested, however, Reuben's search for individual characters and a tellable tale did not end with the end of his novel. Remnants of memories persisted—of Jewish values, Hasidic stories, personal conscience. And out of these fragments, he began to sculpt his own "whole life" into a kind of monument. His everyday existence became, in Leon's terms, both "representative" and "abstract." The inner-city ghetto where he works reminds him of *that* ghetto, and so he does not leave. His self-questioning and self-punishment have precedents, others who have refused to move on or to move out, and through their story he is able to re-create his own. The characters and the whole life he remembers are gone forever. But sometimes dreaming back, or wandering between worlds like a *gilgul*, Reuben can stand with the "Dead Hasidim" almost as though they were still alive, almost as though they were still mourning a single Master around an actual, individual grave.

Thus, in the end, even Reuben retells through the story of a single tragedy, the drama of a single death. And, as for Victor, it is increasingly his own.

BEYOND STORYTELLING

We return to familiar conclusions: the stories survivors tell are made, in large part, out of meanings and memories that persist *in spite of* the destruction. Other pains, other tales, and other graves give form to *those* pains and to that absence of stories and graves. Atrocity is retold in a form that more closely resembles tragedy. This is true even when stories are lived as well as retold: when recounters, consumed by the deaths they strive to convey, begin to resemble the archetypal "ghosts" or "witnesses" we so often expect survivors to be. Even here, a fragment that is tellable and hearable, and still capable of inspiring our empathy, stands for a nightmare that is not.

Typically, our assumptions about survivors' stories are the reverse. It is the destruction itself, survivors' direct experience, which is supposed to make them "storytellers," while "stories" and their retelling have become the summary terms for *all* of survivors' recounting. This is particularly true in recent years, for the terms reflect a broader cultural trend. Storytelling in general has enjoyed resurgent interest—on stage, in schools, in the media, in academia—and programs for and about traditional narrative have appeared everywhere.[10] In that context, Holocaust survivors are also celebrated in the language of stories and storytelling.

Indeed, almost weekly letters from one of the new Holocaust museums or testimony projects invoke the rhetoric. Soon "there will be no one left to tell the stories to the youngsters," says one. "Thousands more stories are waiting to be told and preserved," writes another. "It is in remembering and re-telling these stories that our hope lies" affirms a third.[11] A more extended reflection that could stand for many is this excerpt from the preface to a recent collection of survivors' testimonies. The person referred to as "Howard" is the son of two of the survivors included:

> The stories of Howard's parents were important because they were becoming Howard's stories—and one day they would become the stories of Howard's children.
>
> And not unlike at Passover, when we are commanded to tell our children the story of the Exodus, perhaps we have a similar responsibility here: to tell the stories of the Holocaust.
>
> Maybe that was what was on Howard's face that day—the responsibility of the storyteller. That the story does not stop with those who valiantly died in or survived the Holocaust. That the story is now in the hands of those younger generations—to pass along to others, . . . so that they will under-stand, and continue to tell.
>
> And so for these stories—this book. . . . It is our responsibility to be the storytellers.[12]

Here the model is quite clearly the traditional one, the spirit and imagery of "Mi Y'Malel" precisely. Stories are handed down from one generation to the next. Hope and responsibility lie in hearing the call, taking one's place, retelling the tale.

There is no doubt that these are generous sentiments and reflect projects that are themselves generous. Further, even if it is true, as I have emphasized, that "stories" and "storytelling" do not well summarize survivors' recounting and even less well describe what survivors remember, one would not fairly expect such notions to be represented here. This is, after all, frankly rhetorical writing: images and associations that are *intended* to be ceremonial.

The point, then, is to address that language *as* ceremonial; to consider what *are* the consequences when, intending to be most compelling, we construct our listening to survivors in these terms. As I have emphasized, the greatest casualty of such imagery is the claim of dialogue, the model of recounting as an evolving, deepening conversation. Stories, by definition, are monologues, finished texts.[13] Stories that are to be gathered and preserved—as the Bible is preserved—are more fixed and finished still. On one level, the perpetually *unfinished* nature of survivors' retelling is thereby glossed: the continuing struggle between meaning and memory. But more important for our purposes here, the storytelling model diverts us from the kind of listening that would help us enter into that struggle (which includes discovering how much, as listeners, we are *already* in it). As collectors of stories, instead of being participants in the effort to retell, we are recipients of retelling over and done with.

While survivors themselves sometimes invoke the traditional storytelling imagery, they also question it. Noting the inadequacy of such a model to describe her recounting with her children, Paula exclaimed: "Like I didn't tell them, 'Come on, child, I'll tell you a story—this was hometown, this was Auschwitz, this was my life!'" Also reflecting on what he has shared with his children, Leon commented ironically on the imagery of elders and initiates.

> It comes up from time to time. But there are none of those idyllic pictures— like they approach me in front of the fireplace burning, and say, "Tell me a story about the Holocaust." This never comes up this way. It is *never* done this way.

Victor's private war on traditional narrative and its transmission is perhaps the enacted, and most radical, version of the same critique. He attacks *all* stories that claim to be complete; and especially the most "biblical," the most celebrated, and the most ritually retold.

Still, the traditional imagery is powerful, and the associations it invokes, if misleading in some respects, do convey that recounting and listening are serious tasks, worthy of unusual attention. Further, in borrowing that imagery and those associations, we ourselves make a kind of story—a story about storytelling itself—and it is one that is coherent and compelling. And so the question arises: Can an alternative story about survivors' recounting also seem serious, coherent, and compelling?

In these pages I have tried to tell an alternative story about what survivors are doing when they attempt to retell and what we do as their listeners. The usefulness of that account will have already been tested in the particular instances of recounting and listening that have been discussed. But, before finally concluding, it may at least be useful to return briefly to some of its themes and to consider—I would not avoid the traditional word—its moral.

Chapter 7

On Listening to Survivors: Some Conclusions

While listening to the recounting of Holocaust survivors, we tend to take a part for the whole. We mistake the made story for the full story, the tragedy recounted for the atrocity endured. Celebrating survivors' ongoing lives, we tend to ignore their ongoing deaths. Focusing on survivors' ongoing deaths, we miss the vitality of their ongoing lives; memories and legacies that have nothing to do with the destruction but which allow survivors to recount at all. We confuse the monuments of the present (including one-man monuments) with the rubbish dumps of the past; the iconic images with which we are familiar with a whole world of "private nightmares" that are not in the "public domain." We mistake monologue for dialogue; hearing a "story" for participating in a conversation.

In these pages, I have argued that we follow recounting best when we follow it as a process: when we are able to enter into survivors' struggles for words rather than receiving those words as finished texts. Thus I have traced the fate of some recounters' voices and stories in great detail. I have emphasized that, in their role as recounters, *everything* survivors say about the destruction is part of their retelling, part of their "making stories" and finding forms. I have also emphasized that recounting is always rooted in *two* sets of memories: in meanings and identifications salvaged from recounters' wider life histories and in the reduction and, finally, dissolution of those meanings within the destruction itself. In general, survivors attempt in their recounting to "humanize fate" and to put the "human element" back, even while pointing toward destinies on another scale and agonies of another kind.

To follow recounting as understood here requires sustained engagement. It takes time to get to know recounters, not as abstract "witnesses," but as particular people who bring to retelling their specific concerns, identities, and styles. It also takes sustained participation in recounting to trace the fate of its forms: to find out, for example, why a certain story is repeated; or why a particular set of meanings keeps slipping toward the "worst possible"; or how an enactment may be a story that is lived as well as retold. And time is required to understand what it means to be an "ardent lover"; and why *Ordinary People* or *Cosmos* have been sitting on the table; and why so many friends surround the man who says he is a ghost; and how a tear can have a memory of its own.

It also takes time to discover one's role as a listener, both in its particularity and as survivors' have come to anticipate listeners' expectations in general. Indeed, it is a good sign that a dialogue of recounting is deepening when survivors themselves bring the discourses *about* survivors into the conversation. Of course, those discourses and their presumptions are already there, uninvited but unavoidable. By directly engaging them, however, recounting can escape constriction and dead end. Thus Leon expresses frustration with the "idyllic picture" of storytelling "in front of the fireplace burning" and eventually goes on to talk about the actual role that stories play in his recounting. Paula, wishing to reframe the legacy rhetoric, ironically notes, "I'm not dying yet! I hope I'm not dying yet!," and goes on to talk about what survivors' legacies actually entail. Manny knows I will know what he means when he confides that he can play the hero, and get the recognition heroes get, when he chooses to do so. And, knowing that I am a psychologist, every participant wanted to know early on if I thought they were "crazy," if I thought they had "made their kids crazy," and if I thought there was any "cure" for the brand of craziness they knew. My favorite such comment was Manny's: "Of course, we're crazy! You'd have to be *crazy* to go through something like this and not be crazy!"

All of this kind of understanding—about the vicissitudes of recounting and about the role of listeners—is a result of sustained conversation. But it also all *leads* to deeper engagement. Thus, discovering how limiting and ritualized the general expectations of survivors have been, we, in our own conversations with survivors, are inclined to listen differently and better. Learning the fate of meanings, voices, and stories also implicates us more deeply. For these are, after all, our own meanings, the constituents of our own stories. Viewed in the context of survivors' experience, they cannot help starting to seem fragile to us as well. They cannot help starting to become what all of us have left.

The Moral of the Story

Still, the question can certainly be asked: Why *should* we listen to survivors in this way? Why should we make the effort to enter into their words and into at least a portion of their silences? At a time when there are suddenly so many projects that concern survivors' words—in most cases, gathering them as "testimony"—there also seems to be no shortage of answers. Testimony, we are told, "teaches tolerance." Testimony will help insure that "it never happens again." Testimony will thwart "Holocaust deniers." Testimony documents the crime. Hearing the stories "educates the children." The stories are survivors' "true legacies." Retelling the stories provides identity and hope. "Bearing witness" honors the survivors. "Telling the story" helps survivors "integrate the trauma" and "heal." "Giving testimony" bestows meaning on the suffering and the loss, so that it was not in vain.

Let me speak frankly. I used to believe some of these assertions; I now believe very few of them and those few only with the strictest qualifications. Why that is so will be clear from what has preceded. But the more essential point is this: No such claims about the benefits or consequences of testimony are necessary. And, indeed, it may be a reflection of how ritualized our relationship with survivors and their words has become that we would think we did need such reasons. For the sufficient reason to listen to survivors is to listen to survivors. No other purpose is required. Just as none would be required to listen to any other people who endured what they endured in the world we share; with whom we share everything *except* those agonies and those memories.

In fact, during a brief period shortly after the war, there *was* no other reason needed to listen attentively to survivors. As Paula especially described, for those survivors lucky enough to have a good experience at liberation, the response of their first listeners was direct and unstudied, pure interest and care. Of the former prisoners-of-war Paula met at liberation, she wrote: "We don't understand each other's languages, but we do understand their kindness and compassion. . . . They are interested in our fate. . . . They would like to stay longer but the doctor makes them leave." Leon, Reuben, Lydia, and Manny also found at least some listeners, in the first years, who wanted to hear simply because they wanted to hear. And it is hardly necessary to say that, at this point, no one was doing much thinking about future generations or celebrating the "witness" or teaching tolerance. The (mostly young) soldiers and survivors *were* the future generation; liberation (for those who could celebrate) was celebration enough; "tolerance," like "survivors," were not the constructs they were to become. Instead, there was unmitigated horror and death. And the few who, somehow, remained.

Things changed. And, to some degree, it was inevitable that encounters with survivors would become more deliberate and formal. At the same time, it is clear that some of the formalizing has been in the service of *not* encountering survivors and what they have to retell—at least, not meeting them as particular people, people like us, in sustained conversation, at significant depth. There are good reasons, therefore, to recall the kind of listening that some who survived knew, briefly, at an earlier time. One can still work in its spirit; one can still write in its light.

So I have tried to do here:

In the context of the ways survivors have become symbols of the Holocaust—celebrants of life or archetypes of death—I have tried to present the recounters in this book as individuals, each with his or her particular style and tone.

Against the background of ceremonial and psychiatric "last words"— legacies, testaments, sequelae, and symptoms—I have emphasized barely tellable first words and what all words only point toward.

In the midst of contemporary claims about all we are supposed to "get *out* of" survivors' testimony—its uses and benefits—I have emphasized that it has not become less urgent to think about how we "get *into*" all that survivors have to retell.

Returns

Perhaps no study attempts to re-create more than a single moment. The moment I recall came toward the middle of my first conversations with Victor. Against the background of his initial suspicions about my own potentially "unmasking" or "materialistic" motives, he eventually said this:

> You study me, and I study you. You study me with sharp eyes. I am studying you with dull eyes—through eyeglasses!—but I can see that you go in with a sharp mind and sharp eyes. You look at me with eyes that want to find out what is behind my own eyes. I appraise it. I value it. I am thinking of it. I try to answer you with what is of the heart. And you store it. You remember it. I only make the parallel, the connection between one individual and the other. It is good.

Obviously, I was honored by Victor's comment. But I repeat it here to underline the point that, in these pages, "making the connection between one individual and the other" has been less a methodologic means to a theoretic end than the essence of the end itself. Such conversations, retaining familiar human scale and familiar human terms, are remnants, awakenings, returns.

Notes

INTRODUCTION

1. The dissertation that resulted was entitled, "Who Can Retell?: On the Recounting of Life History by Holocaust Survivors" (Brandeis University, 1985). An important transitional essay was "Lives as Texts: Symptoms as Modes of Recounting in the Life Histories of Holocaust Survivors," in *Storied Lives: The Cultural Politics of Self-Understanding,* ed. George C. Rosenwald and Richard L. Ochberg (New Haven: Yale University Press, 1992), pp. 145–64.

2. Along with the survivors introduced in these pages, there is a considerably larger number with whom I have also spoken. Here, however, I restrict myself to the seven people who were part of the initial study: Leon, Lydia, Manny, Natalie, Paula, Reuben, and Victor. All of these names are pseudonyms.

The emphasis in this work is on the explication of certain themes in recounting, and I do not present all the survivors in equal depth. A second volume is planned that will include more detailed presentations of some of the participants here, while focusing more specifically on survivors' experiences of aging in the context of the recent upsurge of interest in the Holocaust.

None of the conversations with survivors reported on in either volume have been part of any kind of psychotherapy. Rather, they have been research interviews to which, as suggested, I have tried to bring a clinician's habits of attentiveness.

3. A number of literary studies have also emphasized the way the recounter's story becomes the story of recounting itself. See, for example, Sara R. Horowitz's recent *Voicing the Void: Muteness and Memory in Holocaust Fiction* (Albany: State University of New York Press, 1997), especially pp. 33–45.

4. Quoted in *Lodz Ghetto: Inside a Community Under Siege*, ed. and comp. by Alan Adelson and Robert Lapides (New York: Penguin, 1989), p. 276.

5. Aharon Appelfeld, *Beyond Despair*, trans. Jeffrey M. Green (New York: Fromm, 1994), p. 33.

6. Readers who are familiar with psychoanalytic psychology will recognize the role of psychoanalytic thinking in my presentations of each recounter, but no knowledge of psychoanalytic theory is required to follow this text. Thus, when I write about a particular survivor's sense of "special chosenness," some readers may make the translation to "secondary narcissism." When I speak about another's struggles between fidelity and felt betrayal, the outline of an "Oedipal configura-tion" may be noted. But such translating adds nothing to the purposes here. As long as these constellations of meaning serve to help us enter into the process of recounting—here, meanings entirely reflective of "normal" psychology and thus of our lives as much as survivors'—it makes no difference by what terms they are evoked.

CHAPTER 1

1. A transliteration from the Hebrew of "Mi Y'Malel" can be found in Peter Blood and Annie Patterson, eds., *Rise Up Singing: The Group Singing Songbook* (Bethlehem, PA: Sing Out Corporation, 1988), p. 45. There are several English translations of this traditional Hebrew song. The translation given is my own synthesis of a number of versions. For alternatives, see *Rise Up Singing* above as well as Douglas Back, *Folk Songs and Dances of the Jewish People for Acoustic Guitar* (Pacific, MO: Mel Bay Publications, 1994), p. 58 and *The Weavers' Song Book* (New York: Harper and Brothers, 1960), p. 54.

2. Cf. Terrence Des Pres, "The Authority of Silence in Elie Wiesel's Art," in *Confronting the Holocaust: The Impact of Elie Wiesel*, ed. Alvin H. Rosenfeld and Irving Greenberg (Bloomington: Indiana University Press, 1978), p. 54.

3. George Steiner, *Language and Silence: Essays on Language, Literature, and the Inhuman* (New York: Atheneum, 1977), p. 168.

4. Elie Wiesel, "A Plea for the Survivors," in *A Jew Today*, trans. Marion Wiesel (New York: Random House, 1978), pp. 198, 200.

5. Cf. Lawrence L. Langer, "The Divided Voice," in *Confronting the Holocaust*, p. 45.

6. Primo Levi, *Survival in Auschwitz*, trans. Stuart Woolf (New York: Summit Books, 1986), p. 123.

7. Tadeusz Rozewicz, quoted in Yaffa Eliach, *Hasidic Tales of the Holocaust* (New York: Oxford University Press, 1982), p. xvii.

8. T. S. Eliot, *The Waste Land*, in T. S. Eliot, *Collected Poems 1909–1962* (New York: Harcourt, Brace & Co., 1988), p. 53.

9. Cf. Lawrence L. Langer, *The Age of Atrocity: Death in Modern Literature* (Boston: Beacon Press, 1978) and Jay Winter, *Sites of Memory, Sites of Mourning:*

The Great War in European Cultural History (Cambridge, UK: Cambridge University Press, 1995).

10. Eliot, *The Waste Land*, p. 69.

11. Jay Winter has discussed the burial of the World War I dead in *Sites of Memory, Sites of Mourning*. See especially pp. 15–28.

12. Isabella Leitner with Irving A. Leitner, *Saving the Fragments: From Auschwitz to New York* (New York: New American Library, 1985), p. 94.

13. Following a distinction of Charlotte Delbo's, Lawrence Langer analyzes the juxtaposition of the two worlds of memory—and the translation of one into the language of the other—in terms of the relationship between "deep memory" and "common memory." See especially *Holocaust Testimonies: The Ruins of Memory* (New Haven: Yale University Press, 1991), p. 6.

14. Sidra DeKoven Ezrahi, *By Words Alone: The Holocaust in Literature* (Chicago: The University of Chicago Press, 1980), p. 98.

15. Alvin H. Rosenfeld, *A Double Dying: Reflections on Holocaust Literature* (Bloomington: Indiana University Press, 1980), p. 29.

16. Ibid., p. 21.

17. Ibid., p. 33.

18. Ibid., p. 27.

19. The dissolution of the usual transactional relationship between imagination and reality in extremity is discussed in Jean Amery's extraordinary essay, "Torture," in *At the Mind's Limits: Contemplations by a Survivor of Auschwitz on its Realities*, trans. Sidney Rosenfeld and Stella P. Rosenfeld (Bloomington: Indiana University Press, 1980), especially pp. 25–26. In his memoir of Treblinka, Richard Glazar described the particular fascination with which "veterans" of the death camp watched the assault of reality on new victims, no doubt reliving their own initiation:

Early the next day they will take new arrivals off the transports to replace yesterday's dead. Always there is excited anticipation among us—when they're led in, when they begin to understand, little by little. They can't fully comprehend it, they can't really believe it. No one has that much fantasy.

In Richard Glazar, *Trap with a Green Fence: Survival in Treblinka*, trans. Roslyn Theobald (Evanston, IL: Northwestern University Press, 1995), p. 14.

20. Lawrence Langer uses similar language to describe the *simultaneity* of continuity and discontinuity in survivors' experience, an ongoing life together with an ongoing death. "Life goes on," he notes, "but in two temporal directions at once." The result is "a parallel existence . . . two adjacent worlds that may intrude on each other but more often imply a life after 'death' called survival, and a life within death for which we have no name" (*Holocaust Testimonies*, pp. 34–35).

21. As many have noted, while we usually have little difficulty identifying stories "as stories" in everyday practice, it is not easy to define the parameters of stories formally. I have found two recent discussions of these issues particularly informative: Catherine Kohler Riessman, *Narrative Analysis* (Newbury Park, CA:

Sage Publications, 1993) and Jerome Bruner, *The Culture of Education* (Cambridge, MA: Harvard University Press, 1996). Both Riessman and Bruner include reflections on the perspectives of Ricoeur, Labov, Burke, and White.

Within these pages, I emphasize a minimal set of stories' characteristics that seem to accord both with our everyday understanding and with the views of most theorists. These include: some relatively coherent unfolding (the classic idea of sequence through "beginning, middle, and end"); relatively identifiable characters (including, of course, the narrator); a relatively clear context (the development of which may be part of the story's changing circumstances). I repeat "relatively" because it seems to me these are, in fact, relative matters best served by retaining conceptual flexibility.

Along with the outward characteristics of stories, and no doubt reflecting them, the attitude of a narrator *in the role of* storyteller also seems to me to be essential. That is why I emphasize that the very decision to retell memory as a story expresses (again relatively) a recounter's sense of "purchase" on at least that bit of human experience.

22. A number of writers have commented on the challenges to traditional narrative unfolding in the context of Holocaust literature. Sidra DeKoven Ezrahi notes that "the visual arts appear to be more amenable than the literary medium to the representation of violent disruptions in human affairs," largely because "literature like music is a sequence, not a simultaneity, of events" (*By Words Alone*, p. 4). Alvin Rosenfeld comments that Holocaust novels are often "most memorable" when they "approach the condition of poetry. . . . What lingers on frequently has less to do with the narrative elements of plot development and character portrayal than with the presentation of feeling through certain brilliant images" (*A Double Dying*, p. 80).

These insights are complemented by psychiatric studies on the recounting of catastrophic trauma. Most typically, the psychiatric literature reports that traumatic retelling takes the form of discrete images that are detached from each other, from any unfolding narrative, and—seemingly—even from the organizing perspective of the recounter. Thus Richard Mollica describes what he calls "prenarratives" that "have no development, do not progress in time sequence, and fail to actively reveal the storyteller's interpretation of traumatic events" ("The Trauma Story: The Psychiatric Care of Refugee Survivors of Violence and Torture," in *Post-Traumatic Therapy and Victims of Violence*, ed. Frank Ochberg [New York: Brunner/Mazel, 1988], p. 311). Dori Laub and Nanette Auerhahn note that survivors' recounting often seems to take the form of "fragmented percepts," separate from each other and from the person of the recounter (Dori Laub and Nanette Auerhahn, "Failed Empathy—A Central Theme in the Survivor's Holocaust Experience," *Psychoanalytic Psychology* 6 [1989]:387–88). Judith Herman writes that "traumatic memories lack verbal narrative and context" and are more essentially "fragmentary sensation . . . image without context"—like "a series of still snapshots" (*Trauma and Recovery* [New York: Basic Books, 1992], pp. 38, 175;

the image of "still snapshots" is attributed to F. Snider of the Boston Area Trauma Study Group). Finally, Henry Krystal notes that accounts of traumatic experience tend to be "minimal vignettes," detached from the recounter "as if described by a third person" (*Integration and Self-Healing: Affect, Trauma, Alexithymia* [Hillsdale, NJ: The Analytic Press, 1988], p. 152). All of these descriptions suggest how great may be the transformation when recounting takes a storied form.

Indeed, it is a common conviction within the current clinical literature on trauma, influenced by a resurgent interest in the views of Pierre Janet, that "making a story" of traumatic experience is itself essential in the healing process. Thus Mollica describes the "new story" that patients work to attain and writes that "through their storytelling refugee patients regain the world they have lost" ("The Trauma Story," p. 312). Citing a phrase of Janet's, Herman writes:

It appears, then, that the "action of telling a story" in the safety of a protected relationship can actually produce a change in the abnormal processing of the traumatic memory. With this transformation of memory comes relief of many of the major symptoms of post-traumatic stress disorder. (*Trauma and Recovery*, p. 183)

Laub and Auerhahn note that while integrating fragments "in a cohesively narrative personal history is not sufficient for healing to occur . . . it is an essential step" ("Failed Empathy," p. 388).

As I have argued elsewhere ("The Oral Narratives of Holocaust Survivors," in *Texts and Identities: Studies on Language and Narrative 3*, University of Kentucky Department of Communications and Information Studies [1994], pp. 170–76), I am less sanguine than these writers about the possibility of such a full narrative transformation of memory, at least among Holocaust survivors. Rather, it has seemed to me that even for those who have worked hardest to create such accounts—writers like Charlotte Delbo or Primo Levi, for example—recounting remains an oscillation between story and "not-story," expressing strands of memory that are also both storied and unstoried and, ultimately, reflecting the ongoing life and the ongoing death that constitute survival itself. The absence of any final integration does *not* have to mean, however, that survivors remain somehow "ill" or "disabled." Rather, I have argued that many survivors seem, in effect, to be able "to integrate this lack of integration itself"—complexly juggling and balancing the different worlds out of which their recounting takes form ("Oral Narratives," p. 173).

23. Appelfeld, *Beyond Despair*, p. 33.

24. Wiesel, "A Plea for the Survivors," p. 198.

25. Theodor Adorno, "Engagement," in *Noten zur Literatur III* (Frankfurt am Main: Suhrkamp Verlag, 1965), cited and discussed in Rosenfeld, *A Double Dying*, pp. 13–14. Maurice Blanchot has commented on Adorno's formulation in a way that is closer to the sense here in *Vicious Circles: Two Fictions & After the Fact*, trans. Paul Auster (Barrytown, NY: Station Hill Press, 1985), pp. 68–69. I was alerted to this work through Geoffrey Hartman's reference to it in *The Longest*

Shadow: In the Aftermath of the Holocaust (Bloomington: Indiana University Press, 1996).

26. Elie Wiesel, *One Generation After*, trans. Lily Edelman and Elie Wiesel (New York: Avon, 1972), p. 16.

27. Cf. Greenspan, "Lives as Texts," pp. 145–64.

28. I am indebted to Professor George C. Rosenwald for suggesting the com-plementarity between survivors' "making stories" of their memories and our "making stories" about survivors.

29. The concept of enactment has a long history in psychoanalytic and psychiatric theory and has several different senses, including: gratifying an im-pulse or fantasy through "acting it out," re-enacting a trauma in order to master it, or directly reliving the trauma as a kind of behavioral flashback. The notion of enactment as discussed here differs from all of these formulations in at least two fundamental respects. First, with regard to motivation, I am arguing that the *primary* motive behind the enactments I discuss is the drive to retell (as opposed to impulse gratification, ego-integration, etc.). Second, I am arguing that survi-vors' enacted stories, exactly like their spoken ones, always point beyond them-selves—to all that is *not* given form by, for example, enacted guilt or rage.

30. Amery, *At the Mind's Limits*, p. 34.

31. Elie Wiesel, *The Accident*, trans. Anne Borchardt (New York: Bantam Books, 1982), p. 54.

32. Elie Wiesel, *The Town Beyond the Wall*, trans. Stephen Becker (New York: Schocken, 1982), p. 91.

33. Charlotte Delbo, *La Memoire et les jours* (Paris: Berg International, 1985) p. 13, as translated by Langer in *Holocaust Testimonies*, p. 7.

34. I cannot emphasize too strongly that the death that survivors know is known "in their bones"—it is an actual, not a metaphoric death; a body-centered experience, not only a death of "meaning" or "identity" (although it is those things too). With regard to the lethal terminus of trauma, the best discussion is Henry Krystal's seminal essay, "Trauma and Affects," *The Psychoanalytic Study of the Child* 33 (1978):81–116. Even though not fully consumed, survivors enter into a dying process in trauma and retain the knowledge that life, body-centered life, carries the seeds of its own dissolution.

Regarding the "landscape of death" as a "death of creation," see, for example, Wiesel, *A Jew Today*, p. 198; Primo Levi's description of reverse Genesis in *The Drowned and the Saved*, trans. Raymond Rosenthal (New York: Vintage, 1988), p. 85; or Charlotte Delbo's description of "the sun of eternity, the sun before creation" in *None of Us Will Return*, trans. John Githens (Boston: Beacon Press, 1968), p. 125.

35. Wiesel, *One Generation After*, pp. 15–16.

36. Adin Steinsaltz, *The Essential Talmud*, trans. Chaya Galai (New York: Basic Books, 1976), p. 9.

37. Langer, *Holocaust Testimonies*, p. 17.

CHAPTER 2

1. This claim is in contrast with perspectives that have emphasized survivors' need to "give form" or "integrate" their experiences—essentially for the sake of form and integration. Robert Jay Lifton's "formative paradigm" is perhaps the best-known theory of this sort. See, for example, his *The Broken Connection* (New York: Simon and Schuster, 1979). A number of more recent conceptualizations—Laub and Auerhahn, for example—suggest that "integration" emerges out of *both* retelling trauma within a "cohesive narrative" and the experience of being empathically heard ("Failed Empathy"). My own view is close to that of Laub and Auerhahn but would put still greater emphasis on the experience of being heard.

2. On the role of survivors' listeners, particularly in video testimony projects, see James Young's reflections in *Writing and Rewriting the Holocaust* (Bloomington: Indiana University Press, 1988), especially pp. 166–69. On the impact of context, including wider social discourses, on interview dialogues (not only with survivors), cf. Riessman, *Narrative Analysis*, pp. 20–21.

3. Aaron Hass, *The Aftermath: Living with the Holocaust* (Cambridge, UK: Cambridge University Press, 1995), p. 25. See also the discussion of survivor guilt in Terrence Des Pres, *The Survivor: An Anatomy of Life in the Death Camps* (New York: Pocket Books, 1977), pp. 41–54. Wiesel also notes the possible overuse of the concept of "survivor guilt," commenting in his recent memoir, "There is much talk among psychiatrists—possibly too much—about so-called survivors' guilt." (*All Rivers Run to the Sea: Memoirs* [New York: Knopf, 1995], p. 91.)

4. Levi, *The Drowned and the Saved*, pp. 85–86.

5. Ibid., pp. 84–85.

6. This is more fully illustrated in Henry Greenspan, "The Tellable and the Hearable in Holocaust Survivors' Recounting: Survivor Guilt in Narrative Context," *Studies on Language and Narrative 5*, University of Kentucky Department of Communications and Information Studies (1996).

7. Cf. two important analyses by Yael Danieli, "Psychotherapists' Participation in the Conspiracy of Silence about the Holocaust," *Psychoanalytic Psychology I* (1984):24–42 and "Treating Survivors and Children of Survivors of the Nazi Holocaust," in *Post-Traumatic Therapy and Victims of Violence*, ed. Frank Ochberg (New York: Brunner/Mazel,1998), pp. 278–94. Danieli makes the point succinctly: "One of the most powerful functions of survivor guilt is to serve as a defense against intolerable existential helplessness. Being totally passive and helpless in the face of the Holocaust is perhaps the most devastating experience for survivor/victims. . . . Guilt presupposes the presence of choice and the power, ability, and possibility to exercise it" ("Treating Survivors," p. 289). See also Judith Herman, *Trauma and Recovery*, pp. 53–54 and Ronnie Janoff-Bulman, "The Aftermath of Victimization," in *Trauma and Its Wake*, ed. Charles Figley (New York: Brunner/Mazel, 1985), pp. 15–35.

8. Shamai Davidson, *Holding on to Humanity—The Message of Holocaust Survivors: The Shamai Davidson Papers*, ed. Israel W. Charny (New York: New York University Press, 1992), p. 187. It should be said that there has been a significant "minority opinion" in psychology and psychiatry that has taken issue with conventional views of survivor guilt. Members of this group include Yael Danieli, Hillel Klein, and others.

9. Cf. Des Pres, *The Survivor*, pp. 43–47 and Danieli, "Treating Survivors," p. 289.

10. A personal note: When my work related to survivors comes up in general conversation, questions about their guilt are, predictably, the first comments I receive. I am almost never asked about survivors' grief, their rage, or their terror.

11. Cf. Raul Hilberg, "Opening Remarks: The Discovery of the Holocaust," in *Lessons and Legacies: The Meaning of the Holocaust in a Changing World*, ed. Peter Hayes (Evanston, IL: Northwestern University Press, 1991), pp. 11–19. I will have much more to say about the 1970s later in this chapter.

12. Cf. the descriptions of early responses to survivors in Robert H. Abzug, *Inside the Vicious Heart: Americans and the Liberation of the Nazi Concentration Camps* (New York: Oxford University Press, 1985); William B. Helmreich, *Against All Odds: Holocaust Survivors and the Successful Lives They Made in America* (New York: Simon and Schuster, 1992); Alvin H. Rosenfeld, "The Americaniza - tion of the Holocaust," *Commentary* (June 1995):35–40. While this chapter concerns survivors' experiences in the United States, their stigmatization in the very different context of Israel makes for a fascinating comparison. See especially Tom Segev, *The Seventh Million: The Israelis and the Holocaust*, trans. Haim Watzman (New York: Hill and Wang, 1993).

13. Wiesel, *A Jew Today*, pp. 193–94.

14. For comment on the period of the Eichmann Trial, see David Wyman, "The United States," in *The World Reacts to the Holocaust*, ed. David Wyman and Charles Rosenzveig (Baltimore: The Johns Hopkins University Press, 1996). For comment on the publication of testimony immediately after the war, particularly in a French context, see Annette Wieviorka, "On Testimony," in *Holocaust Remembrance: The Shapes of Memory*, ed. Geoffrey Hartman (Cambridge, MA: Basil Blackwell, 1994), pp. 23–32.

15. Levi, *Survival in Auschwitz*, p. 9 and Ferdinando Camon, *Conversations with Primo Levi*, trans. John Shepley (Marlboro, VT: The Marlboro Press, 1989), p. 42.

16. Wiesel, *A Jew Today*, p. 200.

17. On the Holocaust's essential negation of the image of responsive listeners, see Dori Laub's important discussion in "Truth and Testimony: The Process and the Struggle," reprinted in *Trauma: Explorations in Memory*, ed. Cathy Caruth (Baltimore: The Johns Hopkins University Press, 1995), pp. 61–75. See also Shoshana Felman and Dori Laub, *Testimony: Crises of Witnessing in Literature, Psychoanalysis, and History* (New York: Routledge, 1992).

18. Levi's full description of his dream, which I will be citing in segments, is given in *Survival in Auschwitz*, pp. 59–60.

19. Ibid., p. 61. Levi also connects the two dreams in Camon, *Conversations*, p. 42, saying both are "the dream of a primary need . . . a basic need."

20. Screaming may be thought of as the "ur-form" of Holocaust recounting in any case. See especially Des Pres, *The Survivor*, pp. 37–50.

21. Cf. Wieviorka, "On Testimony," in *Holocaust Remembrance*, pp. 23–32. Alain Goldschlager has also noted the flurry of testimony immediately after the war in a preliminary survey of more than 2,000 memoirs he has gathered for a collection at the University of Western Ontario. (Personal communication, February 14, 1997.)

22. None of this and what follows is to suggest that, if survivors only had had willing listeners, all would have been well. The deaths they know would have remained; and their power, though perhaps modulated, would not have been defeated. Primo Levi described a recurring dream he had *after* that ended with the terrifying realization: "I am in the Lager once more, and nothing is true outside the Lager" (*The Reawakening*, trans. Stuart Woolf [New York: Summit Books, 1986], pp. 373–74). Many survivors describe the same return—the sense of never having left—in identical language.

23. Quoted in *Voices from the Holocaust*, ed. Sylvia Rothchild (New York: New American Library, 1981), p. 373.

24. Ibid., pp. 381–82.

25. Edward T. Linenthal, *Preserving Memory: The Struggle to Create America's Holocaust Museum* (New York: Viking, 1995), p. 11.

26. Wyman, "The United States," in *The World Reacts*, p. 721. The earlier date cited by Wyman refers to the appearance of the film *Judgement at Nuremberg*, which premiered in 1961, the same year as the Eichmann Trial.

27. Raul Hilberg, "Opening Remarks," in *Lessons and Legacies*, p. 18. An entirely different kind of development, though not unrelated, was the surge of Holocaust denial activity in the mid- and late seventies, including the founding in 1978 of the "Institute for Historical Review," a center for "Holocaust denial" and other activities of the American extreme right.

28. Cf. Rosenfeld, "The Americanization of the Holocaust." As Rosenfeld also notes, one must not underestimate the importance of survivors' own efforts in all these developments. But these efforts were not new. Only in the late seventies did survivors begin to find a much wider, interested audience.

29. Joan Ringelheim, *A Catalogue of Audio and Video Collections of Holocaust Testimony: Second Edition* (New York: Greenwood Press, 1992).

30. See, for example, Raul Hilberg, both "Opening Remarks" and *The Politics of Memory: The Journey of a Holocaust Historian* (Chicago: Ivan R. Dee, 1996), pp. 123–24; Wyman, "The United States," in *The World Reacts*, pp. 724–28.

31. See Hank Greenspan, "On Being a 'Real Survivor,' " *Sh'ma* 26 (March 29, 1996): 1–3.

32. Christopher Lasch, *The Culture of Narcissism: American Life in an Age of Diminishing Expectations* (New York: Norton, 1979), pp. 2–7, 52–70; Christopher Lasch, *The Minimal Self: Psychic Survival in Troubled Times* (New York: Norton, 1984), pp. 60–129.

33. *The New Yorker*, January 8, 1979, caption by W. Miller, p. 40. In general, I would suggest that the depth of the late seventies' preoccupation with extremity remains unappreciated, a preoccupation that extended from the core to the periphery of the popular imagination. The sudden outbreak of reported satanic ritual abuse, UFO abductions, and the tabloid craze more generally have all been part of the trend, and—in the age of *X-files*—the trend continues. Likewise, beyond the personal choices of Steven Spielberg, America's most successful filmmaker, there is also shared preoccupation that connects films like *Close Encounters* (1978), *Poltergeist* (1982), and *Schindler's List* (1993): a preoccupation with surviving "far out" encounters.

34. Beyond such references to "downsizing," cynicism, and so on, this chapter does not address the question of *why* the wider culture of "survivors" and "survivalism" has itself developed. That discussion, important as it is, would simply take us too far beyond the scope of present purposes. But, along with Lasch's two volumes listed above, I would at least mention the following recent analyses that differ philosophically but, in my view, are all essential on this question: Kai Erikson, *A New Species of Trouble: The Human Experience of Modern Disasters* (New York: Norton, 1994); Donald L. Kanter and Philip H. Mirvis, *The Cynical Americans: Living and Working in an Age of Discontent and Disillusion* (San Francisco: Jossey-Bass, 1989); Charles Derber, *The Wilding of America* (New York: St. Martin's Press, 1996); and Michael J. Sandel, *Democracy's Discontent: America in Search of a Public Philosophy* (Cambridge, MA: The Belknap Press of Harvard University Press, 1996).

35. On the surge of general psychological writing on "post-traumatic stress" since the late seventies, see Dudley David Blake, Anne Marie Albano, and Terence Keane, "Twenty Years of Trauma: *Psychological Abstracts* 1970 through 1989," *Journal of Traumatic Stress* (5 (1992): 477–84. An excellent piece on the association between the general discussion of post-traumatic stress disorder (PTSD) and Holocaust survivors specifically is Ghislaine Boulanger's review ("Psychiatry's Stepchild") of Judith Herman's *Trauma and Recovery* in *Tikkun* (March/April) 1994: 84–85. Both of these articles note that PTSD became a diagnostic entity officially recognized by the American Psychiatric Association in 1980.

36. Gustav Bychowski, "Permanent Character Changes as an Aftereffect of Persecution," in *Massive Psychic Trauma*, ed. Henry Krystal (New York: International Universities Press, 1968), p. 86.

37. PBS, "Holocaust: The Survivors Gather—June 15, 1981," 15 June 1981.

38. The following excerpts from an article about Denver-area survivors who attended the World Gathering speak for themselves:

As international reporters made headlines out of the occasional tearful reunions of relatives or friends, Samuel Silver witnessed the looks of disappointment on the faces of those who found nobody. . . . "All those years, we lived with wounds that stopped bleeding," Silver illustrates. "But the wounds were still there. In Jerusalem the wounds started to bleed again."

Stephanie Gross bristles when told that some observers have said that the World Gathering of Jewish Holocaust Survivors represented a "victory over death." She points to a collection of old family photographs on the wall, showing the faces of in-laws murdered by the Nazis. "How could this be a victory?" she asks. "Everybody loses. This was no victory. It was survival."

From Chris Leppek, *Intermountain Jewish News* (Denver), 3 July 1981.

39. PBS, "Holocaust: The Survivors Gather—June 17, 1981," 17 June 1981.

40. PBS, "Holocaust: The Survivors Gather—June 18, 1981," 18 June 1981.

41. It should be noted that the rhetoric of "legacies" and "stories" is also applied to other groups who have suffered massive misfortune. As a single exam - ple, a prepublication ad for the book, *Polio's Legacy: An Oral History*, was written in a language virtually identical to the fliers one receives for new collections of survivor testimony. The copy stated:

This book shows readers the reality of polio and how it alters human lives. Thirty-five polio survivors open their hearts to explain their experiences. . . . The result is this written t ribute to the survival of the human spirit. . . . Readers will see how polio's legacy reveals itself through these stories.

42. In light of the contemporary fascination with survivors' testimony and their psychology, it is recurrently surprising to read the eulogies for survivors of an earlier time. Discussing the benefits of offering survivors' psychotherapy, Paul Chodoff wrote this in the late seventies, on the very edge of the new interest in survivors that would soon follow:

. . . [W]ith the passage of time, their melancholy tale is almost told. Even those who were small children during the persecution have now reached middle age, while most of the survivors still left are even older. Thus, although certainly they deserve whatever help we can give them . . . the focus of our attention should be shifting to the problems of the secon d generation . . . [the] children of the survivors.

From "Psychotherapy of the Survivor," in *Survivors, Victims, and Perpetrators: Essays on the Nazi Holocaust*, ed. Joel E. Dimsdale (Washington, DC: Hemisphere Publishing, 1980), p. 216.

CHAPTER 3

1. Although a formal gathering of the seven participants never took place, some are acquainted with others. Manny and Paula, for example, are good friends. They both also know Leon and Lydia.

While the participants never met in actual conversation, putting them in imagined conversation with each other—via constant contrast and juxtaposi -

tion—is central to methodological assumptions that are detailed in Greenspan, "Who Can Retell?", pp. 84–121. To excerpt briefly:

> Along with being born in conversation, the central concepts of this study were borne out to the degree that they sustained and deepened conversation. . . . As would be expected, for example, [Leon's] idea of "making a story" of what is "not a story" caused me to listen differently to the stories that other survivors retold. I now listened for the "making" of stories. . . . The result was not simply that Leon's formulation was confirmed or even that I more quickly "caught on" to other participants' recounting. Just as important, as my conversations developed with other survivors, the original concept was revised through their own contributions. . . . I could then turn back and listen to Leon in a new kind of way. . . .
>
> At times I brought this wider conversation into a single interview. That is, within the limits of immediate relevance, I sometimes referred to the reflections of other survivors while speaking to a particular participant. This provided the opportunity for that participant to enter into the wider conversation and contrast his or her own formulations with those of others. . . . At other times, it was only later that I began to realize how the words of some participants "spoke to" the words of others. Either way, the essential principl es of "knowing with" remain the same. They lead less to finished generalizations about what some group of people have (or are) "in common" than to the creation of a "common conversation" among those people. (Pp. 117–19)

The creation of a "common conversation" is illustrated at the end of this chapter. It is exactly the particularity of each that reveals the dimensions of the world they share "on another level." The shared is almost literally "thrown into relief" *because* it is refracted through different perspectives, juxtaposed with each other.

2. Des Pres, *The Survivor*, p. 217.

3. Cf. the discussion of this passage in Greenspan, "The Tellable and the Hearable."

4. See, for example, the description of "camp families" in Kitty Hart, *Return to Auschwitz* (New York: Atheneum, 1982); Livia Bitton Jackson, *Elli: Coming of Age in the Holocaust* (New York: Times Books, 1980); Isabella Leitner, with Irving A. Leitner, *Fragments of Isabella: A Memoir of Auschwitz* (New York: Thomas Crowell, 1978). For a discussion of the role of these kinds of memories in women's memoirs and testimony, see Joan Ringelheim, "Women and the Holocaust: A Reconsideration of Research," in *Different Voices: Women and the Holocaust*, ed. Carol Rittner and John K. Roth (New York: Paragon, 1993).

5. Yael Danieli has suggested that survivors' primary self-presentations could be divided between "victims" and "fighters." While she notes that these categories are not "intended to represent pure and mutually exclusive types," the voices in this study suggest that, as conversations deepen, one usually hears *both* sides of these and related polar themes. See Yael Danieli, "Families of Survivors of the Nazi Holocaust," in *Stress and Anxiety: Volume 8*, ed. Norman A. Milgram (Washington, D.C.: Hemisphere, 1982), pp. 405–21.

CHAPTER 4

1. Elie Wiesel, *Souls on Fire: Portraits and Legends of Hasidic Masters*, trans. Marion Wiesel (New York: Summit Books, 1972), p. 180.

2. The "old man's prayer" that Victor cites is drawn from *Psalm* 71 (I am grateful to Rabbi Robert Dobrusin of Beth Israel Congregation of Ann Arbor, Michigan, for this reference). It is of interest that Leon Wells, who prosecutes God in a different way than Victor, also makes reference to the prayer in his remarkable *Shattered Faith: A Holocaust Legacy* (Lexington: The University Press of Kentucky, 1995), p. 72.

3. Des Pres commented: "In extremity, states of mind become objective, metaphors tend to actualize, the word becomes flesh" (*The Survivor*, p. 205). In his prosecution, Victor re-creates this reductive process. He gives mediated form to the end of mediation.

4. Once again it is noteworthy that Leon Wells makes reference to the same prayer as Victor. See his discussion of the story of Rachel in *Shattered Faith*, pp. 11–12.

CHAPTER 5

1. Sources on Treblinka include Yitzhak Arad, *Belzec, Sobibor, Treblinka: The Operation Reinhard Death Camps* (Bloomington: Indiana University Press, 1987); Alexander Donat, ed., *The Death Camp Treblinka: A Documentary* (New York: Holocaust Library, 1979); Gitta Sereny, *Into That Darkness: An Examination of Conscience* (New York: McGraw-Hill, 1974); Samuel Willenberg, *Surviving Treblinka*, ed. Wladyslaw T. Bartoszewski, trans. Naftali Greenwood (Oxford, UK: Basil Blackwell, 1989); and Richard Glazar's memoir cited earlier, *Trap with a Green Fence: Survival in Treblinka*. Jean-Francois Steiner's novel, *Treblinka*, trans. Helen Weaver (New York: Simon and Schuster, 1967) has been the subject of controversy because of Steiner's inclusion of purely fictional events.

2. I have not found this way of shooting victims confirmed by any other source. The fact that I have not may prove Victor's point.

CHAPTER 6

1. Wiesel, *Souls on Fire*, p. 257.

2. Ibid., pp. 258–59.

3. Lily Edelman, "A Conversation with Elie Wiesel," in *Responses to Elie Wiesel*, ed. Harry James Cargas (New York: Persea Books, 1978), p. 13.

4. Wiesel, *One Generation After*, p. 16.

5. A. M. Dalbray, "Les Juifs du Silence," *Amif* (November 1967): 1771. Cited in Ellen S. Fine, *Legacy of Night: The Literary Universe of Elie Wiesel* (Albany: State University of New York Press, 1982), p. 30.

6. Lawrence L. Langer, *The Age of Atrocity: Death in Modern Literature* (Boston: Beacon Press, 1978), pp. xi—xiv. Cf. also the interesting discussion by Ernest Keen, "Paranoia and Cataclysmic Narratives," in *Narrative Psychology: The Storied Nature of Human Conduct*, ed. Theodore Sarbin (New York: Praeger, 1986), pp. 174–90.

7. Examples of such stories include Elie Wiesel's much cited story of the "pipel," the "sad angel" who was "loved by all" (*Night*, trans. Stella Rodway [New York: Hill & Wang, 1960]), and Leon Wells's account of Marek in his memoir of the Janowska camp (*The Death Brigade* [New York: Holocaust Library, 1978]). The latter is particularly close to the Lieberman story. Marek was also a young inmate, favored by both the guards and his fellows, whose sudden and unexpected shoot - ing proved that *no one* had protection. The one story that Art Spiegelman repeats in *Maus*—and for which he twice illustrates Vladek's emotional response ("It *still* makes me cry!") is also a story of resistance and execution: the hanging of the "black market Jews" in Sosnowiec (*Maus: A Survivor's Tale* [New York: Pantheon, 1986], pp. 84, 132–33).

8. Primo Levi, *Moments of Reprieve*, trans. Ruth Feldman (New York: Summit Books, 1986), p. 10.

9. "Lena's Story," in Alexander Donat, *The Holocaust Kingdom* (New York: Holocaust Library, 1978), pp. 309–11. In keeping with its status as legend, there are a number of variants of Mala's story.

10. There are many manifestations—the popularity of storytelling in perform - ance arts, "narrative studies" across several academic disciplines, the collection of "family stories" in various contexts, and so on. It is of interest that Jerome Bruner dates the emergence of narrative study in the social sciences to the same period as the flowering of trauma study and of what I have called "popular survivalism." He writes: "By the late 1970s and early 1980s, the notion of Self as a storyteller came on the scene—The Self telling stories that included a delineation of Self as part of the story" (*Acts of Meaning* [Cambridge, MA: Harvard University, Press, 1990], p. 111). It is hard to avoid the speculation—in the spirit of Walter Benjamin—that we began to "romance stories," as we began to romance survival, at a cultural moment when coherent life narratives seemed constricted, threatened, or slipping away.

11. These quotations all happen to come from solicitation letters from the United States Holocaust Memorial Museum, but the same language is used in almost all other similar contexts.

12. *And So We Must Remember: Holocaust Remembrances* (Oak Park, MI: Temple Emanu-El, 1992), pp. i-ii.

13. In his study, *Telling Stories: Postmodernism and the Invalidation of Traditional Narrative*, Michael Roemer uses as epigram and opening sentence: "Every story is over before it begins" ([Lanham, MD: Rowman & Littlefield, 1995], p. 3).

Selected Bibliography

Abzug, Robert H. *Inside the Vicious Heart: Americans and the Liberation of Nazi Concentration Camps*. New York: Oxford University Press, 1985.

Adelson, Alan, and Robert Lapides, eds. *Lodz Ghetto: Inside a Community under Siege*. New York: Penguin, 1989.

Adorno, Theodor W. "Engagement." *Noten Zur Literatur*. Vol. 3. Frankfurt: Suhrkamp, 1963.

Amery, Jean. *At the Mind's Limits: Contemplations by a Survivor of Auschwitz on its Realities*. Translated by Sidney Rosenfeld and Stella P. Rosenfeld. Bloomington: Indiana University Press, 1980.

Amery, Jean. *On Aging: Revolt and Resignation*. Translated by John D. Barlow. Bloomington: Indiana University Press, 1994.

Appelfeld, Aharon. *Beyond Despair*. Translated by Jeffrey M. Green. New York: Fromm International Publishing, 1994.

Arad, Yitzhak. *Belzec, Sobibor, Treblinka: The Operation Reinhard Death Camps*. Bloomington: Indiana University Press, 1987.

Bernstein, Michael Andre. *Foregone Conclusions: Against Apocalyptic History*. Berkeley: University of California Press, 1994.

Blake, Dudley David, Anne Marie Albano, and Terence Keane. "Twenty Years of Trauma: *Psychological Abstracts* 1970 through 1989." *Journal of Traumatic Stress* 5 (1992):477–84.

Blanchot, Maurice. *Vicious Circles: Two Fictions & After the Fact*. Translated by Paul Auster. Barrytown, NY: Station Hill Press, 1985.

Bolkosky, Sidney. "Listening for the Silences." *Witness* 1 (1987):66–76.

Boulanger, Ghislaine. "Psychiatry's Stepchild." *Tikkun* (March/April 1994):84–85.

Bruner, Jerome. *Acts of Meaning*. Cambridge, MA: Harvard University Press, 1990.

Bruner, Jerome. *The Culture of Education*. Cambridge, MA: Harvard University Press, 1996.

Camon, Ferdinando. *Conversations with Primo Levi*. Translated by John Shepley. Marlboro, VT: The Marlboro Press, 1989.

Caruth, Cathy, ed. *Trauma: Explorations in Memory*. Baltimore: The Johns Hopkins University Press, 1995.

Charny, Israel W., ed. *Holding on to Humanity—The Message of Holocaust Survivors: The Shamai Davidson Papers*. New York: New York University Press, 1992.

Danieli, Yael. "Psychotherapists' Participation in the Conspiracy of Silence about the Holocaust." *Psychoanalytic Psychology* I (1984):24–42.

Danieli, Yael. "Treating Survivors and Children of Survivors of the Nazi Holocaust." In *Post-Traumatic Therapy and Victims of Violence*. Edited by Frank Ochberg. New York: Brunner/Mazel, 1988.

Delbo, Charlotte. *None of Us Will Return*. Translated by John Githens. Boston: Beacon Press, 1968.

Delbo, Charlotte. *Auschwitz and After*. Translated by Rosette C. Lamont. New Haven: Yale University Press, 1995.

Derber, Charles. *The Wilding of America*. New York: St. Martin's Press, 1996.

Des Pres, Terrence. *The Survivor: An Anatomy of Life in the Death Camps*. New York: Pocket Books, 1977.

Dimsdale, Joel E., ed. *Survivors, Victims, and Perpetrators: Essays on the Nazi Holocaust*. Washington, DC: Hemisphere Publishing, 1980.

Donat, Alexander. *The Holocaust Kingdom*. New York: Holocaust Library, 1978.

Donat, Alexander, ed. *The Death Camp Treblinka: A Documentary*. New York: Holocaust Library, 1979.

Eliach, Yaffa. *Hasidic Tales of the Holocaust*. New York: Oxford University Press, 1982.

Erikson, Kai. *Everything in Its Path*. New York: Simon and Schuster, 1976.

Erikson, Kai. *A New Species of Trouble: The Human Experience of Modern Disasters*. New York: Norton, 1994.

Ezrahi, Sidra DeKoven. *By Words Alone: The Holocaust in Literature*. Chicago: The University of Chicago Press, 1980.

Felman, Shoshana, and Dori Laub. *Testimony: Crises of Witnessing in Literature, Psychoanalysis, and History*. New York: Routledge, 1992.

Ferderber-Salz, Bertha. *And the Sun Kept Shining . . .* New York: Holocaust Library, 1980.

Figley, Charles, ed. *Trauma and Its Wake*. New York: Brunner/ Mazel, 1985.

Fine, Ellen S. *Legacy of Night: The Literary Universe of Elie Wiesel*. Albany: State University of New York Press, 1982.

Friedlander, Saul. *When Memory Comes*. Translated by Helen R. Lane. New York: Farrar, Straus and Giroux, Inc., 1979.

Friedlander, Saul. *History, Memory, and the Extermination of the Jews of Europe*. Bloomington: Indiana University Press, 1993.

Friedlander, Saul, ed. *Probing the Limits of Representation: Nazism and the "Final Solution."* Cambridge, MA: Harvard University Press, 1992.

Gilbert, Martin. *The Holocaust: A History of the Jews of Europe During the Second World War*. New York: Henry Holt and Company, 1985.

Gill, Anton. *The Journey Back from Hell: Conversations with Concentration Camp Survivors—An Oral History*. New York: Avon, 1988.

Glazar, Richard. *Trap with a Green Fence: Survival in Treblinka*. Translated by Roslyn Theobald. Evanston, IL: Northwestern University Press, 1995.

Greenspan, Henry. "Lives as Texts: Symptoms as Modes of Recounting in the Life Histories of Holocaust Survivors." *Storied Lives: The Cultural Politics of Self-Understanding*. Edited by George C. Rosenwald and Richard L. Ochberg. New Haven: Yale University Press, 1992.

Greenspan, Henry. "On Being a 'Real Survivor.'" *Sh'ma* 26 (March 29, 1996):1–3.

Greenspan, Henry. "The Tellable and the Hearable: Survivor Guilt in Narrative Context." *Studies on Language and Narrative 5*, University of Kentucky Department of Communications and Information Studies, 1996.

Gutman, Yisrael, and Michael Berenbaum, eds. *Anatomy of the Auschwitz Death Camp*. Bloomington: Indiana University Press, 1994. Published in association with the United States Holocaust Memorial Museum, Washington, DC.

Hart, Kitty. *Return to Auschwitz*. New York: Atheneum, 1982.

Hartman, Geoffrey. *The Longest Shadow: In the Aftermath of the Holocaust*. Bloomington: Indiana University Press, 1996.

Hartman, Geoffrey, ed. *Holocaust Remembrance: The Shapes of Memory*. Cambridge, MA: Basil Blackwell, 1994.

Hass, Aaron. *The Aftermath: Living with the Holocaust*. Cambridge, UK: Cambridge University Press, 1995.

Hayes, Peter, ed. *Lessons and Legacies: The Meaning of the Holocaust in a Changing World*. Evanston, IL: Northwestern University Press, 1991.

Helmreich, William B. *Against All Odds: Holocaust Survivors and the Successful Lives They Made in America*. New York: Simon and Schuster, 1992.

Herman, Judith. *Trauma and Recovery*. New York: Basic Books, 1992.

Hilberg, Raul. *The Destruction of the European Jews*. New York: Quadrangle, 1961.

Hilberg, Raul. *The Politics of Memory: The Journey of a Holocaust Historian*. Chicago: Ivan R. Dee, 1996.

Horowitz, Sara R. *Voicing the Void: Muteness and Memory in Holocaust Fiction*. Albany: State University of New York Press, 1997.

Jackson, Livia Bitton. *Elli: Coming of Age in the Holocaust*. New York: Times Books, 1980.

Kanter, Donald L., and Philip H. Mirvis. *The Cynical Americans: Living and Working in an Age of Discontent and Disillusion*. San Francisco: Jossey-Bass, 1989.

Kestenberg, Judith S., and Eva Fogelman, eds. *Children During the Nazi Reign: Psychological Perspective on the Interview Process*. Westport, CT: Praeger, 1994.

Kleiman, Yehudit, and Nina Springer-Aharoni, eds. *The Anguish of Liberation: Testimonies from 1945*. Jerusalem: Yad Vashem, 1995.

Krakowski, Shmuel, and Ilya Altman, eds. "The Testament of the Last Prisoners of the Chelmno Death Camp." *Yad Vashem Studies* XXI. Jerusalem: Yad Vashem, 1991: 105–23.

Krystal, Henry. "Trauma and Affects." *The Psychoanalytic Study of the Child* 33 (1978):81–116.

Krystal, Henry. *Integration and Self-Healing: Affect, Trauma, Alexithymia*. Hillsdale, NJ: The Analytic Press, 1988.

Krystal, Henry, ed. *Massive Psychic Trauma*. New York: International Universities Press, 1968.

Langer, Lawrence L. *The Holocaust and the Literary Imagination*. New Haven: Yale University Press, 1975.

Langer, Lawrence L. *The Age of Atrocity: Death in Modern Literature*. Boston: Beacon Press, 1978.

Langer, Lawrence L. *Versions of Survival: The Holocaust and the Human Spirit*. Albany: State University of New York Press, 1982.

Langer, Lawrence L. *Holocaust Testimonies: The Ruins of Memory*. New Haven: Yale University Press, 1991.

Lanzmann, Claude. *Shoah: An Oral History of the Holocaust*. New York: Pantheon, 1985.

Lasch, Christopher. *The Culture of Narcissism: American Life in an Age of Diminishing Expectations*. New York: Norton, 1979.

Lasch, Christopher. *The Minimal Self: Psychic Survival in Troubled Times*. New York: Norton, 1984.

Laub, Dori, and Nanette Auerhahn. "Failed Empathy—A Central Theme in the Survivor's Holocaust Experience." *Psychoanalytic Psychology* 6 (1989):387–96.

Leitner, Isabella, with Irving A. Leitner. *Fragments of Isabella: A Memoir of Auschwitz*. New York: Thomas Crowell, 1978.

Leitner, Isabella, with Irving A. Leitner. *Saving the Fragments: From Auschwitz to New York*. New York: New American Library, 1985.

Levi, Primo. *Survival in Auschwitz*. Translated by Stuart Woolf. New York: Summit Books, 1986.

Levi, Primo. *The Reawakening*. Translated by Stuart Woolf. New York: Summit Books, 1986.

Levi, Primo. *Moments of Reprieve*. Translated by Ruth Feldman. New York: Summit Books, 1986.

Levi, Primo. *The Drowned and the Saved*. Translated by Raymond Rosenthal. New York: Vintage, 1988.

Lifton, Robert Jay. *The Broken Connection*. New York: Simon and Schuster, 1979.

Linenthal, Edward T. *Preserving Memory: The Struggle to Create America's Holocaust Museum*. New York: Viking, 1995.

Mitchell, William, ed. *On Narrative*. Chicago: The University of Chicago Press, 1981.

Ochberg, Frank, ed. *Post-Traumatic Therapy and Victims of Violence*. New York: Brunner/Mazel, 1988.

Rabinowitz, Dorothy. *New Lives: Survivors of the Holocaust Living in America*. New York: Avon, 1976.

Rappaport, Ernest A. "Beyond Traumatic Neurosis." *The International Journal of Psychoanalysis* 49 (1968):719–31.

Riessman, Catherine Kohler. *Narrative Analysis*. Newbury Park, CA: Sage Publications, 1993.

Ringelheim, Joan. *A Catalogue of Audio and Video Collections of Holocaust Testimony: Second Edition*. New York: Greenwood Press, 1992.

Rittner, Carol, and John K. Roth, eds. *Different Voices: Women and the Holocaust*. New York: Paragon House, 1993.

Roemer, Michael. *Telling Stories: Postmodernism and the Invalidation of Traditional Narrative*. Lanham, MD: Rowman & Littlefield, 1995.

Rosenfeld, Alvin H. *A Double Dying: Reflections on Holocaust Literature*. Bloomington: Indiana University Press, 1980.

Rosenfeld, Alvin H. "The Americanization of the Holocaust." *Commentary* (June 1995):35–40.

Rosenfeld, Alvin H., and Irving Greenberg, eds. *Confronting the Holocaust: The Impact of Elie Wiesel*. Bloomington: Indiana University Press, 1978.

Rothchild, Sylvia, ed. *Voices from the Holocaust*. New York: New American Library, 1981.

Sandel, Michael J. *Democracy's Discontent: America in Search of a Public Philosophy*. Cambridge, MA: The Belknap Press of Harvard University Press, 1996.

Sarbin, Theodore, ed. *Narrative Psychology: The Storied Nature of Human Conduct*. New York: Praeger, 1986.

Segev, Tom. *The Seventh Million: The Israelis and the Holocaust*. Translated by Haim Watzman. New York: Hill and Wang, 1993.

Sereny, Gitta. *Into That Darkness: An Examination of Conscience*. New York: McGraw-Hill, 1974.

Spiegelman, Art. *Maus: A Survivor's Tale*. New York: Pantheon, 1986.

Steiner, George. *Language and Silence: Essays on Language, Literature, and the Inhuman*. New York: Atheneum, 1977.

Steiner, Jean-Francois. *Treblinka*. Translated by Helen Weaver. New York: Simon and Schuster, 1967.

Steinsaltz, Adin. *The Essential Talmud*. Translated by Chaya Galai. New York: Basic Books, 1976.

Wells, Leon. *The Death Brigade*. New York: Holocaust Library, 1978.

Wells, Leon. *Shattered Faith: A Holocaust Legacy*. Lexington: The University Press of Kentucky, 1995.

Wiesel, Elie. *The Accident*. Translated by Anne Borchardt. New York: Bantam Books, 1982.

Wiesel, Elie. *The Town Beyond the Wall*. Translated by Stephen Becker. New York: Schocken, 1982.

Wiesel, Elie. *One Generation After*. Translated by Lily Edelman and Elie Wiesel. New York: Avon, 1972.

Wiesel, Elie. *Souls on Fire: Portraits and Legends of Hasidic Masters*. Translated by Marion Wiesel. New York: Summit Books, 1972.

Wiesel, Elie. *A Jew Today*. Translated by Marion Wiesel. New York: Random House, 1978.

Wiesel, Elie. *All Rivers Run to the Sea: Memoirs*. New York: Knopf, 1995.

Willenberg, Samuel. *Surviving Treblinka*. Edited by Wladyslaw T. Bartoszewski. Translated by Naftali Greenwood. Oxford, UK: Basil Blackwell, 1989.

Winter, Jay. *Sites of Memory, Sites of Mourning: The Great War in European Cultural History*. Cambridge, UK: Cambridge University Press, 1995.

Wyman, David, and Charles Rosenzveig, eds. *The World Reacts to the Holocaust*. Baltimore: The Johns Hopkins University Press, 1996.

Young, James E. *Writing and Rewriting the Holocaust*. Bloomington: Indiana University Press, 1988.

Index

About the Author

HENRY GREENSPAN is a consulting psychologist and playwright at the University of Michigan. He originally came to Michigan in 1977 as a Fellow of the Michigan Society of Fellows and began his interviews with Holocaust survivors, and his teaching and writing about their recounting, at that time. His plays include *Remnants*, a celebrated work that also draws on more than twenty years of his listening to survivors.